Analysis of the Under-Five Child

Analysis of the Under-Five Child

Edited by Robert L. Tyson, M.D.

Yale University Press   New Haven and London

Published with assistance from the foundation
established in memory of Calvin Chapin of the
Class of 1788, Yale College

Library of Congress Cataloging-in-Publication Data
Analysis of the under-five child / edited by
Robert L. Tyson.
p. ; cm.
Includes bibliographical references and index.
ISBN 0-300-08764-0 (alk. paper)
1. Preschool children—Mental health—Case studies.
2. Child psychoanalysis—Case studies.
3. Child analysis—Case studies.
[DNLM: 1. Psychoanalysis—Child, Preschool—Case
Report.   2. Psychoanalysis—Infant—Case Report.
WS 350.5 A532 2001]   I. Tyson, Robert L.
RJ504.2 .A53   2001
618.92'8917—dc21   2001002623

Set in Caslon type by Tseng Information Systems, Inc.
Printed in the United States of America.

A catalogue record for this book is
available from the British Library.

The paper in this book meets the guidelines
for permanence and durability of the Committee
on Production Guidelines for Book Longevity of
the Council on Library Resources.

10 9 8 7 6 5 4 3 2 1

Contents

CONTRIBUTORS

Diane Hoye Campbell, M.D.
Robert M. Galatzer-Levy, M.D.
Alicia S. Gavalya, M.D.
Hansi Kennedy
John B. McDevitt, M.D.
Aimee G. Nover, D.S.W.
Henri Parens, M.D.
Katharine Reese, Ph.D.
Samuel Ritvo, M.D.
Melvin A. Scharfman, M.D.
Calvin F. Settlage, M.D.
Martin A. Silverman, M.D.
Alan Sugarman, Ph.D.
Phyllis Tyson, Ph.D.
Heiman van Dam, M.D.

Introduction

Robert L. Tyson, M.D.

PRELATENCY: A NEW GOLDEN AGE
FOR PSYCHOANALYSIS

There is an underserved psychoanalytically accessible population at both ends of the life span. The recently recognized value of psychoanalysis for the elderly has yet to be matched by a comparable insight into the treatability, the suitability, and the need for analytic treatment of many very young children. Case reports of such analyses do exist scattered in the literature, but there is no purpose-made collection of a variety of cases to illustrate this general proposition, to illuminate the developmental and technical issues that arise in the psychoanalytic work with individuals of this age group, and to demonstrate the remarkable therapeutic power of psychoanalysis for them. Also, training in child analysis typically requires supervised experience in the psychoanalysis of an adolescent, thus resulting in the designation "child and adolescent psychoanalytic training" in many organizations, but no such experience is required with prelatency children or children under five. This book is a contribution toward filling the resulting voids. We hope it will evoke interest among psychoanalysts, stimulate both analytic education as a whole and individual candidates to give the subject the attention it deserves, and, finally, alert all those who work with children to the existence of this powerful tool.

Terms frequently used in the book include *prelatency, preoedipal, under-fives,* and *this age group,* which represents a looseness of definition well understood by most analysts who work with children. Readers will find it helpful to keep in mind that a developmental and not a chronological framework underlies most of the clinical work and discussions. Development in children has momentum; it is an intricate process that can be characterized in terms of attainments or achievements, steps, phases, stages, or periods and also in terms of lines of development with regard to object relations, cognitive abilities, and many other psychological dimensions (P. Tyson and R. L. Tyson 1990). Contemporary developmental thinking has itself developed beyond the rigid demarcation of the child's life into a series of sharply defined stages or steps, largely on the basis established by Anna Freud (A. Freud 1965; Edgcumbe 2000) and added to by many contributors.

The 1988 Annual Meeting of the Association for Child Psychoanalysis in New Orleans, Louisiana, provided the opportunity to focus on the subject. Judith Schachter, M.D., Program Chair, and I enlisted case presentations both by seasoned clinicians and by child analytic trainees at various stages in their experience. Designated senior child analysts served as discussants, and two leading child analysts, Melvin Scharfman and Hansi Kennedy, respectively reviewed the salient development and technical issues of psychoanalysis with children of this age group. This book, which contains a selection from among the available presentations and discussions, presents a wealth of clinical and theoretical detail and makes evident the particular interests of many of the contributors. In addition, reports of the psychoanalyses of two little girls with encopresis have been included because of the unique challenges such treatment presents and because of their rarity. The psychological and emotional aspects of encopretic children have been reviewed more recently, with vignettes from work with three boys: two seven-year-olds, one seen in analysis and one in psychotherapy, and a twelve-year-old in analysis (Aruffo et al. 2000). Certainly the much younger children discussed in the following pages vary widely in the nature of their problems and in their responses to them, and in addition to the commonality of their age group, the frequency of traumatic experience—not always recognized as such—will be evident.

To appreciate the clinical work described and discussed in this book, the reader should be aware that analysts historically have had varying ideas about the proper age range within which patients are thought to be suitable for analysis. Freud's ideas on the subject showed that the upper age limit in his judgment tended to increase as he grew older. We know that Dora was eighteen, at the younger end of the age spectrum among his patients. He did not attribute the difficulties he had with her to her age, but to his failure at the time to appreciate well enough the nature of transference and consequently his inability to make appropriate and timely interpretations of it. A present-day supervisor of Freud's treatment of Dora, however, assuming the context to be child analytic training, probably would recommend that he familiarize himself better with how an adolescent's developmental issues affect transference and countertransference manifestations, defenses against impulses, narcissistic equilibrium, and the emergence of resistance. Such a supervisor might make a similar recommendation to Freud about his treatment of Little Hans, a treatment which could hardly be viewed as encouraging the analysis of prelatency children, as valuable as the material was. The father was "in loco therapist" in any event, and the complexities of the transference were essentially missed. So it may be that, as a consequence of these difficulties, psychoanalysts gradually became convinced that the golden age for analysis of children was latency. The latency child suffered neither the impulsivity and instability of the adolescent, nor the younger child's degree of dependency on the parents and the presumed inability to develop transference.

After analyzing a few latency children, however, the child analyst might well wonder whether "golden" was the right term for the situation with this developmental group. While certainly not all of them are reluctant, resentful, and recalcitrant, examination of their developmental histories often enough reveals signs of earlier difficulties which were either ignored or misunderstood as to their import at the time. It is true that many manifestations of early developmental conflict are transient, but a frequent assumption is that, for example, because a fear or a series of nightmares stops, the underlying disturbance is resolved or gone. When such a child is seen a few years later in latency, it is sometimes possible to understand the earlier transient symptoms as clues to an ongoing problem that produces only episodic indications of its presence. That a symptom is transient at such an early age therefore cannot be taken as conclusive evidence that the disturbance producing it is transient also. Only a thoroughgoing developmental assessment will allow the clinician to see past the surface manifestation and to avoid the too-frequent temporizing conclusion that analysis is too big a treatment for such a little child. To make a generalization, one gets the impression that too frequently only the most disturbed prelatency children, and especially those with the most parent-dystonic behavior, are those for whom analysis is considered. In addition, even in this group there appears a preponderance of children who have suffered a known traumatic experience of some sort, as if such an event in itself will justify analysis, while in the absence of obvious precipitating factors, temporizing methods of management are preferred. The underlying disturbance in such cases, while relatively quiet clinically speaking, may also be relatively durable, fixed, rigid, or long-lasting and have far-reaching effects.

Another factor influencing treatment decisions for very young children is how the child's conflicts and symptoms are conceptualized (R. L. Tyson 1991). Prelatency children rapidly and adeptly externalize, so that the observer quite often will see only a conflict with the environment and often enough perceive the mother as disturbed when actually the child's intrapsychic conflict is responsible. Frequently the child's character pathology will surface in this way, and few or none of the typical symptoms of this time will be seen to persist. Furthermore, the professional's reluctance to initiate analysis so early in life may derive from a conviction that the only analyzable conflicts are those internalized ones which stem from efforts at oedipal resolution, effectively excluding many if not most prelatency children from analytic treatment. It is as if there is no recognition of the presence of a capacity for intrapsychic conflict before the Oedipus complex. The presence and importance of analyzable internalized conflicts of preoedipal and early oedipal origin, and the pathogenic potential of the defenses against them, are often underestimated (P. Tyson 1996). Careful assessment of apparently external conflicts is therefore required if a major therapeutic opportunity is not to be missed.

When there is doubt about the best course of action, these distinctions often can be made with greater certainty in a center in which analytically sophisticated observers work in a preschool setting over a period of time and are available to establish the necessary alliance with the family. For example, the preschools at the Anna Freud Centre and the Cleveland Center for Child Development are well able to assess the optimum treatment approach and less often likely to succumb to such temporizing rationalizations as, "Let's see what happens when he gets into latency" or, "It's only transient, and that is appropriate for this age; I'm sure he'll grow out of it." Observers in such settings are much more aware of the dangers stemming from what the child will grow into, when and if he "grows out of" the current problem. Awareness of such issues is a valuable asset also to the clinician who works without the organizational support, as in private practice or a university or group practice setting. It lends a conviction to the clinician's recommendation for analysis that would otherwise be lacking.

Given the decision that analysis is the treatment of choice, the technical issues in the analysis of the prelatency child need to be reviewed. It has long been clear that the technique of child analysis requires special training and that technical requirements differ for the analysis of children of disparate developmental levels. The prelatency child, however, is short-changed in terms of the proportion of analysts who are trained to treat this group, as I've already mentioned. For example, the course of training in institutes affiliated with the American Psychoanalytic Association requires that a substantial portion of the adult work be completed before work with children and adolescents is begun. The already tired candidate faces the usual requirements for graduation from child training, which are three training cases, one each of latency and adolescence; there is no requirement that the third case be a prelatency child. Whatever the rationale, the results are that fewer training cases are prelatency, perhaps adding to the idea that younger children are harder to get into analysis. Supervisors then have less opportunity to supervise the treatment of prelatency children and, perhaps, also become less familiar with the technical issues.

Every aspect of technique is affected by the developmental characteristics of the prelatency child. The greater use of action and enactment in the younger age group, the lesser use of verbalization, the relative cognitive and intellectual immaturity, the

facile externalization, and the closer bonds to the mother especially, all affect the arrangements to establish the psychoanalytic
situation, the technical adaptations required, the child's ways of
bringing material, and the characteristics of the analytic process. Also, the termination process and the analyst's thinking
about it are affected by signs of the advent of latency and its
unique attendant defenses. The therapeutic results among prelatency children, however, have been noted by many analysts to be
more far-reaching and more quickly obtained than in any other
age group. What may be viewed as incidental benefits include
the unequalled opportunity to learn about and work so directly
with the early developmental processes, and also the pleasurable
experience of analyzing such children as reported by almost all
analysts who have treated them. This of course includes Donald
Winnicott, whose extensive writings on this subject are very well
known (for example, 1958, 1965, 1968, 1971a, 1971b, 1977). It is
something of a mystery, then, why a greater proportion of children in analysis aren't prelatency children. It would seem truly
to be the golden age for a psychoanalysis.

Analysis of the Under-Five Child

From the Analysis of a
Thirty-Three-Month-Old Child

Heiman van Dam, M.D.

In his introduction to Aichhorn's *Wayward Youth* (1955), Freud
stated, "The possibility of exerting analytic influence depends
on quite definite conditions which may be described as the 'analytic situation'; it requires the formation of certain psychic structures and a special attitude toward the analyst. When these factors are lacking, as in the case of children . . . the psychoanalytic
method must be adapted to meet the need."

This paper is intended to outline and illustrate, by way of
a case presentation of the analytic treatment of a thirty-three-
month-old preoedipal child, some of the adaptations necessary
in the psychoanalysis of prelatency children.

THE PRESENCE OF THE PARENT DURING
THE INITIAL ANALYTIC HOURS

For most children, the special attitude toward the analyst is of
a quite different nature from that of the adult neurotic patient
who seeks out the analyst for help. In the case of children, including adolescents, most often it is the parent who seeks help
for the child. In addition, the parent gives the initial history, as
viewed by the parent, because most children, especially during
prelatency, lack the observing function of the ego to the extent
that they cannot yet give a coherent history.

Because of his dependency on the parental figures, the prelatency child usually accepts the decision of a parent to go and

I

"talk and play" with the child analyst. If resistances arise and the prelatency child does not want to keep his appointments, he is overruled. His reactions to being overruled are well established before analysis is begun and will assert themselves in this situation of resistance. For instance, in the case to be described, one can see both passive compliance with the parental wishes and also attempts at controlling and rejecting actively the wishes of the parent.

Nonverbal Communication

As is typical of prelatency children, this child required the presence of the parent in the consultation room. She separated easily and early. H. Schwarz (1950) has described rather well her experiences with the inevitable presence of the parent in the consulting room in the case of small children. Particularly cogent are her recommendations of the needs of the disturbed mother and the need of the analyst to utilize the parent as a translator in the case of a child with a severe speech disorder. Neither of these factors was present in the case to be described, and this contributed greatly to the ease of separating the child from the parent. There can be little argument about the desirability of analyzing the child in the absence of the parent. Certain wishes of an aggressive and libidinal nature are easier to elicit if the parent is not present. Additionally, the very young child and his parent are still involved in issues of separation and individuation. For that reason, the prelatency child's analysis should be even more a private matter than at later phases of life. Sometimes it may take interpretations to separate the child from the parent, especially if the child needs the parent's presence to reassure himself that his thoughts have not harmed or killed the parent. It is clear that no rules can be laid down as to when the child and the parent are ready to separate. Part of the separation process is based on educating both of them as to the desirability of eventually having the child come alone into the consultation room. Also, this process deserves an analytic attitude, which employs empathy and tolerance, because partly it is determined by developmental factors and partly by unconscious conflictual attitudes. Countertransference reactions can lead in both directions: either keeping the parent too long in the sessions or prematurely separating child and parent because of the discomfort in the analyst. There is some reality to the discomfort of the child analyst; namely, the child may be ready for an interpretation while it may be difficult, if not impossible, to predict its effect on the parent. The parent often directs the child's activities in the session or tends to take over, as Schwarz described. The rule of abstinence also applies to child analysis, although in modified form. The presence of the parent can also be looked upon as gratification in the analytic situation, which can be resolved by interpretation.

Nonverbal Communication II

Inasmuch as the prelatency child has a different attitude toward the analyst than his adult counterpart, at least during the opening phase of the analysis, the child may not be communicating with the analyst at all. For instance, the child in the case to be described clung to the mother, averting her gaze from the analyst, and did not engage in any verbal communication. Essentially, under such circumstances, the analyst intrudes on what is going on between the patient and the parent. He tries to understand the often nonverbal behavior and treats it as if it is a piece of communication between patient and analyst, while at all times it is abundantly clear that the child wishes to stay with the parent and ignore the presence of the analyst. The tone of the analyst's voice, as well as how he interprets the child's nonverbal behavior, and the analyst's own nonverbal behavior (does he behave in an intrusive way or respect the child's need to remain close to the parent by keeping his own distance?) all contribute in this instance to whether the child can make the transition from parent to analyst. The predominance of nonverbal over verbal communication in this age group is not surprising. A knowledge of the child's current life situation as well as his history can be of considerable help in decoding the nonverbal behavior. Observations of parents may also help one to understand the nonverbal dialogue. Galenson and her coworkers (5) have studied the parallel development of nonverbal and verbal communication in small children. Most nonverbal communication is not preverbal. Even during adolescence, there is much nonverbal communication. While analyzing his adolescent patient Dora, Freud (1905) observed, "He that has eyes to see and ears to hear may convince himself that no mortal can keep a secret. If his lips are silent, he chatters with his fingertips; betrayal oozes out of him at every pore" (77). Nonverbal communication also occurs during adult analysis. It is more prominent, however, in child analysis and particularly with prelatency children because it is phase appropriate. This need for motoric expression is one of the main reasons that the couch is not used in child analysis. Nor does the child need the couch in order to regress. Unconscious fantasies are more readily available. Modes of communication are part of a developmental process, as was discussed by Edgcumbe (1984) and Novick (1983).

PLAY ACTIVITIES

Children's play can be looked upon as a special instance of nonverbal action type of communication. Verbal elements are added to the child's play as verbalization becomes a more prominent feature in the child's development. Certain games can be accompanied by verbal elements, whereas in other games or in drawings verbalization is experienced as an unwanted intrusion. In volume 42 of the *Psychoanalytic Study of the Child*, a large section is devoted to psychoanalytic views of play. In general, as the verbal element in play becomes more dominant during latency and beyond, play is given up and gradually replaced by fantasy. The adaptation analysis makes in the case of children is to accept the child's play as the precursor of later fantasies and daydreams. This is termed a modification of the classical technique because it is phase specific and not case specific. For instance, one would not expect a prelatency child to stop playing as a result of an accurate interpretation or a successful analysis. Solnit (1987) stresses the integrative problem of play: "Play allows thinking and acting (or behaving) to flow into each other with a looser connection, developmentally and experientially, than non-play thinking and acting usually permit" (218). It is the analyst's nonplay verbalizations that provide the integrative functions. For instance, in the case to be described the child's play with her mother's blouse was integrated verbally with her conflict over sharing her mother, and specifically the nursing mother, with her infant brother. The relief that this understanding and insight brought to the child permitted her to substitute the analyst for the mother in her dyadic quest.

Solnit and others have pointed out the care that must be exerted in the phrasing of interpretations in order not to disturb the activity of the play itself. The analyst would lose a valuable source of information about the child's inner life; but even more important is the special relationship of the ego vis-à-vis the drives in play. As Solnit has pointed out, if the drives overwhelm the ego in play, play ceases to be play and may become a drive discharge. If, on the other hand, the defenses against the drives become too strong, as in the repetitive activities of autistic children, then one is dealing with a symptom.

This in-between area is where play is play; it can lead to mastery not only of reality situations, as in the doctor game, but also of the drives, in the sense of its leading to sublimation and neutralization. How well a child plays is a measure of his health.

Heiman van Dam, M.D./5

What differentiates play from the child's motor action behavior lies precisely in this area of the potential for the neutralization of the drives.

The Parents as a Source of Information

Adult patients reveal their own histories and describe current stressful situations. As mentioned before, the observing function of the ego of the child is still poorly developed. Projection and denial still interfere too much for the child to be a reliable reporter. The child may deny that his school problems still exist, or he may project them onto the teacher. For these reasons, most child analysts maintain contact with the parents. This is particularly true for prelatency children, in whom the distinction between fantasy and reality is not easily maintained. For instance, Donald J. Cohen and his coworkers (1987) report an experimental setting with oedipal children. After three sessions, the therapist could still not determine whether this five-year-old child had an actual sister or whether she was part of a fantasy. The way an interpretation about an actual sibling would be stated is quite different from the way an interpretation of an imaginary one would be stated. The younger the child, the more imperative it is to have outside information, that is, the auxiliary ego function of the parent. It is part of the developmental limitations that each child brings with him into the analytic situation. Sometimes children come to a session very upset. It is clear that something has happened that day. Sometimes it is possible to elicit part or all of what happened from the child. Often the child defends against reciting the painful event. The child's play or drawings may be so distorted by the anxiety or by the arousal of aggression or libido as to no longer belong in that in-between area. Instead, the child throws the building blocks around or scribbles instead of drawing. Involving the parents in the child's analysis as a valuable source of information may create countertransference problems. It may make the child analyst feel that he is not doing real analysis. It may reinvoke dyadic or triadic conflicts in the analyst. From the child's or the parent's point of view, being involved makes a great deal of sense. Parents have contact with the teacher and the pediatrician. With adolescent patients, one may not so clearly need as much contact, depending on the capacity of the patient to meaningfully inform the analyst. Similarly, the pediatrician practicing adolescent medicine has much less contact with the parents. The parallel is drawn because one is dealing with similar developmental considerations.

In the case to be presented, there was active, ongoing contact with the parents, particularly during the phase of the treatment in which the traumatic molestation came to light. It should also be kept in mind that the child does not feel the commitment to tell the analyst everything, and in any case is not capable of doing so.

Case Presentation

Betty, the older of two children, was referred by a colleague when she was thirty-three months old. The mother came for the initial visit. The father was invited to attend and wanted to do so, but the requirements of his work prevented it. Later he was involved in the analysis as it progressed. The mother had terminated her analysis with the referring colleague by the time Betty's treatment began.

The main reason for Betty's referral was her virtually uncontrollable aggression toward her three-month-old brother, David. Whenever she had the chance she tried to hurt the baby by pinching him or putting ice in his ear or on his face; hugs would turn into choking and kissing had to be watched carefully or it might turn into biting, and so forth. This aggressive behavior had begun soon after the baby's arrival home from the hospital. It was beginning to spread, however; for instance, she would knock chairs over, break and throw things, and become more violent with her playmate, Emily. Betty would pull Emily's hair and pinch her constantly, leaving marks on Emily's skin, for which Betty, a very verbal and intelligent child, would apologize readily. It appeared, however, that she could not control herself and would repeat the same behavior shortly afterward. The parents reacted at first by reasoning, demonstrating their anger, or on occasion retaliating for what she was doing to the brother. For instance, on one occasion they put an ice cube on her face to demonstrate what it felt like to David. All these measures were to no avail; on the contrary, her behavior seemed to worsen. For instance, Betty loved to attend a backyard observation group, but recently, according to the mother, she had "knocked the air out" of one of the other children. She also had begun to bite and kick her mother, who was very skilled, could be quite firm, and seemed to know how to set limits. Additionally, since the birth of the baby Betty had regressed in that she had taken to sucking a pacifier, which she had never done before. During the mother's seven-day stay in the hospital in connection with the birth of David and a tubal ligation, Betty was taken care of by the mother's fraternal twin sister (they do not look alike at all), Aunt Florence, who was far more strict than Betty's mother. A refusal to eat resulted, as well as a refusal to take her bath after the aunt had apparently accidentally dunked her in the tub water. An identification with the aggressor occurred; she addressed her playmates, especially Emily, in an angry voice using the aunt's language: "You may not do this!" She was overheard to imitate the aunt telling one of her dolls: "Nobody loves you, I am going to beat your butt." In general the mother observed, during the additional two weeks that the aunt stayed after the mother's return home, that Betty constantly "locked horns," to use the mother's words, with Florence. The aunt was a firm believer in letting the child cry it out. On occasion, Florence as well as the paternal grandmother would spank the patient, which the parents had avoided doing because of the already manifest aggression in the child and the readiness to identify with the aggressor. Betty now asked the parents to spank her. Her eating suffered from periodic food refusals. Aside from the aggressive outbursts, Betty did very well in the school situation. Intellectually she was well ahead of all the other children. She had a very extensive vocabulary and spoke clearly. At home, her parents enjoyed stimulating her intellectual capacities. For instance, she was able to play certain board games—Candy Land and Mr. Wiggly, games usually associated with latency children—and follow the rules.

Past and Developmental History

Betty's history contains a number of significant developments. During the pregnancy, the mother, then thirty-seven years old, had noted a relative lack of fetal movements, which made her worry that her child, like one of her nephews who had died as a result, would have Sudden Infant Death Syndrome, or SIDS, also known as crib death. During the last trimester, the mother suffered from preeclampsia. Following the birth, the mother's concerns about Betty's breathing increased to the point that the pediatrician reluctantly agreed to treat Betty as if she had SIDS, by putting her on a monitor at one week of age. Soon, however, the mother's worst suspicions were confirmed, and Betty did develop episodes of apnea and bradycardia. Many of them were life threatening, requiring CPR or vigorous stimulation of the heart area, mainly by the mother. Betty slept in her crib in the bedroom with the mother. In an effort that was doomed to fail, namely, to protect the father's functioning, he would often not sleep in the bedroom because the monitor might go off frequently at night and often did. This situation lasted until Betty was one year old. The mother estimates that she performed CPR on her child between fifty and one hundred times during that year. Sleeping became difficult under these circumstances. Betty would go to sleep twirling the mother's hair, her own hair, or the lead wires coming from the monitor. All these began to assume the status of transitional objects for the child. At the age of three months, her SIDS condition became serious enough that she was referred to the neonatal respiratory division of a children's hospital, where she was considered to be one of their more severe cases. She was frequently seen there on an outpatient basis, while a number of tests were performed on her. Her medical condition gradually improved to the point that she was able to sleep in her own room soon after her first birthday, except when she had transient illnesses like tonsillitis. Any such illness would exacerbate her condition. Essentially from age two on, she outgrew the condition. Medical tests revealed that there was no brain damage. She was breast-fed partly to give her an increased immunity until she was about two years old. It was discontinued on the advice of the obstetrician because the mother was pregnant with David. Soon Betty was told of the pregnancy. She told the parents to send the baby back because she feared that the baby would get into her toys and take up all her mother's time. She was not a thumbsucker but began to use a pacifier after the birth of David. Her eating pattern was erratic and she refused many foods; she was still using bottles.

When she was one year old, on the advice of the grandmother, her toilet training was begun, but she showed no interest. At eighteen months she wanted to wear panties instead of diapers. Encouraged by this, the parents bought a potty chair. Betty put her dolls on the potty chair but did not use it herself. On her second birthday she refused to wear any more diapers, announcing that she would not poopoo or peepee in her diaper any more. She was dry in the daytime and used the potty chair also for bowel movements, though she still wet at night. However, she has awakened at night screaming to be taken to the bathroom, and also she recently has demanded to use the adult toilet.

Three months before she was first seen, when Betty was two years, six months, David was born. The interaction between Betty and her Aunt Florence has already been described. When the parents brought David home, there was a gift for Betty from the new sibling. It was a doll, which she named Debby after a seventy-year-old friend of the family she adores. But she refused to play with Debby, at least until the analysis began. In return, she offered David the one animal toy which she herself had received as a gift from Aunt Florence. She helped the parents dress and bathe her little brother and asked on occasion where her own penis was. The mother told her that boys have a penis and girls have a clitoris and that the clitoris is on the inside, whereas the penis is on the outside. There was occasional manual masturbation. There were no questions about the pregnancy. It turned out that David also had SID syndrome, also in a severe form, creating tremendous stresses for the entire family. Once again, in order to protect the father's daytime functioning, he slept in the same room as Betty. David was attached to a monitor and the mother slept in the parental bedroom. The family went from one potentially fatal crisis to the next, this time in front of Betty, diminishing their capacity to function in a protective way for Betty whenever these crises with the new baby occurred. As a matter of fact, Betty became a participant in rescuing David by watching over him, witnessing the apnea and bradycardia and alerting the parents at times. Betty then became also a sibling of a handicapped child, in the manner so well described by H. Kennedy (6). Many of the findings described in that paper were applicable to this patient. It is not surprising under these circumstances that problems in the area of aggressive drive develop when questions of life and death are a daily quandary. The parents' constant turmoil forced them to seek marital counseling several months before they consulted me about Betty. To relieve the mother and Betty, several times a week Betty would spend part of the day in the home of a sitter named Ursula. Once I had the opportunity to observe what these CPR episodes did to the mother. On the way to my office one day, the baby had gone into a respiratory crisis. The mother pulled the car over to the side and administered CPR while irate commuters honked their horns because she was illegally parked. By the time they got to my office, the mother was ashen gray with fright.

At the end of my interview with the mother, I asked her what she thought would make sense to Betty as far as her coming to my office was concerned. It was decided that she would be told that I would try to help her with her troubles with David and that I had a lot of toys we would play with. Also I anticipated with the mother that the child would not separate from the mother, and that most likely the mother would not be able to stay in the waiting room. I instructed the mother that whatever behavior Betty would show would be useful information to me for my overall evaluation. Especially, I suggested to the mother that she did not need to prompt or direct Betty during the session — the less intrusive the mother was, the better I could study the child.

A few minutes before the appointed time, mother and patient showed up in my waiting room. As anticipated, they both entered the consultation room. Betty was a pretty child, neatly dressed and physically well developed in spite of the medical ordeal in her background. She was totally silent and turned her back toward me, while seated on her mother's lap, digging herself into her mother's chest. The mother, remembering my instructions, remained totally silent. Standing near her, I broke the brief silence by saying, "Hi, I guess you are Betty and I am Dr. van Dam." The child then dug herself deeper into her mother, with her head down into her mother's breasts. I proceeded by telling her that I guessed mother had told her a little bit about me. To my pleasant surprise, she definitely nodded. Perhaps, I continued, she could tell me what she remembered. Obviously, she was not ready to do that, as she resumed digging into the mother. I decided to move a little bit farther away from her, and I sat down behind my desk and said, "I guess mother told you that you and I would talk and play with my toys. My toys are over there, and when you feel a little bit less scared of me, you can go over there and play with the toys." There was little response to this from the child. So after a brief pause I continued, "I don't know what you are scared about, but I think mother probably told you that I only talk and play with children." Now her response expressed ambivalence. She would alternately look and smile at me or dig herself back into the mother. Encouraged, I decided to tell her that I did not know what kind of toys she liked to play with, but that I had dolls, blocks, soldiers, pencils, and crayons. By her nodding it became clear that she was interested in the crayons. So I put them on the floor about halfway between the silent mother and myself while I retreated again behind my desk. Then by accident, my telephone rang twice. She whispered something that I could not understand. When I could not get her to repeat it, I obtained her permission to have her mother say it out loud for her. She had asked a question, namely, Would it ring again? And she volunteered that her brother was home with nanny. With surprise in my voice I said, "Oh, you have a brother, tell me about him." She nodded affirmatively and told me his name is David. When I asked her to tell me more about David, she responded by trying to unbutton mother's blouse. When she succeeded, the mother told her to stop it. In response to the prohibition, she not only rebuttoned the blouse but went one step further, namely, she buttoned the top button, which before had been unfastened. This led to my first interpretation, because I saw in the action her wish for the mother's breasts, alternating with a wish that inasmuch as mother said no to her, the blouse should also be closed off to David. To me, it was reminiscent of Freud's observations on his grandchild with the spool. I told her that sometimes children didn't like it when the baby brother gets fed by the mommy and they don't. She nodded in agreement, got down from the mother's lap and began to work with the crayons. She appropriately corrected me that these were not crayons but colored pencils. She complained that some of them did not work. So I sharpened them for her, explaining that I was here to help her not only with the pencils, but with many other things as well, like her feelings and thoughts about her brother, her mother, and her nana. She nodded in agreement and became curious about the eraser at the end of the pencil. She asked, "What is that?" I told her that I could tell she was very smart and I thought she knew what it was. She said, "No," so I demonstrated to her that it erases. This led to a game in which she made scribbles and I had to erase them. She asked if she could take off her shoes. I told her of course she could, that she could do almost anything here that she likes, not everything, but almost everything, and that I will tell her if necessary what she cannot do here; but of course she can say everything.

At that point the mother, realizing the child had made the transition, spoke up and said that she needed to put money in the parking meter and that she would be back soon and wait for Betty in the other room. The child said it was okay, and the mother looked at me with an *Is it really okay?* look. I said it was fine, and with that the mother left the consultation room—but not for good. The child immediately went to the toy section. There was no more silence or shy whispering; instead she spoke with her usual clarity. The rest of the session consisted of exploring the many choices of toys. She had a special interest in my finger puppets and my guns, less so in a baby doll and some Disney figurines. At one point she handed me a giraffe puppet and called it a cow, confusing the horn configuration of its head with nipples. I was ordered to address her via the cow, which I did, namely, to point out her interest in guns and that the cow thought it had to do with angry feelings. A few times she asked if her mother would be back. I assured her that her mother would, but that "sometimes children don't believe me. The reason is that children sometimes feel they are bad because they are so angry at the baby that they think mother doesn't love them anymore and will bring them and leave them here. That's why they sometimes stay on their mother's lap in the beginning, but of course mommies never leave their children here." As a result she played very well until the end of the hour. At that point I invited the mother in so they both could leave through the usual exit door. When the mother reentered, Betty resumed her whisper and announced the other side of her anxiety over her mother's going to the parking meter. She whispered that she was going to stay with me and that mother should go home without her. I explained that I wouldn't have time to see her until tomorrow. She protested and wanted to come back that afternoon but settled for tomorrow; she wanted to take Mickey Mouse home with her. I told her that if she couldn't be with me, then she wanted something from me with her, and that's why she wanted to take Mickey home with her. I said, "What you can take home are the things we talked about together. It's better that the toys stay here because other children come here and tell me their troubles too, while they play with Mickey and the other toys. Tomorrow I will be here and so will all the toys." With that I stretched my hand out open. Instead of handing me the toy, she put it reluctantly on the couch and left with a very happy mother.

My first impressions were that she had understood the preparation for the session she had received from the mother and that she had responded rather well. In addition, I began to see a hint of her bossiness and stubbornness in the way she ordered me to speak via the cow-giraffe. I also noticed a neatness beyond her years in the way she replaced the toys on the shelves. Her ambivalence was obvious, as was other evidence of internalized conflict. I felt that it was important to separate mother and child during treatment sessions as soon as practicable for the sake of the unfolding of the therapeutic process to afford the child separation and privacy from the parent and to foster her ability to reveal herself with more ease. It is not always possible to assess how an interpretation, aimed at the child, is received and tolerated or understood by the parent. In this instance, one of the parents had been in analysis and both were in marital counseling, which I believed gave me a somewhat wider latitude in regard to making interpretations in the presence of parental figures.

During the afternoon, the mother telephoned asking my opinion about bringing the baby along. Figuring that I might learn something, I said I could see no problem with it, that hopefully Betty would separate well and if not, all three could be in the consultation room. I complimented the mother for her role during the first session and said we would continue in the same way.

The next day the mother had her hands full with a rather fretful baby and dropped Betty off at my office. She explained that Betty brought with her the doll David gave her when he was born. Betty repeated that David gave her the doll when he was in the hospital. I inquired if David was ill. She said no, he was just born there. Just as at home, she did not play with Debby. Instead, she put her in the chair mother had occupied the day before. She then proceeded to the toy section and was upset with me that the giraffe-cow was on the wrong shelf. She put it back on the shelf it had been on the day before. I commented that I guessed that at home, too, she has to put things back in the same place she got them from. She nodded affirmatively, and we played some more with the puppets. Hers and mine rub faces and say, "Hi!" to each other, but she cannot take it beyond that partly because she was not feeling well—she had a cold and her father had given her medicine. She denied that her brother was sick too, although it had appeared to me that way. She spent more time drawing scribbles and what appeared to be a face. Perhaps the most important part of this interaction for her was the sharpening of many of the pencils; the fact that "they don't work" enabled me to point out to her that there are many times when things don't work, and maybe she could tell me about some, besides my pencils. Betty was not ready to do that, however. As she left with the mother and brother at the end of the second session, the mother drew my attention to a belt that the doll Debby was wearing. It was the strap from the monitor the patient had used during her infancy. The mother's comment added conviction to my impression that Betty was trying to convey to me her concerns about illness in herself and her brother, although it was still strongly defended against by denial. In this session, I had commented on the fact that she did bring Debby, but she didn't play with her, perhaps because she was still too angry with her brother. Denial also was used to deal with her ambivalence about leaving me at the end of her second session, evidenced by her flatly stating that our time was not up yet; I interpreted her wish in that denial, and she left relatively easily after that.

After the hour the mother telephoned again to express her concerns about Betty's lying. She had told the mother that she and I had played Candy Land, but the mother knew that I did not have board games in my office. Also she lied, according to the mother, about going to the bathroom. There had been another episode of throwing things, followed by her telling the mother, "Mommy, don't get mad, use your words." Obviously, she had been admonished in the same way when she was throwing things. In addition, she told the mother that her doll Debby needed to wear the belt so it could breathe. Upon my asking, I learned from the mother that Betty sometimes is able to tell her mother that she is afraid to go to sleep because she fears she won't be able to breathe. Recently, she had awakened in the middle of the night screaming. What the content of the nightmare was could not be ascertained.

The next session gave me an opportunity to make an interpretation using information the mother gave me. It began with the mother's announcement that Betty had just wet her panties on the elevator, and that Betty wanted me to fix my elevator. The patient then entered the consultation room willingly, bringing Debby with her. I had observed that both the doll and her brother wore monitor belts and mentioned this fact to her. She told me that her brother had been in the hospital, which was not factual. I commented that sometimes she wished it because she was still so mad about having a brother. She responded that she, her mother, and brother had just come from the hospital, but when I went along with her fantasy she could not elaborate. I then repeated the previous interpretation, "I bet you wished he would go to the hospital and stay there." She nodded affirmatively and told me that her brother gave her Debby when he came home from the hospital. I said that it was very smart of David to give her a doll, because so many girls don't like to have a little brother, so much so that looking at the doll makes them mad and sad all over again, and then they don't feel like playing with the doll. In response she wiggled her shoulders, smiled, and kissed the doll. In this session as in the first one with the button episode, it is sometimes necessary to interpret the language of the action, typically for a prelatency child. Betty's responses are often nonverbal: nodding, wiggling, smiling, or further nonverbal play activity, such as kissing the doll. She played in this nonverbal way with the doll for the rest of the hour; she would hug and kiss it, lie on top of it, drag it off the couch, or change its diapers. Throughout the analysis it was difficult to establish whether she was reenacting her own experiences with CPR or those of her brother or both, because of the relative paucity of verbalization, appropriate for her phase of development. In this particular hour she was at least partly identified with the doll, because she told me that Debby wears the belt on her tummy, whereas she had worn it on her "tiddies." Another nonverbal communication which I interpreted was the episode of the wetting of her panties told to me by the mother. I decided to ignore for the time being its connection to the nonworking elevator or to the colored pencils that needed sharpening in the previous hour; instead I limited the interpretation to her verbal communication of the nonfunctioning brother-in-the-hospital fantasy, namely, her wish to be alone again with the mother just as she was long ago when she still wet herself. Her response was again affirmative nodding. Daytime wetting was unusual for this girl by now, in contrast to nighttime wetting.

After this third session with Betty, I felt it was now time to see the parents, to tell them of my impressions and how I would like to proceed, as well as to learn more about the child, in particular from the father, whom I had not yet met. The parents readily agreed to have me analyze their child. I explained the process and complimented both the mother and child for what had been accomplished so far. However, Betty's symptoms were getting worse; her fear of sleeping caused her to stay awake and out of bed till 10:30 or 11:00 P.M., offering one excuse after the other, particularly claiming she had to go to the bathroom. Also, she would not go to bed if there were wrinkles in her sheets. Her eating had diminished, and she had lost six pounds. In order to get some food into the child, she was allowed to have as many bottles of milk as she wanted. At the time of this session with the parents, they were trying to wean her from the bottles back to table food by bribing her with the promise of rewards. Finally, she had almost managed to turn David's stroller over, with him in it. When he cried she told her parents, "I didn't do it."

The next session began with mother announcing proudly that Betty had given up all her bottles and eaten a breakfast. After the session they would go to the toy store to select her reward. Betty seemed whiney and clung to her mother, obviously competing with David, who badly needed to be nursed. In the waiting room, I interpreted to Betty how hard it is when mother has no time for her, when she is busy feeding David, and that she wants to be with mother too, rather than come and talk and play with me. This fell on deaf ears, except that she pretended to be crying, without tears. At my suggestion, all three came into the consulting room. Once seated there, the mother spoke up, and once again told Betty that she had to go and put money in the parking meter. If she did not put money in the meter, the police would give her a ticket. Then there would not be any money left for buying the toy in the toy store. Betty became upset, wanting mother to stay. Finally, she let her mother go when the mother left her purse in the consultation room as proof that she would return. In the meantime she was trying to "touch" the brother's face, an aggressively driven activity which had to be stopped by the mother because she saw what it was leading up to. Before the mother left, Betty and her mother changed the nightgown on Debby, under my watchful eye. Suddenly Betty yelled at me, "Get out of my way!" It was a clear identification with the frustrating anxious mother when she is engaged in CPR with David. I interpreted to her how bad she must feel when mommy is busy with David when he is sick. She nodded and proceeded to nurse Debby in the identical posture that mother uses when nursing David. (I had not seen mother nursing David, but the mother had told me about her style of nursing and how Betty had adopted it in her play.) She ordered me to get her a pillow. At this point the mother and David left the room, which was very well tolerated by the patient. I then interpreted to her her wish to be "drinking milk from mommy's tiddies again, just like you used to before David was born, and that's why you do not want to eat your food, because you were so much happier then."

The next day it was again difficult for Betty to separate from mother, who brought David as usual. This time she had her unfinished breakfast of Cheerios and a bottle of milk with her. Mother explained to me that the doll Debby had been hurt. Betty had thrown her against a door. The reason was that my patient had been sent to her room for wanting to hit her brother. After some threats from her mother, Betty kissed David and then came with me. I told her that I could see from her kissing how much she loved David, but that at other times she gets very mad at him and wished she could throw him away like she had done with her doll, "but of course you can't do that and wouldn't do that because you love him also." In response she was able to tell me that Ursula, her baby-sitter, had come to the house and had held David on her lap, and not her. I agreed that she must have been mad at Ursula and David both, and if she could throw David away she would have mommy, daddy, and Ursula all for herself. Her response was to play with her doll, undressing her, bathing her, spanking her for making a poop, spanking her for not making a poop while sitting on the toilet (my couch served as toilet). When she decided to dress the doll again, she made me do the buttons, to which I readily agreed, stating that doing buttons is very hard when you are little. This she angrily denied and began to unbutton her own clothes. She made it clear that she wanted me to give her a bath. I suggested that I give the doll a bath, because "it is better not to take your clothes off here. We can just pretend, or give the dolls a bath." She accepted the limit setting fairly well and let me bathe the doll. It did not occur to me then to ask her if she ever played with anyone where they did take their clothes off. However, when I announced the end of the hour she protested that we had not played with the building blocks yet, and so on. Also she had to "read" three books to the doll before it could go to sleep, and so on. I pointed out it was as hard to leave me as it was at night to leave her mother when it was bedtime. By this time, it was well past the fifty minutes, so I brought the mother and David in. When she refused to leave in spite of my assurances I would play with her again tomorrow, the mother threatened to leave without her. She decided to go with the real mother, rather than stay with the idealized mother of the transference. She left in tears.

Obviously, many more details could be given. Suffice it to say that the problems of the dyadic relationship to mother and also father continued in the transference, as well as in her behavior outside the analytic situation. This is not surprising, not only because of the phase of development this patient is in. It should also be recalled that Betty was breast-fed, and frequently, for two years; as for so many youngsters who are nursed that long, for Betty the mother and her breasts became transitional objects and breast-feeding itself, perhaps, a transitional phenomenon. She even developed a fantasy that Ursula, her sitter, was going to have a baby; from the mother I learned that Ursula was sixty years old. Her death wishes toward David reached a point that she would pull electric cords out of the wall sockets, including the electric cord of the brother's monitor. In the sessions with me the wish to regain the earlier relationship with the mother was reenacted as well. For a while she would drink only from bottles and stay up till all hours fearful of going to sleep and competing for parental attention; in her sessions she would yell at me as her distressed parents did at her on occasion, or she and I would engage in nursing and bathing scenes with several of her dolls. What toys to bring to her sessions would become as much of a ritual as her bedtime routine or the endings of her hours with me.

By the end of the first month of analysis, enough of the dyadic conflicts had been worked through that triadic material started to emerge. It began with a game in which we were making cheese; it was followed by a doctor game, and then a report from the mother that she pulled her panties down in order to masturbate at home. It culminated in a game in which she and I went to bed on make-believe beds on the floor. Castration material emerged as well. When it was time for me to prepare her for my vacation, she readily accepted it by announcing that she was coming along.

With the shift to oedipal triadic interests her relationship to her brother improved. The bedtime situation, however, at best remained unchanged. It should be kept in mind that the father slept in her room. In the transference I was either the father or her. The flow of the material occasionally would be interrupted by external events, especially episodes of the brother's apnea, which then would become the subject of the session. It led to her fantasy that she had put coffee in his milk bottle, which made him so sick. It became clear that one reason for her bedtime difficulties had to do with her fear and wish to see if David would stop breathing. When that was interpreted to her, Betty responded with, "I know that." I became the brother on the monitor, and my fate was in her hands. Sometimes she would come and fix the monitor; at other times she would pull the plug on me. It also became evident that she confused the words "monitor" and "monster." It is the monitor in her that can kill.

As the medical situation at home began to improve temporarily, the triadic material reemerged. It was the mother now who appeared as the monster in the triadic situation, and oral sadistic fantasies about the primal scene emerged.

In a session toward the end of the second month, I suddenly had to sneeze. Although I had covered my mouth, she yelled out, "Cover your damn mouth!" With it her facial expression changed radically. It became distorted in an extremely angry fashion that I had not seen in her before. I told her that was probably what her mommy and daddy said to her if she sneezed near the baby. She nodded, and once again we played monitor. I was the sick baby and she refused to fix the beeper, as she told me, "I'm sick of it; go ahead and die." From there her comments included that I had "ruined her damn sandwich," and she called me a "turkey" or a "damn buzzard," and sent me to my "damn room," and so on. The rest of the session we returned to her oedipal fantasies—"By eating the wedding ring you make babies," as she protruded her abdomen. I connected it to her refusal to eat foods. In the next session her swearing returned; this time it was about "the damn fucken room." With it, she displayed again such an angry sadistic face that it made me wonder what experience or fantasy was being (re)enacted. For the first time in the three months she had been in analysis, she had to go peepee during a session. That night she wet her bed and was awake at least ten times. Since she had used the swear words in front of her mother, I felt free to discuss it with the parents in their next session. I learned she was using the same language with the same affect at home as she was using with me; the parents were as much at a loss to explain it and the sudden upsurge of her anxiety as I was. Further, her behavior had regressed again in most areas: refusal to eat solids again, physical abuse of her brother and her playmate Emily, regression in toilet training, and hitting the baby-sitter, Ursula. Her relationship with her father, however, was improving, as was her ability to go to bed at night.

In the subsequent sessions her language and emotions continued as before; she called me a "pisser," a "fat shit," and so on. She threatened to cut my belly open if I didn't take a pee. The same was by now going on at home. In the grocery store she addressed a woman shopper as "you goddamn dirty bitch." The parents had become very alarmed over her behavior and language; it became more and more evident to them and to me that she learned this language at the sitter's house, where Ursula also took care of her twelve-year-old granddaughter. This girl had boys come over and occasionally substituted for Ursula in taking care of Betty. It appears that this girl and her boyfriend made her undress, tickled her abdomen, and may have forced her to urinate by frightening her with their language. This episode never was fully worked out to my complete satisfaction. Gradually, as it could be reconstructed, her language and behavior returned to a more normal pattern: her eating, temper, and ability to play with peers were much improved again. The material in the sessions resumed where it had left off before this episode. She told me a fantasy, namely, that when she was thirteen she was a boy. She went to a doctor who cut her private parts so that she became a girl.

At this point, five months into the analysis, the father lost his job. It was agreed to decrease the frequency of the sessions from five to two a week for the time being. Betty reacted to the reduced frequency with anger toward me, accusing me of not wanting to play with her. I interpreted it, on the basis of previous material, as feeling to her as punishment over her pleasure of sleeping with daddy because David was so sick. I assured her that the reason she was coming less often was because she was doing so much better. Her response was a game in which she was ill and there was a baby in her tummy. We telephoned the pediatrician on a play phone; she preferred that he come over, and then the baby came out of the belly button. In the next hour she was able to tell me about her brother's latest episode with breathing and that the parents had taken him to the hospital. From there her thoughts wandered to starving children in Africa dying and that she was giving her money to these children. I told her that she also worried about David and herself dying. She readily acknowledged this and talked about a time when she was a boy and ate playdough. Her mother had spanked her for it. I linked her fear of dying with her sense of guilt, especially about her anger. At home she had been afraid of flies and other insects biting and killing her. This had receded and was replaced in the transference by the idea that a fly would come in my office and bite and kill her. I linked it to her guilt over her death wishes toward her brother. Her response was, "I don't like David."

A few days later the father phoned me to say that he had found work in another city and that there would be only one more session. I pointed out it was too quick for Betty. He was obviously quite upset and needed to be firm. In the last session I told Betty that we wouldn't see each other anymore because she was moving away, but that I thought she had learned a lot and that I was sure she would be all right. She responded by drawing me her phone number and asked me to give her mine, which I did. In addition, I gave her a farewell gift, a musical doll. She told me that she was going to sleep with it.

SUMMARY

This case demonstrates the modifications necessary for the analysis of a prelatency child. The child analyst interprets the play, the behavior, and the verbalizations of the child, as if they are communications; free association and the commitment to reveal everything are compromised. The couch is not used because of the child's need for motor expression. Also the defensive organization in the child is sufficiently fluid so that regression can occur in the presence of the equidistant attitude of the child's analyst.

The child still relies on external auxiliary controls to maintain a balance between the various forces operating in his psychic apparatus. The tolerant atmosphere of the child analytic situation suffices to induce controlled regression. The role of the parent during the initial and later phases of the analysis is discussed.

Heiman van Dam, M.D./27

Discussion of van Dam Presentation

Calvin F. Settlage, M.D.

Dr. van Dam presents us with a beautiful and enviable example of child analysis in the case of Betty, a thirty-three-month old girl with the very unusual development history of having had Sudden Infant Death Syndrome. There is much that one would like to explore further in this fascinating case, but what it invites in particular is consideration of the application of the analytic method to the preoedipal-age child. With Betty as the case illustration, my discussion will include (1) some observations on the analysis of the preoedipal-age child, and (2) some comments on the pathogenesis and resolution of the patient's problem of "virtually uncontrollable aggression." I will explore the concept of preoedipal structure formation through therapeutic and developmental process in the analytic situation, as exemplified by object and self constancy.

ANALYSIS OF THE PREOEDIPAL-AGE CHILD

McDevitt (1979) postulates that "the formation of sufficient psychic structure following the resolution of the rapprochement crisis . . . makes analysis possible during the fourth subphase of separation-individuation" (338–39). "If the child is fortunate, identifications will help him to resolve the ambivalence and conflicts of the rapprochement crisis and to begin to attain object and self constancy" (340). This structuring "partly explains why reconstruction based on analytic (primarily verbal) data cannot, as a rule, go further back than the rapprochement subphase"

(339). He also notes that the formation of psychic structure at this time may be expressed by neurotic symptoms and defenses (338).

I understand McDevitt to say that internalization and structure formation, by about twenty-four months of age, include sufficient structuring of the ego and precursors of the superego, and the separately defined representations of self and other, to allow the child to participate in the analysis of intrapsychic conflict. I would add, though, that the young child's analytic capability is supplemented, and structure is further developed, in the interaction with the analyst as an external auxiliary ego and a developmental object.

Betty's analysis began when she was thirty-three months old and ended when she was thirty-eight months old. Agewise and also in her generally good ego and cognitive development she met the structural criteria for analyzability.

Both psychosexual theory and separation-individuation theory see the child as being ready, biologically and psychologically, to enter the oedipal stage at about three years of age. Betty's age during the analysis thus also meant that her analysis, and her development, straddled the move from the preoedipal to the oedipal stage. Because an analysis begun after age two will usually continue beyond age three, this is the usual condition in the analysis of preoedipal-age children.

Because preoedipal and oedipal issues can be represented in the same or closely intertwined analytic material, interpretation often involves judgment as to whether the issue of one or the other developmental level is more in focus in a given hour. This is illustrated by Dr. van Dam's interpreting Betty's wetting her panties in the elevator as expressing the dyadic stage wish to be alone again with her mother, rather than interpreting the triadic castration concerns represented by the patient's references to the nonworking elevator and the pencils that needed sharpening, of the previous hour. Another illustration is the interpretation made when Betty reacted angrily to the decrease in sessions from four to two a week and accused the analyst of not wanting to play with her. Although the reduction in sessions posed the threat and the actuality of separation and loss of relationship, Dr. van Dam interpreted her reaction to the reduction at the oedipal level: it felt to her like punishment for her pleasure of sleeping with daddy because David was so sick.

Dyadic stage conflicts reflect unresolved issues as they are conceptualized by psychosexual and separation-individuation theory. Psychosexual examples in Betty's case are the continuance of breast-feeding to age two years, the breast becoming a transitional object; and the oral sadistic fantasies about the primal scene. Separation-individuation examples are the rapprochement phase issue of autonomy versus helplessness which Dr. van Dam so sensitively respected in his technique; and the problem of regulation of aggression, which is first addressed frontally in the disciplinary interactions and the fear of loss associated with the heightened separation anxiety of the anal stage/rapprochement subphase (Mahler 1972; Settlage 1980, 1988). Commonly, separation-individuation and psychosexual conflicts are interrelated (Settlage 1971). For example, the primal scene experience includes both loss-separation and sexual-aggressive fantasies and anxieties.

Dr. van Dam makes it clear that he and his young patient were addressing internalized conflict: "Her ambivalence was obvious, as was other evidence of internalized conflict." Because he is addressing internalized conflict, Dr. van Dam's focus is on the child and on the past experience of the child as revealed in the analysis, not on the current interaction between the mother and the child. He therefore seeks to work with the child separated from the mother and to interpret the transference in the usual analytic model.

At the same time, there is the question of how well internalized and structured Betty's conflicts were, and how much they also were still interpersonal. At the developmental level in question, internalization and preoedipal structure formation are still in process as the necessary preliminary to adequate structuring during the oedipal stage (Settlage 1980, 158). In addition, it is to be expected that Betty's uncontrolled aggression would seriously interfere with the amalgamation and integration of maternal and paternal images into well-structured object constancy (see below). Conversely, her symptomatic behavior would reflect the pathology of these preoedipal structures (Settlage 1980, 157–58; 1988). To the extent that Betty's internal conflict was not firmly structured and was still being shaped pathogenetically in the child-parent interaction, would it also be indicated to address the interpersonal conflict by involving the mother in the treatment?

I think further that psychic conflict, at this age, involves the defense of denial as well as repression. At times the very young child's affirmative response to interpretation suggests that the conflict was not firmly repressed and unconscious but more within preconscious awareness, with a part of the conflict being warded off through splitting and denial. An apparent example is Betty's response, "I know that," to the interpretation that her fear of sleeping was due to her wish/fear that David would stop breathing. This perspective suggests that repression, made more effective by rapidly accruing ego development, has a greater play and is the central defense in the resolution of the oedipal conflict and the pathogenesis of more strictly neurotic conflict.

Also related to the preoedipal and early oedipal level of development is the rather transparent nature of the patient's symbolic representations and the forthrightness of Dr. van Dam's interpretive technique. For example, in response to the analyst's asking Betty to tell him more about her brother, David, she unbuttons her mother's blouse and in response to mother's disapproval rebuttons it one button higher than before. Dr. van Dam interpreted this nonverbal "language of action" as expressing Betty's double-edged wish for access to her mother's breasts and for them to be closed off to David. As a second example (I condense), the first part of a treatment session involves Betty's clinging to mother in competing with David, who badly needs to be nursed. It is interpreted that she feels bad when mommy is busy with David. Betty then proceeds to nurse her doll Debby in the identical posture mother assumes when nursing David. Dr. van Dam interprets that Betty wishes to be drinking milk from mommy's tiddies again, just as she did before David was born.

From my own experience in the analysis of preoedipal-age children, it is my sense that their symbolic representation and associative processes tend to be quite literal and not very disguised. For example, a three-year-old girl took one look at a plant in my office, a vine climbing up a stick, and excitedly declared, "Jack and the Beanstalk!" Another three-year-old girl represented her vagina by various slotlike openings, including the mouth of the TV puppet Cookie Monster. I think it is this directness of representation and association that accounts for a good deal of the pleasure we experience in working with very young children. Their symbolism is easy to read, and it gives refreshing confirmation to Freud's discoveries in the realm of infantile sexuality.

I understand this age-characteristic functioning to reflect (a) the still limited capability for abstraction, (b) the relatively simple, uncomplicated defensive capability and personality organization, and (c) the openness and permeability of the developing psychic structure. In addition, the preoedipal-age child is much involved in the categorization and organization of experience. A prototype for categorization and organization generally could be the formation of object and self constancy. Their structuring is conceived to proceed from affectively determined, separate, good and bad categorizations of object and self representations to the amalgamation or organization of these categories into a single, but two-faceted, unified representation of the object and the self.

As Dr. van Dam so sensitively demonstrated, our technique must respect the child's sense of autonomy and fear of emotionally disturbing intrusion, and the related tolerance for interpretation-aroused feelings and fantasies. This principle applies not only to the preoedipal-age child, in whom internal boundary formation and defensive function are developmentally not yet firm and easily breached. Particularly in the case of preoedipal pathology, it applies in child and adolescent analysis generally and in adult analysis as well (Settlage 1979, 824–27). Within these constraints, though, it seems that the postulated characteristics of the preoedipal-age child may require less of the usual preliminary exploration and the defense analysis technique of carefully peeling back one defensive layer after another.

THE PROBLEM OF UNCONTROLLABLE AGGRESSION

With regard to Betty's "virtually uncontrollable aggression," Dr. van Dam observes that it is not surprising that problems develop in the area of the aggressive drive when questions of life and death are a daily quandary. The mother's preeclampsia during the last trimester of the pregnancy and the occurrence of the Sudden Infant Death Syndrome (SIDS) with its repeated episodes of apnea and bradycardia in both the patient and her three-month-old brother indeed created unusually stressful internal and environmental conditions for the fetus and the developing child. The concepts of organismic distress and annihilation anxiety immediately come to mind.

The variables in the pathogenesis can be conceived to include (1) an excess of infantile aggression reactive to the impact of the Sudden Infant Death Syndrome and the necessarily intrusive, resuscitative interventions of the mother; (2) the mother and child's inability to achieve an adequate mutual regulation of the child's aggression; (3) such inability's overwhelming of the rudimentary ego in the early phases of its development; and (4) the later interference of the hyperaggression with the formation and integration of the object and self constancy structures.

As background for the discussion of these variables, I offer the following review of the theory of the development of object and self constancy, largely excerpted from Settlage 1988. As initially conceived, object constancy meant simply that the parent has become represented in a lasting way in the child's psychic structure (Hartmann 1952, 15). The concept subsequently has undergone increasing elaboration (A. Freud 1965, 64–68; Mahler and Furer 1968, 222–25; Fraiberg 1969) to reach a detailed delineation on the basis of the understanding provided by clinical work (Kernberg 1966; Settlage 1977) and direct observational research on early development (Mahler, Pine, and Bergman 1975).

Object and self constancy are outcomes of the separation-individuation process. They are comprised of integrated representations of emotional experiences in the child-parent interaction. Mental representations of the mother and the self are initially closely intertwined. They are sorted out through the process of self-object differentiation enabled by the infant's advancing cognitive development. The representations thus differentiated are conceived to be organized at first by the child's subjective sense of emotionally charged, contrasting, good and bad experiences in the mother-child interaction. At this early level of cognitive development, the child is thus seen to have a disjunctive sense of unintegrated good representations and bad representations of the mother on the one hand and of the self on the other. It is the subsequent amalgamation and integration of these sets of good and bad representations that result in a conscious, unified representation of the mother and the self as separate entities, each having good and bad features. As a consequence of this integration, the earlier tendency to deal with uncomfortable, contradictory feelings through the defense of splitting yields to ambivalence.

The attainment of object constancy means that the parent is now represented in a lasting way in the child's psychic structure. In this sense, the parent now is always available to the child. Separation can thus take place without the former high degree of separation anxiety. The amalgamation of affectively charged object images into object constancy means also that the child has the expectation that the love relationship will survive hostile feelings and episodic angry confrontations. The internal "presence" of the parent tends further to diminish the need for the external presence of the parent in support of the developing regulatory functions. As a psychic structure, object constancy serves the establishment, maintenance, and regulation of object relations generally. Early psychic structure formation has culminated in a definitive step toward independence and autonomy.

Self constancy is developed through entirely similar, codetermined processes and has analogous outcomes. In addition to the sense of a single, integrated self, there is the confidence that the self will survive separation from the love object. There also is the expectation that the integrated, predominantly good self will survive a temporary resurgence of the bad self. The self constancy structure serves the regulation of self-esteem and maintenance of the sense of self.

Importantly, the effective structuring of object and self constancy takes place under the aegis of a predominance of loving feelings over feelings of anger and hostility in the child-parent relationship (McDevitt 1979). The predominance of love is the glue, if you will, of the unified representation.

To return to the topic of pathogenesis, the reenactment of the episodes of cardiopulmonary failure and resuscitation in play and the transference allows us to infer something of the child's subjective experience of them, as more or less revised by later defensive and developmental processes. But we mostly can only speculate about the specific determinants and actual nature of this experience as it occurred repeatedly from the first weeks of life until age two years (fifty to one hundred times during the first year).

With regard to the child's experience in the interaction with the mother, I assume that the life-saving mouth-to-mouth breathing and the sternal thrusts would nevertheless be experienced as aggressively intrusive and evoke an aggressive response. If so, the images of such a mother are juxtaposed to the contrasting images of the soothing, care-giving mother. If the aggressive images are severe, they pose a problem for the amalgamation of the positive and negative object representations into well-structured object constancy, and thus for the identificatory regulation of aggression. This problem was complicated by the fact that the negative images of the mother were reinforced at age thirty months, when the brother was born, by the seven days in the care of Aunt Florence. Aunt Florence was aggressively strict and intrusive both physically and verbally. There appears to have been a similar reinforcing experience with the baby-sitter, Ursula, and her twelve-year-old granddaughter.

In this same regard, Dr. van Dam mentions Betty's "readiness to identify with the aggressor" in the context of the parents: their deliberate avoidance of spanking Betty in contrast to Aunt Florence's and the paternal grandmother's willingness to spank her. This defense can serve separation-individuation in normal development, as exemplified by the child's identification with the mother's prohibitions by the use of the word "no" (Spitz 1957; McDevitt 1979, 332). Under pathogenic circumstances, however, this defense can result in the internalization of "an unassimilated, disassociated foreign body, as a hostile, 'bad' introject" (McDevitt 1979). McDevitt conceives that this introject preserves the relationship with the actual mother, who is thereby protected from the child's hostility (334–35). Pathological identification with the aggressor poses a problem, then, for the amalgamation of the positive and negative representations of the self into well-structured self constancy and thus for the regulation of aggression.

Dr. van Dam saw the mother, I think correctly, to be very skilled, quite firm, and seemingly knowledgeable about how to set limits. I note, though, that the mother invoked the imagery of getting a ticket from the police in support of her leaving the treatment room to put money in the parking meter. Such a reach for external, adjuvant authority often indicates parental discomfort with the use of aggression. It seems possible that the ability of Betty's mother to function at her best level in helping regulate Betty's aggression was impaired by her fear of her own aggression in relation to Betty's vulnerability.

It is noteworthy and important for Betty's overall development that the mother did not defend against the threat of loss of her child through death by withdrawal of libidinal cathexis. In my experience, such a threat commonly causes a diminution of material emotional involvement and availability. Betty's good cognitive development was no doubt due to the mother's continuing to be available to her as a developmental object. At the same time, the threat of loss can heighten the parental valuation of the child and sometimes interfere with appropriately aggressive limit setting. This may have been a contributing factor in the regulation of aggression in this mother-child pair.

In any given SIDS episode, the mother was patently stressed and frightened. On the one occasion when Dr. van Dam saw the mother immediately after a SIDS episode with the brother, she was "ashen gray with fright." The combination of the mother's acute fright and the ongoing dire threat of the episodes, and their unpredictability, must have created a more or less omnipresent aura of parental anxiety. We can assume that this anxiety was felt by Betty and in turn aroused anxiety in her. Later, Betty experienced this anxiety in relation to the brother's cardiopulmonary episodes.

The developing ego thus had to deal with an excess of both aggression and anxiety. It seems likely that this circumstance impeded development of the ego capacity not only for control but for delay of response, and thus for conversion of reactive anxiety into signal anxiety. Although the analysis of Betty was terminated after only five months of treatment because of the family's move to another city, the therapeutic process was substantial. In highlighting the progression of the therapeutic process, I first of all note that Betty made a quick "latch" to Dr. van Dam and formed a good therapeutic alliance. I see this as testimony to the mother's sufficient emotional availability as a developmental object for her SIDS-afflicted daughter. To my understanding, based on similar experience with a number of children, Betty's removing her shoes indicates comfort with the analysis. This may already be reflected in her early play of making scribbles which she then has Dr. van Dam erase.

An initial exposure of Betty's anxieties and conflicts, including the problem of control, is represented in her concern about things not working and needing to be fixed. This is expressed, for example, in her wetting herself in the improperly working elevator. This concern is pointedly conveyed in her having her doll wear the belt from the SIDS monitor. Her concern about and denial of her own loss of control are symptomatically expressed in her lying about her misbehavior.

The SIDS experience and the involved feelings are reenacted, reexperienced, and analyzed in play with the analyst. At about the same time, Betty engages in the play of nursing Debby, the doll given to her at the time of her brother's birth. This fantasy play, in identification with the nurturing mother, is especially crucial to the process of change. It serves the amalgamation of the bad representations of the mother and those of Betty herself under the aegis of loving, good representations (McDevitt 1979; Settlage 1988).

The reenactments and expression of anger and rage then begin to escalate in intensity. For example, Betty yells angrily at the analyst. At the same time, there are libidinal reenactments of nursing and bathing scenes. Here, too, good and bad in external behavior and internal representation are juxtaposed. Betty then plays monster with the analyst. A scene in which the mother is the monster suggests the relationship between the introject of the bad mother and Betty's repressed hostility in the determination of Betty's sense of herself as monster. Next, Betty swears and expresses her anger with a sadistic-looking face in an extremely intense, distorted fashion.

Dr. van Dam notes that both he and the parents were at a loss to know just what is being reenacted. My sense is that they were witnessing the release of the previously repressed and otherwise defended anger and hostile rage stemming from the experiences associated with the SIDS and with David's arrival and his SIDS, both embodying for Betty the threat of loss of relationship with the mother. The repression of anger is invoked in order to maintain the love relationship with mother. The intensity of the behavior, all the more so because of its not having been fully expressed when first experienced, no doubt reflected identification with the aggressor. The abreaction also allowed Betty to experience the full range and dimensions of angry feelings in the safety of the analytic relationship. In a sense, the feelings were detoxified by the analyst's empathic, nonreactive reception of them and by the fact that the patient and the analyst, and the analytic relationship, survive their expression. The feelings are thus brought within the purview of the conscious ego, where they can begin to be controlled in a modulated rather than a repressively rigid way.

Enabled by the undoing of the pathology, a parallel developmental process accounted for some of the favorable change in Betty. I refer to such factors as turning passive into active, striving for mastery, reaction formation (as in wanting to help starving children), and the "objectification" of very early experience enabled by advances in cognitive and fantasy capability. Repressed and denied experiences, in part through developmental processes, thus come to be represented in the play and the transference, where they are accessible to the analytic method.

But I also refer to the patient's use of the analyst as a new and different developmental object, particularly so as interpretation removes the initial transference-distorted view of the analyst (Loewald 1960). The function that the analyst serves for the patient—more precisely, how the patient can use the analyst—has several facets. As reported from the dialogue with Anna Freud (Sandler, Kennedy, and Tyson 1980, 107), the child can use the analyst as a transference object, a new person, a new love object, an auxiliary ego, a new object for identification, or an object for externalizing inner conflicts or the splitting of ambivalence. In an elaborating paragraph, the authors state that "if the analyst is used as a new person, as a new love object, he can also be used as a new object of identification, as happens in children's lives all the time." Parenthetically, I would add that the same can be said for adult patients and adults in their lives (Settlage et al. 1988).

The interaction with the analyst qua analyst can result in identifications that contribute to the revision of psychic structure. In particular, in a child of this age, identification with the analyst's regular availability, consistency of caring and helping attitudes, and nonreaction to the transference—in short, the analyst's emotional constancy—contribute to the structuring of sound object constancy in the patient (Settlage 1988).

After family circumstances require the reduction in the frequency of sessions, Betty reacts angrily toward the analyst, accusing him of not wanting to play with her. When her behavior was interpreted rather than reacted to, the relationship with the analyst thus being assured, she plays a game in which she is ill and there is a baby in her tummy which shortly is born through the umbilicus. In reaction to the actual and threatened loss of relationship with the analyst, the illness and birth of a baby fantasy can be seen to express the wish to hold onto the "doctor" analyst. The fantasied baby could represent both the patient, "reborn" or "rehatched" through the analysis, and the oedipal baby of the patient and the analyst father. In either case, the fantasy would appear to defend the reality threat of loss of the analyst.

In the hour following the latest SIDS episode with David, the patient has thoughts about starving children in Africa and her giving money to them. Dr. van Dam interpreted her worry about David and herself dying, also connecting the fear with guilt about her anger. As noted above, I think the patient's thought about helping starving children could also reflect normal repression and reaction formation. In the next-to-last session, Dr. van Dam linked Betty's speaking of killing her (fantasied) baby to her guilt over her death wishes toward her brother. Her response was to say, "I don't like David." The advent of normal repression and my perception of the progress of the analysis make me feel that Betty's response was a moderated one, reflecting a significant amelioration of her initially uncontrolled aggression. These changes suggest that the problem with aggression had been substantially analyzed.

In conclusion, I thank Dr. van Dam for the opportunity to "witness" the analysis of Betty and to offer some thoughts about the pathogenesis and resolution of her problem and the analysis of preoedipal-age children generally.

Johnny: The Analysis of a Prelatency Boy with a Gender Disturbance

Phyllis Tyson, Ph.D.

Johnny, age four years, five months, declared he would like to be a girl so he could marry a man. His parents' anxiety that he might become homosexual led them to seek treatment for him. Toward his father he was clingy, demonstrated sexualized behavior, staring at and wishing to touch his father's genitals, and wanted to shower and sleep with his father. He was competitive with his stepmother for his father's attention and was prone to depressive moods.

Johnny's developmental history is plagued with trauma. When his mother's pregnancy with him reached six months, she had a brain tumor surgically removed, which left her with a relatively impassive nature. Although a constant presence, she could not care for or relate to Johnny in any affective manner. She gradually deteriorated and died when Johnny was just over two. This period was marked by chaos and several changes of caretakers; the very attached father provided as much affection as he could, but without extended family support from either mother's or father's family. Johnny finally had to be placed in foster care for two months when the now-depressed father was hospitalized with a back injury just before his wife's death. Following this, a punishing, neglectful caretaker entered the scene, and the depressed father often worked late, unable to face conditions at home.

When Johnny was two and a half, his father met the woman

who was to become Johnny's adoptive mother. She immediately responded to the needs of the almost mute and non–toilet trained boy whose life seemed chaotic. She took care of him whenever possible to get him away from the punitive and possibly seductive caretaker. She attempted to modify the highly stimulating showers and toileting interactions between Johnny and his father and tried, at least when she was present, to end Johnny's sleeping with his father. When Johnny was three, she married his father, bringing her two girls, ages six and ten, from a previous marriage. The first year and a half she spent trying to organize and structure Johnny's life. He was used to eating junk food and had no regular mealtimes or fixed bedtime. In fact, getting him to bed often took up to an hour and a half.

While this history of trauma and neglect left certain remnants —impulsive behavior, tongue thrusting, problems over eating, problems going to bed, and a certain "shadowing" of his adoptive mother—diagnostic evaluation showed primarily a neurotic organization. Johnny was a very intelligent little boy who was highly critical of himself and of others. Although his impulse control was weak, he suffered guilt, self-criticism, and low self-esteem following episodes particularly of aggressive behavior. He longed to have friends but feared no one would like him. He viewed men as wonderful and women as punishing, unreliable, and not especially nurturing or supportive. Although Johnny was clingy with his adoptive mother and intensely jealous whenever she paid any attention to either of her daughters, as soon as his father came home he treated her as if she didn't exist. Then he was competitive with her for father's attention.

The diagnostic evaluation also showed a very anxious, over-controlling, and critical adoptive mother who was, at the time, in twice weekly psychotherapy. Formerly a teacher, she had given up work when her children were born. After marrying Johnny's father, she devoted her life to helping Johnny and frequently expressed her profound disappointment when he did not show the gratitude she felt she deserved and did not love and admire her as she thought an oedipal-age boy should and would. Johnny's father appeared as a somewhat passive, retiring, although affectionate man who seemed to be able, at times, to temper the effects of the stepmother's anxiety. At other times, he became annoyed by Johnny's intense hunger for him and withdrew to his newspaper, tuning out all activity around him and making Johnny and his adoptive mother all the more anxious and hungry.

Johnny and his family were initially evaluated by a male analyst who recommended analysis for Johnny and referred the family to me. The stepmother had difficulty with the idea of a female analyst because of her intense competition with women, but the parents finally agreed, in the hope that treatment goals would be accomplished within two years. A four times weekly frequency was established, and the parents were seen monthly; at periods during the analysis the stepmother was seen alone weekly or bimonthly.

To capture the flavor of this little boy's analysis, I will report some sessions in detail and sometimes summarize several sessions. The necessary condensation may make the pace of the analysis sound faster and somewhat smoother than it actually was.

Johnny greeted me the first session by commenting, "I don't like you; I only like men; Why do I have to see you anyway?" He commented, "Superman watches; he's always watching what you do." He attempted to tease me and tested limits, then sang a song: "I'm Popeye the sailor man, I eat from the garbage can; I put on the heater, it pulls off my weiner; I'm Popeye the sailor man." Then he said, "I'm afraid my weiner will come off." I commented on what a big worry that must be.

By the fourth week Johnny smiled in a flirtatious way and said, "I'm beginning to like girls a little." The following Monday, while drawing a figure, he questioned, "Is it going to be a girl or a boy? What if their heads get cut open?" He said, "I don't see how anybody could like you." He wondered if he and I could both draw a picture of a man, but then he worried that mine would be the better drawing. He told me a story about the Incredible Hulk: "He is strong, he can pick up the world with his pinky. What if his pinky breaks? Oh, he'd put it back on with magic." I commented on his wish to be strong like the Hulk, then he wouldn't have to worry about his pinky or head or weiner or any other body part. He paused and said, "Maybe I'm beginning to like you, but only when I'm at home, when I think about you." I said that he seemed so determined not to like me that perhaps he was worried about whether I liked him. He said, "Oh, I don't care." He paused and said with a big smile, "Daddy has fur around his weiner. Daddy is strong, but he's not as strong as the Incredible Hulk." Later that session pensively he asked, "Does Dr. Tyson go and leave you and not let you come along? Does Dr. Tyson say go away, and say I want to be alone now? Do you cry?" I commented that I thought he was wondering if I would understand how it feels to be shut out, like he feels when his daddy reads the paper and ignores him, or goes away with his mommy and leaves him behind, or when I say go away, our time is up.

Two days later he told me a story: "I got run over by a bad guy, then I threw his car up and broke it to pieces. Not really, because I wasn't the Incredible Hulk. Do you love me? I don't love you—I'm not going to marry you."

Johnny's parents went away for a weekend, leaving the children with a baby-sitter. The following week he told me about her and about how much fun he had had jumping on the bed, but complained that she did not read him a bedtime story. For several days, however, he seemed remarkably regressed, rubbing his legs and hair, thrusting his tongue, and looking like a two-year-old. His words became confused and mixed up. He made up a game in which I was a little person and he was big. After several repetitions of the game I verbalized his wish to be big so he could be the boss over who left and who got left. I added that he may be wondering if I could understand how it felt to be left without mom and dad, even to tell him a nighttime story. He smiled. Then he suddenly jumped into my lap and questioned, "Did I step on your penis?" He grinned and said, "You have one behind your butt." Concern about what would hurt me and what would hurt him occupied him throughout the week, and he became increasingly concerned about my other patients, wondering if I liked them better than I liked him.

He began the eighth week by describing a memory of playing with his poo when he was little and pensively said, "I had a lot of toys in the old house; I'm not sure I didn't lose some of those old toys when we moved." (The house he referred to was his adoptive mother's old residence, where he spent long weekends whenever father had to be out of town.) The next day he again mentioned the memory of playing with his poo and became excited and laughingly said, "I put my head down the toilet." He then started playing with pens and was disgusted that others had left the tops off. He became focused on whether or not I had a penis, and said, "You must have one, you just have it hidden, poopy-face." He became silly, asked for a drink of water, and proceeded to "spill" most of it on the floor. On leaving he wondered who else I was going to see.

Johnny began the next session by commenting that "God is everywhere, he sees what you do." I commented that he might have been worried about getting silly the day before and worried not only about God but about me, whether I would help him not to do silly things and whether I would like him even if he did silly things. I added that I knew his parents were away for a few days and that he was probably feeling left out and worried about whether or not they liked him. He then played with horses. The daddy was bigger, the baby had a room of his own all alone but it's the biggest room. But the baby wants to be with the mommy and the daddy. "Just like Johnny wants to be with his mommy and daddy," I added.

Back from the short trip the next day, his stepmother brought Johnny, and he did not want to separate from her. She had errands to do and left immediately, and he watched at the waiting room window for a long time, not wanting to come into the consulting room. I said I thought that when his mommy and daddy leave him it makes him feel like the baby in the story, left out, wanting to be with his parents, and feeling that even if he had the biggest room, it didn't make up for feeling left out. I added that when he does "silly things" (our label for impulsive behavior) he worries about how well his parents like him, just as he worries about whether or not I like him. I added, I thought that when his mother leaves it makes him feel unliked, sad, and lonely. After these interpretations he chose to play Candy Land, making sure my character and his stayed in close contact, disregarding the usual rules. When it was time to go, he asked, "Will you be here tomorrow? I'd like to play this." He added, "But what if I feel like I felt today?" During the next week it became increasingly difficult for Johnny to leave at the end of sessions, yet he frequently had trouble separating from his stepmother; demonstrating his remarkable capacity for self-observation, he said, "Huh, funny, sometimes I don't want to come and sometimes I don't want to leave."

We can see from the material already presented that Johnny felt sad and angry over being left out. In the opening phase of his analysis he had various ideas about why he was left out, many relating to his difficulty in controlling his sexual or aggressive impulses, most of which were contrary to the demands of his critical superego. Several defenses against drive expression are apparent, but they seem not to function well, as demonstrated, for example, by his excited discussion about his feces. Only after the fact did his reaction formations come into play, making him judgmental of the messy children who leave the tops off pens and anxious about my regard for him. This material also shows that early in treatment Johnny's growing affection for me became an area of increasing conflict as he maintained he only liked boys and men; he periodically tried to deny the conflicts by insisting that I had a penis. His denial not only helped him rationalize that his attachment to me did not conflict with his wish to be loved by an idealized male figure, but it also served as a defense against castration anxiety. Yet, his heterosexual attraction toward me was becoming increasingly apparent. The material presented also shows Johnny's capacity for self-observation and his capacity to form a treatment alliance.

Johnny made up a game using two dolls, one to represent each of us. My doll was to phone his house and he pretended his father answered the telephone, saying, "Johnny's taking a nap but after that you can come and play." My doll then visits and the two sit together, go to bed together, and play the piano together. He decides that my doll can stay in their family because he has a mother and a father and I don't. The more open expression of affection and positive libidinal attraction aroused two painful feelings in Johnny. First were loyalty conflicts; Johnny feared his stepmother's jealousy of our relationship. Second, it made the end of sessions and weekend separations all the more painful, and Johnny again defensively expressed his wish not to come, maintaining that he did not like me.

While working on these conflicts, now after six months of treatment, Johnny's parents again went away for four days, leaving him sad and very angry. His sessions were not interrupted, although it was a very difficult week in which he complained about everything I said and did, displacing his anger at his parents on to me. He said, "My parents love me, but I'm mad at you." He wanted to kick, pinch, and punch me. His parents returned on Wednesday night, and his stepmother again left abruptly after dropping him off for his Thursday session. Johnny looked really depressed and cried silently in the waiting room. He angrily accused me of making his parents go away. It wasn't because they didn't like him. I said I could understand how sad he feels. He told me to shut up. I reminded him of how he often feels sad and kicked out when our time is up and then figures I don't like him. I suggested he felt with his parents like he feels with me, sad and left out, but to be angry may risk further loss of love so it was best to blame me for their going away. I then made a reconstruction. I said the feelings he had now of being with me instead of being with his mommy like he wanted were like the feelings he had a long time ago when he used to be with Ann (the abusing baby-sitter) but really wanted to be with his daddy. He looked up and said, "And she locked me out sometimes and I didn't have anyone to feed me or put me to bed."

The next day he told me he was worried about his teeth being too long (presumably as a result of tongue thrusting, his front teeth protrude). I elaborated on the interpretations made earlier, saying that sometimes when his parents go away, he feels it's because they don't like him, and he looks for all the things he thinks may be wrong with him. He told me a dream: "My parents were going away in a car with Jane [his stepsister]. They were leaving me and Debbie [his older stepsister] with the baby-sitter, but I ran after them and I was trying to jump in the car and they wouldn't stop, so I fell off, but I didn't cry." I verbalized how sad he feels when they leave him and wishes he could be big and brave, then maybe they would not leave him.

Throughout this period Johnny was intermittently provocative, messy, and angry in the analytic sessions. He would try to start fights with me by deliberately throwing something on the floor. If I did not take the bait, he might become more openly aggressive and impulsively try to kick, spit, or punch me. He called me names or became giggly and silly. His difficulty in controlling this behavior became an ongoing theme as Johnny transferred on to me a current conflict in his relationship with his stepmother, a conflict associated with anxiety that he would be rejected.

Johnny began a session in the seventh month of treatment by trying to provoke such a fight. He threw tissue on the floor and demanded that I pick it up. Later in the session he drew a picture. In the center he drew a box with a frowning face inside. He put bars across the box. To the left he drew another face, this one smiling. "This is the robber," he explained. The robber was happy, he had tied up the man inside. But then, the policeman came from the other side of the box and tied up the robber. The man in the center was now happy and out of jail. I said I thought he was drawing a picture of himself, that he has robber feelings and policeman feelings inside, and he, the man in the center, has the job of pleasing the policeman and controlling the robber. The robber does mischievous things, tries to pick fights, is silly sometimes, and at other times gets out of control. When he doesn't stop his robber, his policeman is mad at him and punishes him by making him feel bad, or feel that other people don't like him. He then feels sad and alone, as if he were in jail. I added that I thought he wished that his inside policeman could be in control of his inside robber. He said, "Silly, I don't have anyone inside." He erased the picture, all but the policeman and said, "Watch" and threw an airplane. He said, "I was going to throw it in your face but my policeman stopped me." Policeman and robber feelings became a useful treatment metaphor, Johnny at times playfully commenting, putting his feet up on the table, "The policeman is taking a coffee break!"

Johnny's anger and jealousy toward anyone who demanded his father's attention and his resulting fear of rejection became an increasing transference theme, and transference interpretations sometimes led to the revival of early memories. He dreamed that his parents drove away, leaving him behind. He also dreamed that he was left at school all night while his mother was at home with his sisters. He played a game with character dolls. The girl is with the mom and the boy is with the dad. When the boy is with the mom, he wonders what the dad is doing with the girl. Does he like her better? He played with horses. The baby and the dad were together. The mother got lost. "That's okay because the baby had the dad, so he didn't have to be sad," he said. He wished I could give him a piggyback ride like his dad used to when he was little. He felt angry with me when our time was up for the day, and he wondered who else I had to see. He tried to kick me on leaving.

He began the next session by declaring that he was mad and didn't want to come. He said he didn't like me and that his head hurts when he comes. I began to interpret the underlying themes by saying that I thought his feelings were hurt yesterday. He had been telling me of how he felt with me like he feels with his daddy, he wanted us to be together, but instead he felt I kicked him out to see someone else, which is why he had tried to kick me. He feels someone else is always interrupting, which makes him mad and he then worries that he will not be liked if he gets mad. "How do you know about my worries? Does my mommy tell you?" he asked. "She doesn't like me," he added. I said that he had felt yesterday that I didn't like him because I said he had to leave. "Shut up, I don't like you," he said. I commented on his affect, saying how his mad feelings seemed to make him feel terrible. Brightening, he found two big empty water bottles and said, "Can you see me looking at you through here? I don't want you to look at me; watch how strong I am." He then set up the game with the horses, using the bottles as houses. There was a daddy, a baby, and a mommy. The daddy and the baby go off and leave the mommy. Then the daddy and the mommy leave the baby with the farmer. Next the mommy gets lost. He looked up and said, "My mommy died. Pretend in the game the mommy died. The baby and the daddy went off for a walk. They both cried. Then the new mommy came and surprised them. That's what happened, but I got to sleep with daddy before my new mommy came with her girls. I still got to for a while because she liked me, but not now." I said, "So you felt you got kicked out of bed because she didn't like you, like you felt I didn't like you yesterday and you got kicked out of here." "Don't talk," he said, "Let's play with the horses, but they have to be nice to each other, not nasty, they work together to kill the monster."

Among other things, this material illustrates how Johnny displaces on to me current and past conflicts related to his parents. It also shows his involvement in the analytic process. Following this interpretive work it was possible to reconstruct how conflict and projected anger had distorted object and self representations. This offered Johnny the opportunity to resolve painful conflicts and the possibility of finding new ways of relating to others. This process elaborated the transference as old and ongoing neurotic conflicts became reactivated.

Johnny became increasingly concerned about whether I liked him. "Do you like me if I'm silly?" he questioned, as he aggressively teased and tested, and increasingly felt sad and left out during weekend separations. When I attempted to verbalize his feelings, he commented, "But you weren't lonely, you have Dr. Tyson." He said he'd like to be big like his daddy, then he'd really be strong. "Did you ever want to be a boy when you were little?" he asked, as he tentatively conveyed his feeling that maybe his father would prefer him if he were a girl. He said that if he were a girl he could kiss the boys. Increasingly the transference reflected his wish to have an exclusive relationship with his idealized father, but, I want to emphasize, as a son, not as a daughter. It soon became clear that to become a girl meant not only the loss of his precious penis but also the loss of the growing affectionate heterosexual relationship with me. Yet a heterosexual relationship brought fears of abandonment derived from earlier trauma, as well as fears of being belittled, controlled, and rejected, that is, castrated, as he felt currently with his adoptive mother, so his compromise was the idealized father-son couple. He made an elephant and a man, each on a raft. They were friends, but they kept getting lost from each other. Attempting to consolidate the transference in preparation for a future interpretation, I said I thought he was telling me how he felt he and I were always getting separated, lost from each other, and how sad he sometimes feels about that.

He made up a game, "friends," with two boys and two dads; their mothers had died. They took turns visiting each other. He thought about their names; he could use his middle name and my middle name. Then mine would be a girl, I commented. Then he said with a sheepish smile, "They could be married" but, looking embarrassed, he said, "Don't ask me what I'm thinking, just silly thoughts, come let's play."

Johnny's fantasy games continued. Father and son were working on the road. The father makes dinner for the son, the mother is dead. The boy admires his dad's strength. "Does anyone else really come?" he questioned me.

He pretended that Superman, Superboy, and Spidy live together. Superman talks to Spidy, and Superboy feels jealous. He knows that Superman loves him best, he is his son, but Superboy still feels jealous. Just like he feels when his daddy talks to one of his sisters or his mother. "And like he feels when he thinks of my seeing other children," I added.

Johnny described how Superboy can do anything Superman can do except fly. He grinned and said, "I think I know how Superman gets his power, his power is in his penis!" Superman and Superboy decide that they are never going to have another mom, they have each other. I said that I thought he wished he were Superboy, then maybe his dad wouldn't have needed another wife, he would have wanted only him.

Johnny's game began to shift. He pretended that he and I were on a boat, cooperating with the various tasks at hand. He became flirtatious and put his arms around me. He found some nail polish and wondered if I would let him put some on me. He smiled, looking fondly up at me, and said, "I can see me in your eyes." On leaving the session he ran back to hug me but stopped and turned the hug into a slug. This affection seemed to represent, first, a transferred father-son relationship and, second, the beginnings of a developmental step toward a positive oedipal position. Such a position, however, was threatening to Johnny because it threatened his idealized father-son relationship fantasy. Thus the slug represented an instance in which the reality of my gender confronted him with this conflict.

Movement toward a positive oedipal position became more obvious with a new game Johnny made up. "Let's play Popeye, he's strong, and pretend Wonderwoman is Olive." They were asleep, and a robber comes in to steal Olive; Olive screams; Popeye beats him up and takes him to jail. He repeated this game for several weeks with variations in which he was strong Popeye overcoming the robbers who try to steal Olive. The robbers get sent to jail and endure various sorts of punishment, and Olive admires Popeye.

Johnny reintroduced the friends game. Superman and the Hulk lived together, but Johnny wanted the Hulk to be David, that is, not mad. Superman and the Hulk compare and admire each other's strength. "Go get the crew," he suggests and brings Supergirl and Wonderwoman into the game. The robbers also want to marry the girls, but they can't share. They tell lies and try to steal the girls, but the Superheroes had the girls first.

The robbers are put in jail, then killed, and made into pie and eaten. I commented that I could see why he was so worried about his own robber feelings if the robbers get killed and eaten. He smiled and said, "Remember the time you were mad at me?" I said, "You were worried I wouldn't like you; maybe you were also worried that I would hurt you, like the robbers in the game got punished." "You wouldn't," he insisted. "Remember the time I didn't want to come on Monday?" he continued. "Yes," I said, "You thought I didn't like you because you had to leave at the end of our time and you didn't want your feelings hurt again."

Johnny proudly brought me a picture of himself. He set up the house with Popeye and Olive, who were to admire the picture. Popeye is strong and likes Olive, but the robbers want to marry Olive too. Again they get put in jail because they can't share. He grinned. "I'm thinking of marriage; do you like me? Love, who do you love?; do I have anyone who I love?; Love is gross, you probably love Dr. Tyson." At this point I continued interpretive work begun earlier and said, "And you feel left out; you feel like you'd like to be the robber and take me for yourself. Instead Dr. Tyson gets me and you worry about what he'll do to you: Will he be able to share, or will he put you in jail and chop off your head," I said. He replied, "I don't feel left out," he denied, but increasingly his friends game reflected his conflict over whether to be with a man or with a woman, with his idealized father or with me.

He pretended that Superman and Wonderwoman got married, and they have Superboy; Superboy grows up and marries Superwoman, and Spidy is their son. "No! No girls," he suddenly demanded, defending himself from mounting excitement, with increasing awareness of his affection for me and increasing oedipal conflict, "because I can see Superwoman's boobies! The mothers all died; the fathers wanted to be with their sons; the mothers die because that was what the boys and dads wanted." His play returned to the idealized father-son constellation, expressing the wish for an exclusive relationship with his father with fantasied total gratification. I could do nothing right, and he felt disgruntled and dissatisfied with everything he attempted. He questioned why I did not see him on Fridays— but denied his wish for more time. I said that I thought he was disappointed that we did not spend more time together. I knew he sometimes felt like Popeye and wanted me to be Olive, but when I make him leave he feels his love is rejected; then he concludes that I don't like him. "But," I said, commenting on the role of his superego in maintaining his low self-esteem, "look at yourself, you expect yourself to be perfect and figure that we don't have more time because you are not good enough for me. Then you get mad at me because I'm not perfect. That policeman inside is a pretty hard guy to please, both you and I have to be perfect." I continued, "The only trouble is, the policeman also knows about the robber feelings, all those feelings of wanting to steal Olive or of wanting to kill the mom; the policeman doesn't like those feelings, so he makes you feel that nobody likes you." He responded by putting the toys neatly away and asking, "Do you really have somebody else to see?"

Gradually a new game emerged after nine months of treatment. He pretended that his family and mine go on a trip together but in separate campers. My family keeps getting lost in the jungle, and he rescues me. Then he brought in a toy boat, large enough for both his family and my family. He positioned himself next to his dad in the story, mused that he and his dad look alike. I was given the task of speaking for his dad, as he could not make his voice low. He pretended the dad was making chicken pot pie, with meat, peas, and rice. I had to announce dinner in a low voice, and, misunderstanding, I announced that dinner was chicken, peas, and rice. "No, stupid! Meat!" he said furiously. I commented on the intensity of his anger for what seemed like a small mistake. "Well, I said meat and you're wrong and I'm right!" Returning to the fantasy game—the people were fishing and the boat was going to sink, my family was thrown overboard to be eaten by the whale. He then had to go to the bathroom. On his return I suggested he needed to interrupt the play at that point because he was afraid of how angry he was and afraid of the power of his anger. "What a punishment for being wrong, being thrown to the whales," I said, and continuing, said that I could see why he feels he needs to be perfect all the time. He smiled and threw a rope to rescue me.

The boat game continued, as did his bossy, perfectionistic mood. He wore a new shirt with a picture of the Hulk but claimed he was not the Hulk, it was just a shirt. Ordering me around, he said I should take the people out to do something in the garage (a tissue box). Again I displeased him because I did not play out all of the action in the tissue box. He yelled, "No— do it in the garage! Why can't you do it right, don't you ever listen to me?" I commented on how angry he becomes when I make a mistake or misunderstand him, when I am not perfect. With a sheepish smile he went to the window, hiding behind the curtain. He asked, "Can you see me, can you see me now? Come here." He told me a dream. "I was mad at you, we were here. I threw you out the window, you were holding on with your fingers, then you fell, hit your head on the sidewalk and you were dead." I asked how he felt in the dream. "Really mad at you." I commented on his fear of his anger, linking my interpretation to his earlier story, that is, how Superman and Superboy killed the moms because they wanted it that way. I suggested that his anger makes him worry because he also likes me and is afraid if he hurt me I'd be gone forever, like his first mommy. I said that maybe when he was little he felt his mad feelings were magic and could kill, and he may have wondered if he killed his mommy with his angry feelings. I added that perhaps that was another reason he stays close to his dad, he feels safer with his dad because dad is stronger; he feels he will not hurt his dad with his anger, but he worries that he could hurt or even kill me, like in his dream. Johnny responded, "I don't know how my mommy died, but it was me, mommy, and daddy, and then it was just me and daddy."

Experiencing that I could survive his rageful attacks increased Johnny's trust in me, but he began to experience weekends and separations as more painful. In anticipation of our next separation over a holiday, Johnny asked to have a pen, which I granted with a comment about its transitional function of maintaining a link between him and me. On his return, now after fourteen months of treatment, he could best be described in Mahler's terminology as "low key." Following several sessions in which he played a game relevant to his feelings of being left, I made a reconstruction. I said I could see how sad he feels when we are separated, and how he wants me to know how that feels. But I wondered if not only does he feel now with me like he felt several months ago when his parents left him, but also that feeling so sad was a way of remembering a time when he was very little when he was left all alone; a time when he didn't even have his dad. But when his father returned he was so happy that he forgot all about his sadness. Now, I continued, perhaps he remembers the time with dad as more wonderful than it really was and thinks of the idealized relationship as a way of coping with sad or mad feelings. Johnny responded by continuing the game. "Now look how big I [the elephant] am, you have to go to this island, you don't have a raft, and I'll pick you up." I said as a part of the game dialogue, "But I'll feel so alone, I won't know anyone, and I won't know when you are coming back." I was instructed to be very happy when he arrived to pick me up. I then commented on a piece of reality, that is, his stepmother had to cancel the remainder of the week. Johnny looked sad, then, employing his usual defensive anger, he hit my man, broke him up, then hit out at me. I said I could understand his anger; here he was telling me about how he wanted to be the one in control, show me how big and strong he was and rescue me, and make me feel less sad, and instead I remind him that neither he nor I are always in control. He broke up the rafts, saying, "I'm never going to play this again." I pointed out how his anger seems to ruin his happy feelings about me. "Let's play cars," he suggested, "and you get lost in the jungle and I come and find you. I need two vans, a fighting van and a fun van." "So you can put all your fighting feelings in one and leave them behind so you only have the good feelings," I replied.

This narrative covers several themes in the first year of analysis. While not including all themes, I have tried to convey a sense of the analytic process. As Johnny's analysis continued, his ego grew in strength, giving him greater control over aggressive outbursts, greater capacity to use affective signals more effectively, and greater satisfaction in relationships with others. For the first time he began to play well with other children, using as a model the reciprocity he had employed in our friends game. The predominant themes now were Johnny's tenacious idealization of and sexualized attachment to his father, his fascination with penises and fear of castration, and his difficulty in integrating his penis into his total body and self image. This paved the way for exploration of positive oedipal fantasies, and for several weeks Johnny played narrative games, using a dollhouse, in which he pretended that he and I were married. Resistance to the analysis of the idealization of his father, however, continued to be an obstacle to his establishing a firm heterosexual position, and the game shifted to one in which he lived alone and I was his girlfriend. He played variations of this game for months, experimenting with various kinds of living arrangements, using me to represent first his girlfriend, then his wife or a male friend.

I noted in the beginning that Johnny's parents wanted treatment to be completed in two years. While he had made considerable progress after two years, clearly more work was needed, and I was able to extend the treatment for one year longer. However, his adoptive mother's ambivalence toward him remained considerable. She had wished that treatment would put her in the position of being the loved and admired parent, and she often behaved in a competitive manner with her husband for Johnny's love and competitive with Johnny for her husband's love. She had an enormous problem with penis envy and in spite of her own treatment and sessions with me, she found it very difficult to tolerate Johnny's phallic exhibitionism. Her castrating behavior toward Johnny reinforced his close bond with his father and with me, and she found it difficult to see that she had any role in this continuing pattern. She frequently reacted to my efforts to help her respond differently to him as indications that I did not take the potential of homosexuality seriously, and she would feel unsupported by and angry with me. The technical difficulties of juggling her negative transference and Johnny's positive transference in a way that remained therapeutic and enabled the analysis to continue were considerable. Eventually she rationalized that the time involved in Johnny's treatment was preventing her from giving her girls the attention they, too, needed, and she decided that treatment would have to terminate. So, after three years, Johnny's analysis ended.

The termination phase was very difficult for Johnny. To introduce the termination issues, I present a session from the thirty-first month of treatment. This material particularly illustrates Johnny's struggle and resistance in dealing with his idealization of his father. His stepmother had recently reported to me that Johnny had said that although he knows it is wrong, sometimes he thinks that he likes men better than ladies.

Johnny began the session wanting to play ball. He suggested

that we pretend I was his daddy, recognizing how he enjoyed the attention I gave him and our comfortable sense of reciprocity. He told me the story of Hansel and Gretel, announcing that the dad in the story was mean. He told the story fairly accurately, emphasizing the wickedness of both the stepmother and the witch, but also the passivity of the father. Johnny happily reported that the father had finally gotten rid of the stepmother and so was able to welcome his children back. He particularly enjoyed the part in which Hansel also brought back jewels so that he could now support the father. I commented on how both the ladies were mean. "My mom is sometimes mean," Johnny said and continued, "Maybe you could be my mom; no, then you would be mean." I asked what he meant by mean, and he claimed that I was mean when I made him come on Wednesday at a time he disliked. He elaborated on his mother being mean and said, "You know what, I used to lie to her. She used to get mad if I didn't eat all my lunch, but I didn't want all my lunch. So I'd lie and tell her I ate it, but she'd still get mad at me." I said that it seemed the person is mean when they made him do something he didn't want to, and that if I were his mother he is afraid that he and I would also battle over what he should do, which he fears would spoil his good feelings about me. "My mom and dad fight over me," he volunteered. "One time at the airport my mom was saying 'He just doesn't know how to behave,' and my dad said, 'Oh, he's ok, he's not too bad.' Another time I wanted to go to my friend's house and they won't let me walk over alone and my mom said to my dad, 'We've given him lots of attention all day.' But my dad said, 'Oh, it's ok, I'll walk him over.' My dad never gets mad at me." I said that when his mom says things like that it makes him worry that his mom is like the stepmother in the story. "But," I questioned, "earlier you said that the dad in the story was mean, what did you mean?" He avoided my question by describing a neighbor boy's father who gets angry. "But," he said, quickly revising his story, "mostly to older boys, not to us little ones. He protects us." I commented that although the dad in the story seemed nice, he didn't protect the children from the stepmother and didn't come to find them. I noted that Hansel may have been mad at the dad but felt the dad was all they had left; if they were mad at the dad they'd be all alone. "So," I suggested, "the story makes the women look like the bad guys and the dad look like the good guy, just like you feel that mommy is the bad one and daddy always nice, and you stick close to your father because you know he will always like you. Sometimes you wish you could be like Hansel and bring jewels for your dad, then you know he'd like you." "Sometimes he gets mad at me," Johnny admitted. "And how do you feel?" I questioned. Hanging his head, Johnny admitted he feels very sad when his father is angry with him. I suggested that he mostly protects himself from ever letting his father get angry by idealizing his father, never disagreeing with him, and always doing what his father says so as not to feel those sad, painful feelings.

As our work on this theme continued I was able to interpret how Johnny displaces his anger from his father to his mother so as to maintain his idealized view of him. Through the analysis of his continuing though less frequent provocative behavior toward me, along with his self-reports of how he provokes his mother (telling lies, deliberately not eating a portion of his lunch, and so on), I was able to show him how he provokes his stepmother to confirm his view that she is the mean one. In my sessions with the stepmother, we did considerable work to help her not to respond in such a competitive manner when he sought attention from his father and to help the father take a more active role in disciplining Johnny. All this helped Johnny come to view his father in a more realistic manner. Although he remained emotionally close to his father, he was able to a considerable degree to transfer his closeness with me to his mother, and they finally began to establish a closer reciprocal relationship.

During the termination phase, Johnny oscillated between two themes. At times he could openly express sadness that we would no longer be meeting. At other times he reverted to his old, now not very effective stance of saying he didn't like me because I was a girl. Work around the sadness theme contained also sadness that I could not be his mother and that I had not been able also to help his stepmother to like him better or at least to be more lenient with him. Through experience with me and also from contact with the mothers of his friends, he had begun to come to terms with the fact that sometimes his stepmother also had problems. This work entailed working through of an idealized fantasy of the mother who died, and some mourning for the mother he didn't have. Work with Johnny and also with his father enabled his father to share some of the details of his mother with Johnny. In that way the father, too, was able to at least begin a mourning process that he had been thus far unable to confront.

While Johnny's relatively sophisticated level of insight was often available, he remained vulnerable to reengaging the provocative sadomasochistic interaction with his stepmother. Work with both parents had helped his father to be more aware of how his withdrawal reinforced the pathological mother-son inter-action, and he was able more consistently to take a more active role, first, in disciplining Johnny, which made the stepmother feel more supported, and also in more frequently supporting Johnny and protecting him from the stepmother's criticism.

This concludes my report of Johnny's analysis. Of necessity, a number of themes have been omitted in the effort to convey the process of the analysis. There are many theoretical and technical implications of this material which I have not been able to consider here. I am sure the discussion will take them up from various vantage points. I hope I have shown, however, that in spite of difficult family issues, many of which treatment was not able to modify, the opportunity to have an analysis afforded this little boy the opportunity to resolve a number of intrapsychic conflicts. Through the analysis he was able to displace old and ongoing conflicts with his parents on to the analyst. The analysis of these revived conflicts within the transference helped this little boy to revise his denigrated self-image and to revise representations of objects. He was able to establish a reciprocal relationship with me as a father figure and as a mother figure, and the analysis of the transference enabled him to make developmental progress in establishing a positive oedipal configuration. In the eventual transferral of our reciprocal relationship to his adoptive mother, their relationship improved. He was then able to modify the exaggerated idealization of his father while continuing to love and admire him. The analytic process took into consideration a multitude of issues — gender development, choice of love object, choice of gender role, ideal formation, superego development, the role of superego criticism in maintaining low self-esteem, the role of the ego in relation to superego and drive conflicts, defensive functioning, and so forth. The result was a restructuring of his personality and much greater ego strength and capacity for self-observation. His ultimate object choice, whether it be heterosexual or homosexual, remains a question to be resolved finally in adolescence. But by the termination of the analysis he had returned much closer to the path of normal development.

Discussion of Tyson Presentation

John B. McDevitt, M.D.

From the beginning of his analysis Johnny spoke of two concerns. The first was the fear of the loss of the love object. The second was the fear that his weiner would come off. The expression of this concern—castration anxiety—alternated with the expression of the first concern. Later in the analysis a third concern appeared: sadness and feelings of inadequacy—not living up to his ego-ideal and his fear of his superego, the policeman inside him. In view of the traumatic experiences in his life, the extent of Johnny's concern about being liked or being left is not surprising. These experiences caused Johnny to believe that he would be disapproved of or abandoned in any close relationship, especially when he misbehaved or was silly or when he felt angry or sexy.

It is surprising, however, that Johnny had advanced as far as he had in his development. He was in the phallic-narcissistic and early oedipal phase of development. Although his longing for love was excessive, he had a strong attachment to Dr. Tyson. He also cared for her and was able to express concern about her. He was open, self-observant, and willing to listen. He seemed to understand that his excessive fear of the loss of Dr. Tyson's love at the end of each hour and over each weekend was the same fear that he experienced with his parents and, furthermore, that this fear began in the past and existed in the present in the form of an internal policeman.

This discussion will be about Johnny's second concern—his

castration anxiety. He announced in the first session that he was afraid that his weiner would come off. After this, in the first eight weeks, his flirtatious manner and his mention of marriage clearly suggested that Johnny's fear of losing his penis was directly related to his genital excitement and his fantasies about Dr. Tyson.

In order to lessen these fears, Johnny, early in the treatment, turned passive into active by playing that he was the boss who did the leaving and that he was as strong as the Hulk so that he need not worry about losing his weiner. Another defense used to lessen anxiety may have been an overemphasis on one fear in place of another, on loss of love in place of castration anxiety. In the first part of the analysis these two fears came up in the material one after the other. For example, in the Popeye and Olive game, Popeye and the superheroes put the robbers who tried to steal Olive, Supergirl, and Wonderwoman in jail. They then killed the robbers and ate them. Dr. Tyson told Johnny that she could understand why he was so worried about his robber feelings if the robbers get killed and eaten. This worry appears to be an expression of Johnny's castration anxiety in regressive form.

A major defense against this anxiety is seen in a subsequent game. Superman and Wonderwoman get married and have Superboy. Superboy grows up and marries Superwoman and Spidey is their son. Suddenly, while experiencing mounting excitement, Johnny exclaims, "No, no girls, because I can see Superwoman's boobies! The mothers all died; the fathers want to be with their sons; the mothers died because that was what the boys and dads wanted." Dr. Tyson interpreted this dramatic shift from oedipal excitement to the wish for an exclusive tie to the father as follows: "The only trouble is, the policeman also knows about the robber feelings, all those feelings of wanting to steal Olive or of wanting to kill the moms; the policeman doesn't like those feelings so he makes you feel that nobody likes you." This interpretation is correct, but Johnny at this stage in his analysis was much more concerned that Dr. Tyson's husband would castrate him for looking at Dr. Tyson's boobies with such excitement. It was Johnny's inner concern, the fear of his superego, that caused him to believe that such terrible punishment would occur to him because of his oedipal wishes. In the face of intense castration anxiety, Johnny retreated to the idealized father-son relationship, from castration anxiety to the concern over being liked, from a triadic to a dyadic relationship. We see here patterns of defense as they are being formed in statu nascendi.

Johnny may have used another defense to diminish the guilt brought on by his superego and by the feeling that he failed to live up to his ego-ideal. For example, he said, "Why can't you do it right, don't you ever listen to me?" Was he saying that it was Dr. Tyson who deserved to be punished and who was inadequate rather than himself? And was he turning passive into active when he threw Dr. Tyson and her family overboard to be eaten by a whale in contrast to his earlier fear that he would be killed and eaten because of his robber feelings for Dr. Tyson?

At the end of the paper Dr. Tyson writes, "Resistance to the analysis of the idealization of his father continued to be an obstacle to his establishing a firm heterosexual position, and the game shifted [from playing that he and I were married] to one in which he lived alone and I was his girlfriend." I think the real obstacle was Johnny's castration anxiety, which forced him into an idealized relationship with his father and at the same time prevented him from achieving a firm heterosexual position. The central issue was not simply sad or mad or bad feelings, not fears of rejection, but the fear of castration.

Although Johnny's parents brought him to treatment because

he expressed a wish to be a girl and showed a sexual interest in his father, nothing in the material suggests that his castration anxiety might also have been the result of negative oedipal wishes. The wish to be a girl appeared only once in Dr. Tyson's paper. Johnny wondered whether he would like to be a girl who could kiss the boys or whether he would prefer to be big and strong like his father. We know nothing more about his wish to be a girl. Possibly it began after Johnny's father married a woman who had two daughters. At no time in the analysis did Johnny play that he was a girl or express such a wish in his play. Instead, in his play he clearly wanted to be a boy. In the analysis his interest in the father's penis was because the penis represented strength.

Johnny's analytic material is not at all like the analytic material typical of boys his age who want to be girls. Five of these boys expressed this wish repetitively in their play, a wish which had begun between two and a half and three years of age. In these boys the mother for one reason or the other—the wish for a girl, hostility toward the male, fear of phallic sexuality—shaped their sons in a feminine direction. Late in the second year and in the third year, these boys shaped themselves in a feminine direction by identifying with the phallic mother as a defense against their marked castration anxiety. The fathers of these boys played a minor role in the analysis, as they had in their lives.

By contrast, Johnny was interested in both his father and Dr. Tyson. There was a gradual shift in the course of the analysis from a tentative interest to a very definite interest in Dr. Tyson. Johnny, however, had to retreat from his oedipal wishes because they were too frightening.

At the end of his treatment he alternated between oedipal wishes and idealized father wishes, just as he had alternated in the beginning of treatment between the fear of loss of love and fear of castration. In treatment he was able to move forward, but his castration anxiety repeatedly caused him to regress to establish fixation points—to the phallic-narcissistic phase in which he had a unique relationship with his beloved father, a father who had been both a mother and father to him.

The Analysis of a
Four-and-a-Half-Year-Old Boy
with a Feminine Identification

Henri Parens, M.D.

Four-year-old Emmett was referred for evaluation because he persistently wished to be a girl, pretended to be a girl, and acted in an exaggeratedly feminine manner. Emmett's psychoanalysis began at age four years, seven months, was conducted in four sessions weekly, and lasted almost four years.

EVALUATION

The only son of a young professional couple, Emmett was very interested from age two and a half in long hair and dresses and insisted that things like his shoes be pink. At age three, he dressed like a girl at play, pretended he was a girl, and was fascinated by dolls. Although verbally aggressive, he never hit his peers. He was physically timid but needed to "run the show" and control others. Once Emmett refused when two boys wanted to tie him to a tree. His father suggested that the boys would stop bothering him if he let them tie him up once, and Emmett complied. Briefly, Emmett seemed to have a problem with aggression, with a need to control the environment, and with a pressured and already stabilizing feminine identification.

Emmett had no signs of stranger anxiety in his first year, but a disconcerting facility in befriending people, often strangers, became apparent during his second and third years. By age two, Emmett's parents had gone on two two-week vacations without him. Shortly after his second birthday his father had a brief extramarital affair while the mother and Emmett were away. For several months afterward, his father's depression and the dread of his mother "collapsing" surrounded Emmett, and she felt puzzled that her son showed no signs of being upset by this crisis.

At the time of the evaluation Emmett's mother was becoming increasingly angry both with her husband and with Emmett. Speaking of her marital problems, she said, "I didn't want to be a masculine female, but I don't want to be put down." In preparation for the analysis, the mother agreed to change her open bathroom policy, which permitted Emmett to see her nude at all times. Emmett's father tended toward depression as a teenager. He met his wife-to-be at age eighteen and married seven years later. Happy when his wife became unexpectedly pregnant, he always felt close to Emmett, though seldom paid attention to him. The father couldn't set limits or modulate his own aggression so that, as he described it, he would let Emmett push him until he had gone too far and then he would "explode."

The mother dressed seductively and reported feeling uncomfortable when Emmett touched her. There was much physical closeness between them, Emmett being fascinated by his mother's dressing and hair combing. His father alternated between caressing Emmett and pushing him away. Both parents were made anxious by Emmett's declarations that he wanted to be a girl, and they feared that he might become homosexual. Early in Emmett's analysis, both parents began affairs, rationalizing that their marriage would benefit. Soon their guilty feelings led to secretiveness, and Emmett did not challenge them with his unavoidable discovery of the deception. Thus his first analytic year was accompanied by much conflict at home owing to parental strife and separation, and the analytic work centered on the fantasies he derived directly from this aspect of his life.

During the evaluation sessions Emmett displayed major conflicts of ambivalence. For example, a witch wanted to kill her father because he didn't come home from a trip, and then she wanted to marry him. There was also identification with and rage at the mother and a wish to seduce the father. Love for the mother was surprisingly absent. I saw Emmett as involved in a negative Oedipus complex, possibly already stabilized for nearly two years. His ego functioning was appropriate for his age, with indications of capacities for sublimation and artistic expression. His feminine identification had a stabilizing cohesiveness which, while pathological, suggested satisfactory ego functioning. I felt little warmth from Emmett, and his anger seemed to impede his interpersonal relationships to some extent. He fantasied being punished in such a way as to suggest harsh superego precursors, and identification with the aggressor was prominent in those fantasies. A pathologic identification with his mother seemed central in the development of his neurotic disturbance.

Opening Phase—First 100 Hours

Emmett's provocative, counterphobic, and masochistic maneuvers were noteworthy. He set up "being bad games" in which provoked parents retaliated by beatings; he demanded that I beat him and got angry when I didn't comply. I said I could help more if we "talked" what he wanted me to do rather than to actually do it. He began resisting entering the office, seemingly convinced that he would get hurt there. I thought he feared I was a doctor who would "straighten him out" by some drastic treatment. I considered but did not interpret that his masochistic defense in the being bad game arose from efforts to master castration anxiety by actively inducing its regressive equivalent, being beaten.

Emmett gradually accepted my talking proposition and began

to use puppets, repeating the coming-to-office theme, saying he'd comply but then refusing to come in. Then the mother and analyst puppets got very angry with him. Soon, Emmett's office behavior changed. He came happily, the excessive provocativeness stopped, and he was less impulsive and more creative and productive. He now showed a pseudofondness for me behind which there was little emotional investment.

In one persistent theme in Emmett's fantasy play the dominant character was a girl or a mother; much pleasurable attentiveness was given to the mother's dress, "bonnet," or hair, suggestive of identification with the female. Another theme contained the expression of a great deal of hostile destructiveness of self and objects. Thus father, mother, boy, and girl often fell into the water and drowned or fell off cliffs and died. The bad wife tricked her husband into getting killed or being called to her and then rejected; or the bad mother tricked her children into climbing up a cliff and then she pushed them off. In these fantasies I took the boy and the girl to represent Emmett's sexual identities. The most frequent participants in his fantasies were the boy-girl (either or both) and the mother. Father was vague, often absent and weak.

Near the end of this period Emmett's pants were frequently unzipped, and he would leave behind some little thing he had brought—a ring, a top, a plastic fish or troll. He often leafed through a picture book about families, excited and anxious on seeing "people's bottoms." He looked under the dolls' skirts, and in fantasy play, destructive feelings toward the females led to their getting their legs broken. Once he secretly took home pieces of crayon that he put into his underwear. I mused privately that perhaps he left various items behind and took crayons with him in his pants as a kind of female-male exchange, and I noted that some "boy play" and phallic castration material surfaced at times when the "girl play" became expansive and persistent.

At times Emmett asked me to make the dolls out of tissue and clay because, he let me know, he wanted me to join in defying his parents' dictates that he not play with dolls. I saw this as a secondary structural conflict (ego/superego) arising out of the initial negative Oedipus. I thought that he first protected himself against the threat of castration by reassuring his father, "You have nothing to be angry about with me since I am only a little girl," but then he had to confront his parents' dictates *not* to act like a girl. Analysis added a complication for him when his parents accepted his playing with dolls and puppets in the office. His efforts to integrate this confusing discrepancy may have loculated his neurosis and the analysis from his life at home; while his parents reported better peer relations and much less interest in dolls, hair, and pink things, these were his predominant preoccupations in the analysis.

Emmett now began building with Legos, as if to say, "You want me to play with dolls, but I don't want to play with girl's things." This thought led me to wonder out loud, "What was it that made you feel I wanted you to play with girl's things?" I now thought that an additional confusion associated with his defensive feminine identification derived from an ego/ego-ideal conflict, that is, shame at wanting to be a girl, indicating the internalization of parental disapproval.

HOURS 101 TO 222

Play themes became more focused, and I understood them as depicting more clearly the defensive operation of the negative Oedipus complex. Emmett's material evolved from scenes of general destruction and abandonment, such as earthquakes, people drowning or falling off cliffs, and car crashes to dread of bodily damage and then to a clear castration fear, which, during this period of analysis, stood out as the dominant source of anxiety, though fear of abandonment persisted. Emmett explicitly voiced his fear that his father would leave, and he dramatically displayed fear of his mother's abandonment when she was absent from the waiting room after sessions laden with anger and provocativeness. A transference fear of abandonment appeared when Emmett learned that I would be away for a week. However, he showed no fear of loss of the object's love, possibly because of his strong defenses against it.

Emmett became preoccupied with the female's broken legs, with fetishlike interest in little treasured items, and with physical dangers that would lead to death or gross maiming. He insisted in fantasy play that the doctor fix the crippled. In one session he expressed the thought of giving his penis to his mother, that somehow he had castrated her. Later he wanted to solve this dilemma by eliminating sex differences—both male and female have a baby in fantasy play. A few months after this, he showed me a puppet scene repeated several times: the baby is being loving and tickling with his mother and in mother's bed. Suddenly he screamed in fear at the sight of mother's not having a penis; then just as suddenly the angry tiger-man appeared and cannibalistically destroyed the boy. From here, Emmett's material evolved progressively to vivid allusions of castration, including the bloody loss of an arm, leaving a large hole, and a father who severely scolded a boy who then looked at his bottom and "doesn't even see a blob." This led me to interpret that he was very worried about the way girls and his mother are made because they have no penis. At this point he took over the interpretation by declaring that he knew they have a vagina and never had a penis, only to reveal his resistance to this knowledge then and the next day by adding that the mother's bosoms, which have come off (in fantasy play), are inside her (as must be her penis). I understood that Emmett was bringing to his awareness that he acted like a girl because feeling and acting like a boy led to unbearable castration anxiety.

Transference   My initial observation about Emmett's cool-
ness was clarified as he showed a defensive distancing, a kind of
"freeze" on object love that seemed to arise in part from fear of
loss of the object's love as well as loss of the object. He seemed
to want closeness but was afraid of it, a fear that only gradually diminished. I felt that the development of positive feelings
toward me was prerequisite to the unfolding of the castration
fears I described above, derived from feeling that I could help
him fix things and limit his chances of being destroyed in the
office and at home. Further elaboration of transference feelings
appeared when he shifted from the wish for me to take him home
and the expression of anger toward the children that he guessed
I had, to saying, "I hate your wife!"

A note on technique   At the outset, Emmett obliged me to
structure and limit his actions because of such behavior as throwing things, pushing chairs over, and scraping the wall. As he
gained progressively better control, I didn't need to restrain his
mess making and did not ask him to help clean up. Along with
this there was a shift in play content: whereas it had been the girl
who was the aggressive, nasty, bad child and the boy the helpless,
passive recipient of her abuse, now even the boy could be aggressive, nasty, and angry. This step allowed the emergence of the
positive component of his Oedipus complex defended against
by his tenacious feminine identification. That is, when the boy
could be aggressive enough and not feel endangered or dangerous, he could allow himself to experience his positive oedipal
wishes.

Analyzing Emmett's defense of confusion and unclarity contributed significantly to this result, as did interpreting his reaction formations and blandness of affect. My interpretations of
his recurrent defense of turning passive into active were useful
particularly when he was coping with the anxiety created by his
parents' actual separation and in relation to his dread of being

castrated. Emmett's use of my interpretations was well illustrated when he said at an appropriate moment, "And don't think I'm singing a happy song because I'm sad!"

Treatment alliance An unspoken contract evolved between Emmett and me. When he said something like, "Don't tell me," or "Stop saying that," I knew that he was not prepared to hear that confrontation or interpretation. When he asked me to start a story, however, as from a drawing he made or to do a puppet play, I understood this to be his way of asking for a commentary or interpretation. The clarity of this aspect of our work together proved invaluable to me.

Hours 223 to 440

When I had to leave for a week, Emmett revealed his dread of being left with the hostile, oedipally rejecting mother, who actually was having an affair at this time. In a play scene, the mother laughed and had fun at the neighbor's while her child suffered alone at home, riddled by anxiety and fear. The play child became angry; with this, Emmett became angry, then he feared his mother wouldn't return to get him after his appointment. Back into the play, Emmett burned down the house with the child inside and said that the mother, returning happy from the party, would be devastated by finding him dead. In a fresh wave of anger he slapped the mother puppet and cut off her leg. He then complained that my sessions were too short and that I see too many patients. The last session before I left he gave me a chance to connect his anger with me for going away with his dread that I would abandon him. This led to his expressing fears that his parents would leave him because he was bad and doing bad things.

On my return, Emmett dramatized that he wanted to be a girl and have mother's baby; he then revealed that in my absence he gave his mother an elaborate drawing that he and I had started together at his initiative. The material in the next session showed that he dreaded being castrated, and he whined that he wanted my pen. I learned that Emmett had once again seen his mother nude in spite of my earlier arrangements to prevent such exposure. Emmett went on in play to depict that he was upset by the mother's penisless state, wanting the doctor to fix her insides. In a bathroom hide-and-seek game he played at hearing and seeing things in the bathroom, letting me know he was worried about "mother's bleeding." He then excitedly presented his concern about sex differences and reexplored the idea that girls have vaginas and do not have penises. In puppet play he presented a girl who wanted to know what happened to her penis. In reaction to the excitement stirred up by this material, Emmett had a puppet crocodile scold me for telling children such things and using "such bad talk." But then the baby boy puppet persisted and wanted to know why he didn't have hair on his penis like his father. In working on his criticism of my "bad talk," I was able to interpret the underlying loyalty conflict, which led to his fear of being caught while peeping. This was followed by another transference element—he wanted me to stop him physically from jumping up and down on the couch, and as I approached him he squealed erotically. After several such episodes I commented on the sequence, and he immediately dropped to the floor, thumb in mouth, making infantlike sounds, and angrily messed up the toys. My subsequent interpretations took up Emmett's anxiety, with which I understood he was attempting to cope by this regression.

I believed that we were dealing with negative aspects of his Oedipus complex manifested by the wish to be grabbed and penetrated, the attendant anxiety defended against by the rapid regressive collapse to the floor. Positive oedipal components, such as the wish to have a penis like his father and the impulse to peep, also led to transference anxieties such as the time when he threw a crayon at me and exclaimed, "I was afraid you were going to hurt me!" Following this he broke off the chimney of the house he had made and said, "You better fix it; I'm dying!" At this point I interpreted his fear that I would hurt him because in his mind he wanted to hurt me, and that he then feared I would break off his penis, which was so important to being alive. The following hour he threw the girl doll into the waste basket, but soon after he seemed compelled again to defend against positive oedipal strivings. The mother and her daughter are having a fine time while I live in California (I had been away recently), where my house is getting repeatedly destroyed. He knew, he said, that I would say that this made me think of his mother and father living in separate houses. I said yes, he was right, and also I thought he was telling me that he had a fine time with his mother while I was away, which made him worry for some reason that I might be angry and forget about him. In subsequent fantasy play, I was a boy to whom he said, "I think your lady likes me," and then he attacked me.

Now Emmett's phallic narcissism became prominent in our sessions, in which he behaved in an insistently domineering fashion. At one point he wanted to throw away a drawing he had made, and for some unclear reason I retrieved it. We both recalled a time when he threw away so many of his early drawings and then another time he threw away a girl doll. I said maybe he was telling me that he wanted to get rid of some of his old ways of drawing and of needing to play with the girl doll, an interpretation he did not deny but seemed to accept. I said he was testing to see what would happen, just like he worried that his parents had separated because he felt he had been so angry and bad.

At this point, well into the second year of analysis, Emmett's parents said that his girlish behavior had notably decreased and that he was more assertive in activities with both boys and girls, while with his father he seemed more fearful of being hurt. With me Emmett became more controlling around breaks in treatment, and once he wanted to take off my wedding ring and to go away on a vacation instead of me.

When I returned from that vacation Emmett seemed more angry and distant than when we had parted. In addition to his reaction at not being able to control my going away, I learned that he had been infatuated with a pretty baby-sitter who dealt him yet another disappointment in love. At the same time he began first grade with a full day of school, and his mother arranged for someone else to bring him to his appointments. At home his parents reported a return of some of the girlish behavior that occasioned his coming to treatment, a regressive move that I understood to be in reaction to these events; but I could not tell whether any one event was more important than the others.

The emerging analytic material shed new light on Emmett's anger and resentment at the man and woman who hurt him, and it was clearer that his own hostility and hate were a large source of his feeling hated. In play with doll figures he became enraged and blew up the dollhouse. Everyone was killed. Dismayed with Emmett's palpable sadism, the play mother wept bitterly and died heartbroken. Then the parents privately talked of how they hated their children. Subsequently the mother is in heaven but kills her husband so he can come to heaven with her. Once there they are happy, but then the husband takes his robe off and allows the wife to see how small he is. She becomes disappointed and kills him, then feels guilty and decides to kill herself. Emmett said he felt mixed up.

I understood this material to be primarily an oedipally based fantasy that contained elements of wish-fulfillment, reality, hostility, and guilt, together with identification with and projected destructiveness. Emmett continued this theme with the wish that he were big and I little; then he'd be the helper, and if I did nasty things he'd slap me. Feeling optimistic, I said that he wished to control me so that I could help him better control his own hate feelings. He responded by showing me that to be aggressive and masculine is dangerous: he loves a beautiful queen; then he is racing a car, although the driver is invisible (he cannot yet see himself so) and crashes.

At this point the parents reported that Emmett had recovered from his regression and that he was quite happy with school. In further external corroboration of analytic progress, Emmett told his father that he used to be afraid of how his father really felt behind his friendly face.

Emmett was similarly forthcoming in the analysis. Once when he bossily told me to draw for him, I didn't but instead told him I wanted to understand what made him so demanding. "Okay," he said, "I'll do it myself." I saw in this an increased assertive vigor and a decrease in his narcissistic vulnerability. Emmett elaborated on this theme when in fantasy play he wanted to retain the parental throne he occupied while the parents were away and a storm developed. I clarified the nature of the tempest, saying that the children imagined their parents would be so angry with them for sitting on their throne and not wanting to give it back that they would cause a terrible storm. Emmett responded by saying that he thinks people have bad dreams because they've done things they shouldn't. Shortly after this session, Emmett engaged in some fantasy play that clearly showed an aspect of his castration anxiety. A queen has her legs cut off. She orders everyone in town to have their legs cut off too. I eventually wondered aloud if the queen was angry because she didn't have a penis, and she wanted all the men and boys to have their penises cut off. Mildly annoyed, he said, "Oh, don't say that." He then combed her long, beautiful hair with much ado and sensuality. I wondered, again aloud, if she had beautiful long hair to make up for not having legs. He said, "That's exactly the point!" I interpreted then that his great interest in mother's long hair was to be connected to his fear that she would be angry—the angry queen—because she has no penis. He told me calmly that he knows a lady has no penis.

Following this session Emmett appeared quite confused, a defense we had previously worked on that, when now reinterpreted, led to further working through of oedipal themes. In the course of this work, his mother reported that Emmett told her after his bath that her pubic hair had frightened him and that it reminded him of a witch. The mother then said that Emmett had given her an abstract drawing in which she detected an explicit erect penis. In the next session I wondered if Emmett had any thoughts about my visit with his parents. He suggested that I make an abstract drawing. Given our long-standing understanding that this gave me a chance to say what I was thinking, I complied and added in clear outline an erect penis and sac in the lower left corner. Emmett glanced at it and said with an anxious smile, "Don't draw what I drew." Because Emmett occasionally used his mother to give me messages that made him too anxious to say himself, I had taken the mother's communication as such a message and used it, hoping thereby to permit Emmett's masculine claims to elaborate further in the transference. Whether because of my action or not I could not tell, but in subsequent sessions Emmett went on to make clear that he experienced his further identification with his father as pleasurable.

As Emmett developed more capacity for self-observation, less commentary from me was required. While more affectively responsive with me, his rivalrous father transference feelings came more to the fore. For example, he often had each of us make a drawing, and he would take mine and give me his, carelessly drawn. We then set up shop where people bought his paintings but ridiculed and teased me about mine. I interpreted that he sometimes feels not lovable, or good, or strong as with the drawings, that he wishes he could draw well instead of me, and that the lady would then like him and not me. Following this he became bossy and assertive (to my mind in these circumstances, phallic-aggressive) and demanded that I be passive and weak. He jailed me and wanted to tie me up. I interpreted how mixed up he must have felt, being angry, but still sort of liking it, when his father told him to let his peers tie him to a tree. He did not remember the incident, and I did not press for recollection.

A little later, during our working through of his phallic competition with me as father and after enacting the sadistic father, he said, "Everyone's nasty a little bit, right?" I agreed and pointed out that he had been very worried about what would happen if he were angry, because sometimes he felt so very angry with his beloved parents that it scared him. In the course of this work Emmett became more tolerant of his own hostility with greater control over hostile acts and remarks, less projection of dreaded feelings and wishes, and diminished anxiety. His tragedy fantasies not only decreased in frequency but began to include reunions as endings.

I now learned that Emmett's mother was going away for ten days. Although calm at home, in the analysis he was furious with her for leaving him. In his rage, he expressed the early latency boy's hateful rejection of what he experiences as the "penisless" girl: "Girls, ick!" In a puppet depiction of a positive oedipal fantasy, Emmett arranged for the mother to become furious. While the father was enraged because the boy was in bed with the mother, the most feared object was the mother, who became a vampire. The many play storms that followed led me to interpret that the storms showed how Emmett felt so much anger in and around him, and that his anger caused the storms in him and the people in his life. Emmett also had to deal with my impending departure for three weeks; thus more anger toward women evolved in his fantasy play as well as toward me in the transference. I linked the fantasy girl's wish, to be pretty outside so as to hide how angry/ugly she felt inside, with Emmett's wish that I help him get over having very angry feelings toward me and his mother. He angrily retorted, "There is no connection! I am not a girl!"

Upon my return, Emmett described the feminine love-object as very pretty, very bossy, and very mean. "In my imagination that's the way she is," he told me, a priceless bit of evidence of his growing self-observing capacity. I pointed out how very mixed up a boy would feel with such a lady because she feels so attractive but also so mean and frightening. This led to a bit of fantasy play regarding Queen Elizabeth I, who, he told me, destroyed her husband and family. Soon thereafter, the fantasy boy became very angry, then feared his mother would kill him, cried, and killed himself. I wondered aloud if he killed himself because, when he was so angry with the mother he loved, he felt he was so bad, and I linked it again to Emmett's feeling that he had destroyed his own family by having bad thoughts and feelings. The next day he arranged a puppet play in which a boy said urgently to his mother, "Mommy, I want you, I want you, mommy!" and he hugged her. He repeated this and told me it was my turn to do a play. I presented the same boy who said the same thing to his mother, but then I added that he thought his daddy wouldn't like that and so he got very frightened and angry. Emmett said, "Don't do that; that's not another play, that's the same as mine." Then he became quite controlling and did not want me to go on.

Shortly after this session, Emmett's destructiveness appeared clearly in a depiction of a boy sadistically and mercilessly beating a girl. This outburst suggested to me that Emmett had defenses against his own intense hostility, including the perception of the maternal introject as hostile, by means of a passive reaction formation and by a pseudofemininity. I also considered the possibility that the beating might be an aggressive defense against sexual wishes experienced toward the oedipal mother (who, like the girl in the fantasy, was at times seductively dressed). For the first time, Emmett could separate from me before I said good-bye at the end of this session. Subsequently Emmett brought into his play the reality of his parents' extramarital affairs with much to say about jealousies, rivalries, and fights. Perhaps out of countertransference, I permitted myself the intrusion that I was glad Emmett's fantasied couple had no children because a child would be so confused and upset by it all. This he acknowledged.

Next Emmett said that he had asked his mother how long he would have to come see me. He answered his own question—he thought this would be his last year. He then played out a couple making love with quite positive feelings, but a wreck followed. After that a frankly negative oedipal theme appeared in which a boy pretended he was a girl because he was afraid his father would be angry. Here he revealed in fantasy the mother's lying to him about her transgressive activities with a man other than father, and the jealous boy punishes the mother for her transgressions. But then the boy is punished because he also transgressively loves his mother.

A series of sessions followed in which a lady had long hair and fancy clothes, but this time the source of the maternal introject's anger was more clear. The queen in Snow White wants the diamond belt the princess has and kills her for it. Emmett indicated by talk of penises and vaginas that this was the source of the queen's being as angry as a witch and why she had such beautiful clothes. He seemed then to try to get rid of the witch-queen doll by externalizing the hostile castrating introject who died repeatedly in play.

Emmett now revealed with anxiety, pleasure, and shyness that he was going to sleep at his "girlfriend's" house. He clarified with some help that he meant he really liked this girl as a sexual object. In puppet play he showed his conflicted relation to the internalized oedipal and preoedipal mother, who was beautiful and loving on the one hand but witchlike and frighteningly hostile on the other. He is pursued, seduced, and tortured. Man and woman have intercourse with the woman as aggressor. She has a baby, tortures the man, and kills herself in self-punishment. He finished the session by projecting blame onto me, asserting that the mess was mine to clean up (since I let him make it). I felt perhaps he was blaming me for putting him in what he perceived to be a position of danger by not prohibiting him from going to his girlfriend's house.

At this time Emmett's father reported his new relation to his son: "It's really good; he's strong and sure of himself, and he can let himself go and play like other kids his age." Two weeks later Emmett succeeded in riding his bike. He was also getting along well with his peers, being more assertive and active, and they were not pushing him around as they did before. He was playing football and soccer and was doing well in school. Emmett told his mother he now had only one more thing to do "to be like the other boys," and that is to stop going to see Dr. Parens.

Meanwhile, in the analysis Emmett's aggression turned the corner into frank oral sadism with biting of breasts, behinds, penises, and vaginas, all by a monster lion. Phallic competition with me followed with car racing. He returned then to the frequently played out primal scene in which the mother and father are kissing, the father tears the mother's dress, and a fight begins. They will get a divorce. The children stay with mother because "a son is supposed to love his mother more." The father gets thrown out; the children blame the mother, who feels bad. A hurricane threatens. Emmett sums up, "You know who this lady is? She's the same as all the others, ever since I came here. And I know what you'll say, that it has to do with my mother and me. Right? Don't say any more."

Henri Parens, M.D./87

The parents reported that Emmett talked with new ease, even about his not wanting them to get divorced. The father wondered if Emmett's occasional difficult behavior now was connected with the end of his analysis and that this made him feel anxious, regress, and want to hold on. For the first time in nearly two years, the mother reported that Emmett's zipper had been open as it also had been during a recent analytic session.

In the next session Emmett calmly went over his accumulated old drawing-story materials, mentioning soberly which were his and which were mine. In the following few sessions Emmett brought into focus in fantasy play, that in a fit of anger as a girl out of control, he killed his mother and then missed her terribly. Everyone hated the girl and returned at night to hit her. And she knew, I said, as did Emmett, that this was her punishment for how bad she felt she had been by having fits of anger and wanting to kill her mother. I could see that Emmett's feelings of anger were evoked by jealousies arising from his rivalrous fantasies and feelings about his father and about me in the transference. In the course of our work this sequence of feelings came to include how his feelings of guilt resulted from his rivalrous fury and the associated murderous fantasies. His progressively greater tolerance of sexual and destructive wishes and further consolidation of a more benevolent superego seemed evident. I was convinced of this when Emmett detailed a fantasy in which a robber wanted to abduct and forcibly penetrate a woman. As he played it out, the manifest erotic feeling belied the defensive aggression in which the fantasy was cloaked, confirming my impression that the primal scene appeared to be only a hostile battle in order to defend against Emmett's anxiety aroused by his erotic wishes. And yet again as he played out the fantasy, his anxiety appeared to interrupt the play. He declared that he was tired of that game and wanted to know when he could stop coming to analysis.

Emmett's parents reported at length on his notably improved relationship with them, including a much warmer and stronger emotional involvement. A parallel improvement in his other relationships supported my view that important changes in his inner life had stabilized. In the analysis, Emmett behaved consistently in a masculine manner typical of boys his age, and he showed no evidence of his former feminine identification. Signs and symptoms arising from his dread of castration and of abandonment had faded. The extensively analyzed introjects were much less harsh, and the hostility in his fantasies much mitigated. Although I could have wished for even better progress and stability in his interpersonal relationships, I concluded that Emmett's development had gained momentum along usual or normal pathways, and so I decided to agree with the proposal to terminate. We settled on a date in four months.

Following this I saw a marked decrease in the intensity, sharpness, and pervasiveness of his hostility, especially in regard to the maternal introject, along with a clearly lessened tendency to regression. Emmett went over old materials, revisiting conflict areas. I was impressed with his last efforts to eject and to rid himself of the unassimilated part of the hostile maternal introject. I felt that in the transference he had successfully externalized aspects of that representation on to me, thereby facilitating his separation from me.

Emmett terminated his analysis in a dominantly positive relation to me, but at the same time he was glad not to have to come anymore, and he showed only minimal signs of object loss, less, I felt, than I did. However, he did set things in order before leaving. I thought his attaining a revitalized libidinal relation to his now-separated parents was yet another factor that eased his separation.

Henri Parens, M.D./89

DISCUSSION

Why did Emmett wish to be a girl? I know personally about the analyses of two other such boys. One is Billy, analyzed by McDevitt (1985), and the other is Stanley, analyzed by Haber (1991). I will draw on Emmett's material and that of Billy and Stanley to develop a hypothesis about the factors that play a role in the boy's wish to be a girl.

Emmett's mother was the firmer, more emotionally available, stable, and dominant of his parents. Both Billy's and Stanley's mothers were also much more influential in the family than their fathers. Highly narcissistic, sexual feminine identification material presented in the analysis of all three boys. Emmett's mother, in contrast to those of Stanley and Billy, tended to dress seductively. Emmett's father, somewhat like Stanley's, was oppressed and withdrawn, suffered from reactive depressive episodes, and seemed vulnerable. Billy's father also was not involved with his son. As Emmett's analysis progressed his father seemed to grow stronger at home and in his relationship with his son. Billy's father, too, became more parentally involved as Billy's analysis progressed.

Stanley's and Billy's mothers would have preferred that their sons be girls. According to McDevitt, Billy's mother feared that "a boy would be too sexually aggressive" (1985, 2). Emmett's mother showed no evidence of wishing that he be a girl. Emmett's parents, like Stanley's and Billy's mothers, were troubled by his wish to wear girl's clothes, to wear pink shoes, and to have long, blond, flowing hair. Stanley's and Billy's fathers were less troubled about these matters than were their mothers.

Stanley's mother had tantrums, screamed, cursed, threw dishes, and walked out during some outbursts. Emmett's mother did not have tantrums, but she was overtly enraged with her husband; they eventually separated in the course of their son's analysis and later each remarried. I gained the impression that her rage toward her husband, which had antecedents in her rage toward her parents, emerged in Emmett's fantasies of the bad witch/queen who was enraged with and destructive of her husband. Billy's mother seemed unable to tolerate his demands or expressions of anger. He did not dare defy his mother, she told McDevitt. He was much too subdued and reasonable.

The dread of loss and of abandonment played a large part in the early lives of all three boys. In Emmett, this fear led to his distancing in attachment, perhaps related to the parents' having gone on two two-week vacations without him. His parents were upset but didn't understand the implications of Emmett's not recognizing them on return from the first of their vacations. McDevitt also reported a separation of this kind that was traumatic to both Billy and his mother.

I have found similar constellations in children who develop quite different symptoms, exemplifying the problems of specificity of experience and psychodynamics as etiologic determiners of symptom choice. I agree with McDevitt (1985) that some congenital disposition facilitates this choice of symptom, be it explained on the basis of temperament (for example, Thomas and Chess 1977) and/or drive endowment (for example, Alpert, Neubauer, and Weil 1956), expressed in the "basic core" (Weil 1970) as a suppression of "activity" or of aggression.

I do find two factors common to these three boys which may play a substantial and perhaps a specific role in such boys' choice of symptom. First, in my analysis of Emmett, I was puzzled by the centrality that the omnipresent threatening bad witch or queen occupied in his fantasies. In the many contacts I had with his parents, I found no evidence of such a threat or of sadism in his mother's attitude toward him. She let me know she was furious with her husband, but I never found any hint that she was vicious and mean with Emmett. The unfolding of his transference furor and hate toward me led me to infer that its origins lay substantially *in his own rage and hate*. I concluded that Emmett's fantasy of an omnipresent, sadistic, bad witch/queen was not shaped by the reality of his mother, but rather *that the mother became a witch/bad queen through the influence of his own rage, the rage generated in his relationship with both mother and father, and that this became specifically invested in the mother representation.* As his analysis progressed, the threat of castration was at first attached to the bad witch/angry queen, not predominantly to the king-father, as is usual in the boy in the positive Oedipus complex. In Little Hans, although his mother threatened castration, Freud's report (1909) suggests that Hans experienced the dread of castration as coming from his father. Did this difference play a part in Little Hans's and Emmett's choice of symptoms? In both Stanley and Billy, the mother featured quite specifically as threatener of castration. Like Haber (1991), McDevitt (1985) found that Billy's mother unconsciously wanted her son to be a girl, although both mothers were very troubled by their sons' compliance with that wish. The first factor, then, is that the mother as castrator, or as the perceived initiator of castration, is experienced by the boy as especially alarming and as more dangerous than the father as castrator.

The second factor is the frightening experience of some young boys that their hostile destructiveness is unmanageable. I am convinced that much and varied psychopathology results from the generation of hostile destructiveness (Parens 1979a, 1984) in the very young. As a consequence of such excessive and protracted hostility, the child's ambivalence (Parens 1979b) toward objects and self is heightened, and in efforts to cope, a variety of pathologic compromise formations such as defensive splitting (Kernberg 1966; Mahler, Pine, and Bergman 1975) of self and of object representations are produced.

In Emmett and Stanley, expressions of rage were densely

woven into the transference. Emmett's sadism was rampant, but he clung to me in equally intense despair when his mother was late in getting to the waiting room to pick him up. Haber tells us that Stanley would walk out of sessions in outbursts of rage like those his mother had at home. McDevitt reports that he did not know enough about Billy's first eighteen months, but he inferred that Billy manifested either a low endowment of aggression or a marked inhibition of it during that early period. He also knew from the history that Billy's mother could not tolerate his assertiveness and hostility and that he quickly learned not to be defiant. But how might heightened hostile destructiveness play a specific role in the symptom formation we found in these boys?

Inhibition in the face of unmanageably intense hostile feelings toward the mother is a major defense employed by children beginning at about ten months of age (Parens 1979a). I suggest that such inhibition, whether derived from actual or fantasied sources, is a critical factor in the boy's wish to be a girl. Specifically, the male child needs sufficient access to his nondestructive aggression in order to allow his phallic aggression, when it differentiates, to give character to his oedipal elaboration. The boy's experience of sufficient phallic aggression is essential to the experience of burgeoning masculinity.

I have found no difference in nondestructive aggression (that is, assertiveness) in infant boys and girls under two years of age (Parens 1979a, 1984, 1989). That is, girls are equally assertive, equally aggressive as boys at that time. The striking difference between them occurs from about the beginning of the third year of life on, not so much in the amount or degree of aggressiveness as in the characteristics of the aggression expressed, in the *modes* or *patterns of aggressive discharge,* when phallic aggression in boys far outweighs that in girls, and gender-behavioral distinctions between male and female can now more readily be seen.

The question arises whether the inhibition of aggression that results from the child's efforts to contain excessive hostile destructive feelings toward the mother carries with it the inhibition of phallic aggression. Speaking of Billy's shifting bisexual identification, McDevitt (1985) wrote, "Following the onset of castration anxiety (in analysis) . . . *once his rage at his mother had subsided somewhat,* Billy turned toward me with interest" (22, italics added). In my work with Emmett, "the analysis of his rage toward his mother and the freeing up of defended-against aggression, especially phallic aggressiveness, was a cardinal factor that allowed his masculine identity to be experienced more fully and freely."

Thus a review of reports from the analyses of these three cases lends more support to the conflict/defense hypothesis of gender disturbance in boys as proposed by Meyer and Dupkin (1985) than to the nonconflictual identity hypothesis earlier put forward (Stoller 1968). I assume that the biological/imprint hypothesis of gender disturbance (Gadpaille 1980; Green 1982; Meyer and Dupkin 1985) undoubtedly has a meaningful place; I propose that in addition the confluence of two factors embedded in other etiologic codeterminers plays a key part in such boys' choice of symptom. The experience of unmanageably heightened hostile destructiveness not only intensifies ambivalence in them, but also becomes attached to the mental representation of the mother, who, rather than the father, is experienced as the object who threatens castration. At the same time this heightened hostile destructiveness toward the mother must be inhibited, leading some boys to significantly inhibit the phallic aggression that is a necessary ingredient, if not organizer, of their emerging masculinity.

During the phallic phase there may be a further vulnerability in boys in that their phallic aggression and narcissism are both in jeopardy as they navigate a course between overidentification with (or insufficient disidentification/separation-individuation from) their mothers on the one hand, and mother-attached castration anxiety on the other, at the point in development when their masculinity emerges. This factor may well lead to the gender problems we find in boys like Emmett, Stanley, and Billy.

Further Comparative Notes

Emmett, Stanley, and Billy each had a central fantasy in which the self-representation was a girl, and each wanted to wear a girl's clothing and walked with body undulations that caricatured a feminine mannerism; but each boy enormously valued his penis.

Haber (1991) observed that his patient Stanley had strange but analytically accessible "switch" fantasies in the direction of being a boy to being a girl. I was impressed with the degree to which Emmett resisted psychoanalytic collaboration in our efforts to understand the fantasies that led to his switching. When he experienced the witch/queen as especially hostile and powerful, he seemed to retreat from masculinity. When he could express hostility toward the "Lady" or when he could be assertive with her, he usually represented himself as a boy. There were two types of women in his fantasies—the hated witch or queen who was frightening, commandeering, or threatening, and the Lady, who emerged later in analysis and who was neither hated nor experienced as threatening. Enlightening, too, are the fantasy conditions under which Stanley (Haber's patient) could maintain a male self-representation. When feeling secure he would be the doctor and Haber would be the patient who got shots to get well. "When danger was perceived, he *switched* to being a nurse" (17), or he was "a detective who figured out clues and always won in the end" (17); he might then occasionally rescue a beautiful, rich woman to whom he *had* (that is, someone already possessed) made love, or he "was the richest man in the world and had contact with presidents and kings." A critical shift occurred when Stanley fantasied a woman in danger who then was saved by a fearless man. This led to positive oedipal thematic material. It is interesting that a pivotal element of the shift was the woman being perceived as being in danger, a circumstance associated with a man who is capable of being fearless (cf. Person 1986).

QUESTIONS OF TECHNIQUE WITH
PRELATENCY CHILDREN

In my experience, prelatency-age children are more capable of verbalizing (or in play to give evidence of) their experiences, emotional and cognitive, than seems to be generally assumed; analytic interventions with such children are effective when they facilitate the child's *verbalization* of their own fantasies. Even with three-year-olds, a nondirective, nonsuggestive, and analytically neutral approach takes priority, thus minimizing the assumption of meanings, the direct interpretation of the sign-function behavior, and the guessing of interpretations. The major exception is in setting limits, which is virtually unavoidable in the analysis of prelatency-age children, though this, too, needs to be analyzed.

From the clinician's viewpoint, there are some questions to be addressed in conclusion. In the course of Emmett's analysis I was able to observe the evolution of his conflict-derived defense of being a girl to his age- and gender-appropriate wish to feel that my lady likes him better than me. Stanley's fantasy evolution led to his wish to be a superman hero saving a woman in distress. Perhaps such changes could have occurred spontaneously, but what would it have required from Emmett (or Stanley), from his environment, or from chance experience? Could it have occurred by therapeutic means other than psychoanalysis? Could some behavior modification technique be devised that would undo his dread of abandonment and of castration, the dread of his own hostility and that of his hostile mother representation, and the overriding fantasy that integrated all these factors? Could such a behavior modification procedure be achieved, sustained, and be development-promoting in a young child? And would it protect against symptom recurrence if the underlying wishes, fears, and conflicts were not resolved? I have yet to see such results accomplished by means other than by psychoanalysis.

Could the desired results be achieved by means of psychotherapy once or twice a week? I believe not, though some mitigation of symptoms may occur. Or by a mother-child psychotherapy modeled on psychotherapy conducted with infants (Fraiberg 1980) or treatment of the child by way of the parents (Furman 1957)? My doubts about the efficacy of these forms of treatment for prelatency children suffering gender disorders are based on seeing that children are often unable to verbalize central issues when they are in an analytic session with the mother present. Evidence of this has been reported from direct child-parent observation as well (for instance, Parens, Pollock, Stern, and Kramer 1976). For example, one nearly three-year-old girl was mortified when a student observer asked her to repeat in her mother's presence who it was she said she was going to marry.

Furthermore, in doing mother-child psychotherapy from two years of age on, I have seen many moments when issues emerge that could lead to transgressions of the child's private fantasies if brought up with the mother present. Overall, these kinds of observations seem to me to be strong evidence for certain crucial issues being inaccessible to intervention when a parent is in the session. I have also found this in psychotherapy preparatory for psychoanalysis, when the mother or father is present in the session. For example, a four-year-old boy several times became resistant to pursuing a line of thought that he himself had initiated, saying, "This is for later."

Why psychoanalysis at four years of age? Could we not have waited to see if Emmett "outgrew" his problem? Discontinuity theory notwithstanding, we have much evidence from decades of clinical and direct observational work that children's efforts at resolving rapprochement and oedipal conflicts during the two- to six-year-old period lead to the emergence, establishment, and stabilization of psychic structures that strongly influence all subsequent personality development. I am convinced that the prevention of maladaptive psychic structure formation made possible by psychoanalysis of prelatency-age children is less costly in all dimensions than later efforts at undoing and cure.

The Analysis of a
Frightened Little Boy

Robert M. Galatzer-Levy, M.D.

Psychoanalytic work with very young children holds many rewards and surprises. The case described below illustrates some of them. The rewards included the opportunity to get to know an extremely interesting youngster in depth and to help him move from a state of great psychological distress and blocked development to a joyful engagement with the internal and external world. The surprises came with the personal rediscovery that severe psychopathology can arise in the context of a rich and highly developed psychological life and that the psychoanalytic method is genuinely self-correcting in the sense that the psychoanalyst's theoretical prejudices need not bar his finding central themes in analyses that are contrary to his predispositions. He has only to take the method of psychoanalytic exploration seriously.

To understand this last point the reader must know that the author's training and conceptual thought have been deeply influenced by the concepts of self psychology as developed by Heinz Kohut and his followers. Psychopathology, as conceptualized in this framework, is primarily the result of deficiencies/incapacities to perform necessary psychological functions that support a cohesive and vigorous self. This incapacity is believed to originate in disturbances of the patient's early environment that interfere in the internalization of these functions, which are ordinarily earlier performed by caretakers. Either primarily inadequate provision of these "selfobject" functions or their traumatic interruption may lead to self pathology (Kohut 1984). Thus confronted with a young, seriously disturbed child, I tended to assume that the fault lay in some inadequacy of psychological capacity rather than in internal conflicts. Finding myself to be mistaken carried with it far more conviction about the validity of the analytic work than I would have had if my prejudices had been confirmed.

This case report is meant to be a polemic and a seduction. My clinical experience with the boy I here call Johnny, as well as my direct and vicarious experience of the analyses of several other young children, convinces me, first, that they can often enter into psychoanalysis, second, that psychoanalysis offers them opportunities for emotional growth available in no other way, and, finally, that these analyses provide extraordinary opportunities to enrich psychoanalytic experience. Many youngsters like Johnny, even when they come to the attention of psychoanalysts and psychoanalytically sophisticated mental health professionals, are treated through such environmental ameliorations as parent education and less thorough-going psychotherapies in the belief that a child so young cannot have developed a sufficiently stable internal psychology to warrant analysis. I believe these ideas arise from wishful thinking that defends against the full psychological force of the inner life of the young child. Regardless of their origin, I think they are mistaken and that many young children could not only benefit greatly from psychoanalysis but will be left crippled and deprived of their full capacities without it. While we will never know with certainty how Johnny would have developed without analysis, it seems to me highly improbable that the development he exhibited could have occurred in any other context. Nor could the rewards for all involved have been as great with any other type of work. I hope the analyst reader will be moved to attempt similar work with appropriate patients and that the nonanalyst reader will learn that there are young children for whom psychoanalysis is the treatment of choice.

The Case of Johnny

Background   Johnny at age three years, six months was referred to me by his mother's psychiatrist. For approximately a month before the referral he often seemed terrified. He cried inconsolably. He complained bitterly to his parents about hundreds of tiny cuts on his fingers and insisted his parents put bandaids on them. There was no physical evidence to suggest injury, but the intensity of the boy's demands and his abject terror when his parents failed to tend to the "cuts" led the parents and the housekeeper to comply with his demands. His fingers were thus regularly covered with bandaids. Johnny was horrified at the thought that eating his food would hurt it. He avoided biting into food but instead swallowed it whole. He panicked when he accidentally bit into a piece of food, spat it out, and cried. Not only did he not want to hurt his food by biting it, it was essential that the food on his plate be in perfect order.

At the beginning of his illness Johnny was satisfied if various foods were neatly separated, but by the time I saw him he required that each grain of rice be in a row on the plate before he would eat any of it. The parents were particularly frightened because Johnny's weight had fallen from thirty-three to twenty-nine pounds in the month before I saw him. Johnny's nights were haunted by "fire eyes," entities he could not describe except that they were "the most dangerous things in the world." Johnny's parents described only two remarkable features of his development. Johnny always loved books and started reading at age two and a half. After a brief time he insisted on reading to himself. Within a short time he could read anything he chose. There had been occasional struggles when the parents offered to read to him and he would not let them. Generally they were pleased with his reading and supported it with a seemingly unending supply of children's books. Though his parents thought little of it, Johnny always insisted on having several books with him wherever he went.

Attempts at bowel training had been resisted from their inception, also when Johnny was two and a half. When I saw him, he enjoyed urinating in the toilet. But as he stated clearly, he preferred to "make poops" in a diaper and withheld his feces until a diaper was provided. When he was about three, at the pediatrician's recommendation, Johnny's parents refused to put him in diapers. Though obviously very uncomfortable he did not defecate for a week until they gave in and provided him with a diaper. The parents were not particularly concerned about Johnny's refusal to use the toilet except that they were worried that he could not attend school if he required diapering to defecate.

Johnny's parents were both slightly odd. His mother's face seemed always neutral in expression. Though she was well groomed there was something unintegrated in her appearance. She reminded one of a painting by Braque. It was only some time into the treatment that I discovered that she was capable of a brightly radiant smile. She said she had been depressed since the death of her father six months before the start of Johnny's treatment, which was the reason for her being in treatment herself. Johnny had not been close to his grandfather but spoke openly of missing him. He worried about his grandmother. Her grief concerned and frightened him, and he wanted to make her stop crying.

Johnny's mother was also much distressed by her husband's fascination with a young male business associate. The manifest content of this preoccupation involved a high-risk business deal that seemed to Johnny's mother to threaten the family's financial security.

The incongruous sense of Johnny's mother was intensified when she was in the company of her husband. She is tall and fair, whereas he is short and swarthy. They seemed not to go together. His manner was coarse, especially when he spoke of bodily functions in a way that seemed out of keeping with his middle-class background. When mother said, "Johnny sometimes masturbates in the bathtub," father broke in saying, "Yeah. The kid just grabs for that pecker and goes for it."

Johnny's father was mildly disappointed with the boy. He had looked forward to having an athletic and playful son. But Johnny was a solemn youngster, uninterested in and frightened by rough and tumble. Though father spoke of an appreciation of the boy as he was, particularly his intellectual abilities, he knew of his disappointment. Sometimes when Johnny became frantic, the father became enraged at the mother or the child, but he later regretted this reaction. The young man whom mother found so threatening was described by father as merely a business associate—"but boy is he a pistol."

Johnny was the much-wanted and only child of this couple, who had married in their late thirties. The pregnancy, delivery, and development were unremarkable as reported by the parents, except for the absence of stories and fantasies about the pregnancy and Johnny's infancy. That is, with the exception of the matters discussed earlier, the parents seemed to have no stories or ideas about the child's history and attempts to elicit such stories were unrewarding. The family history was negative for major psychiatric illness.

Initial interviews   When I first met Johnny he was a sad, tiny child with a solemn adultlike manner. His fingers were covered with bandaids. Invited into the office, he sat in a chair that seemed utterly enormous for him and said nothing. He did not look around the room or at me. After a while he started to tap his hand rhythmically. I asked whether he was thinking about a song. He said he was but he didn't know what its name was. It was a sad song. I said he looked sad, and he said that he was because he was thinking about a fire eyes. I asked what that was, and he said he couldn't explain but that it was "a very very bad thing, the worst thing." I asked whether it made him sad, and he said no, that it frightened him. He thought about fire eyes a lot. He went on that his mother explained that I was a doctor who helped people with their feelings. That I didn't give shots. But his trouble was his imagination. "Are the fire eyes parts of your imagination?" I asked. "Yes," he said. "Well, then," I said, "maybe we can figure out why you imagine them." "No," he said. "Why not?" "Because I don't imagine them." "I thought you said they were in your imagination." "I did." "But you don't think we can figure out why you imagine them?" Tears welled up in Johnny's eyes and he looked miserable. He said, "You don't understand. I don't imagine them, they're in my imagination." "Oh," I said, "I think I see. When you say something is in your imagination you don't mean it's something that you thought up." "That's right, it's something that got into my imagination. Fire eyes are very real you know."

Johnny was very willing to tell me a great deal about his inner world—a place dominated by terrifying beings, the worst of which was the undescribable fire eyes. But for Johnny this was a trip to an actual place. His imagination was in no sense a mental playground or differentiated from the external world. Rather, internal and external reality were undifferentiated objective realities.

Though Johnny was courteous toward me and everyone else I saw him with, his attitude was that of a master toward a servant. He courteously informed one of how things were to be. For example, in coming into the office, he announced, "Bring my books." He made no demands of me that felt onerous. But when his mother or the housekeeper brought him, commanding yells emerged from the waiting room when they did anything contrary to his wishes.

Additional sessions quickly confirmed the observation that Johnny was severely depressed. He had a major deficit in reality processing but was highly intelligent and verbal. The intensity of his fantasies, coupled with their lacking special status as fantastic, often left him in a state of terror which was inadequately controlled by obsessional and grandiose defenses. His own subjective distress motivated him toward treatment, and I felt I could work with him.

My recommendation of psychoanalysis was greeted with enthusiasm by both parents. Mother said that if his symptoms continued much longer she did not think she could bear it. Father, who had seemed aloof and skeptical until the recommendation, became tearful. He said he hoped I could help his son because he loved him more than anything in the world.

The beginning of treatment Johnny quickly fell into a routine in our sessions. He brought six to eight books with him to each hour. Sometimes he told me their stories; sometimes he read them to me. The stories deviated little, if at all, from the books' contents. I could discern no clear pattern except that he brought many versions of the Wizard of Oz. In these books his attention was often focused on witches.

Attempts to interpret the content of Johnny's readings in terms of himself, for example, by observing that characters in the stories resembled his experiences of family members, were met with denials and, more important, little elaboration of the stories. When I discussed the anxiety Johnny experienced, however, or that characters in the stories might experience in various situations Johnny calmed and elaborated ideas.

For example, when I talked about the good and bad witches in the Wizard of Oz as they represented a split image of his mother, little of value emerged. Interpreting this split met with bland denials and a return to the narrative as it appeared in the book. Yet comments on how confused and in need of help Dorothy must have felt when confronted with this strange new world were readily related to Johnny's terror in confronting the alien world of his own experiences. Increasingly he spoke of Dorothy's helpers, who clumsily, yet ultimately usefully, assisted her.

Despite the seemingly impersonal content of what he said, Johnny was engaging. Though the contents of stories he repeated were well known to me I never found him boring or difficult to listen to. His sadness, fear, and precocious manner stimulated a sense in me of being with a worthwhile person capable of strong feelings. But to a surprising extent for such a young child, he elicited few fantasies in me of protecting him or relieving his suffering. Only on rare occasion, when I misunderstood him and his eyes filled with grief laden tears, would I suddenly be struck by how very little he was and how inordinately he suffered. As Johnny became less terrified, the stories he told deviated increasingly from the strict text of the books that he carried with him. References to his deviations initially led to flight back to the books' text.

Beginnings of an analytic alliance   After several repetitions in which my observation that he had deviated from the printed text in telling me a story had resulted in his terrified withdrawal, I commented to him that he was afraid that if I noticed his own thoughts I would push him too far and leave him feeling very frightened. He began to cry and told me how sometimes he was "so scared." He said he really liked me and didn't want to be scared here. I said that he saw me as like the helper in the Wizard of Oz, well meaning but unable to protect him. He said my beard reminded him of the scarecrow. I also told him there were two ways to feel less scared—you could turn away from scary things and try to pretend they weren't there or you could look at them and understand them. Sometimes it was easier to look at things if you had someone on your side to help you look at them. He said he understood that from the Wizard of Oz. But there were some things—like fire eyes—that were so bad that they would destroy anyone who tried to help him. Gradually, in the context of repeated interpretations of his anxiety about telling me his thoughts and his use of the printed story as a means to protect himself from the dangers of such revelations, he came to tell his own stories. Of his own characters the first to arrive was the Gump, a salty, gruff man who was forever threatening this and that and becoming irritated and angry.

Somehow the Gump never acted on his threats. Despite his gruffness there was something appealing about him. The Gump quickly developed a wife—the Moym. The Moym tended to worry frenetically or, sometimes, with a burdened sadness about her husband's whereabouts. Eventually the Gump would show up, usually irritated by the Moym's failure to have his dinner promptly on the table. Johnny played the roles of both Moym and Gump, each of whom answered my questions about their activities and feelings. The Moym sometimes confided in me how difficult it was to live with the tempestuous Gump. But despite her difficulties it was clear that the Moym and the Gump were extraordinarily fond of each other. They had gotten together, so the story developed, because both of them were "weird" and though they were dissimilar in many ways their shared experience of being outsiders drew them close to each other.

They were both slightly ludicrous characters who when asked about having children said that they very much wanted one but had no idea at all about how to take care of a child. "Where do you put the fuel in?" asked the Gump. "Do you put it in the closet at night?" "How much soap do you put in the dishwasher to clean it?" inquired the Moym.

Robert M. Galatzer-Levy, M.D./107

Though the Moym and the Gump transparently represented Johnny's parents, the power and psychological accuracy of the portrayal suddenly became apparent to me in an interview with the parents about a month after Johnny began telling me these stories. As I sat listening to their discussion of Johnny, I suddenly realized that, though wanting to be good parents, neither of them had any spontaneous notion of what to do with a child. Mother, in fact, who like Johnny always had a book in hand, had systematically read many books on child rearing hoping to make up for her conscious sense of ignorance about child care. I had the overwhelming sense that I was interviewing the Moym and the Gump and barely suppressed an urge to laugh.

Although I had previously offered the idea to Johnny that the Moym and the Gump represented his parents, it got nowhere. Although I never said it in so many words, I believe that my attitude when I made this interpretation communicated something like, "Out of your own psychological needs you have constructed a picture of your parents in which they are well intended but not very competent or well put together." After the interview with his parents, despite my awareness of the counteridentification with Johnny that would lead to my agreeing with him, my sense was that his caricature had captured central elements of his parents' personalities. During the session following the meeting with his parents I said to Johnny, "You know, your parents do really have a lot in common with the Moym and the Gump." Johnny laughed and said, "They do, Dr. Levy. Only you and me know that—that's our secret."

The full intensity of Johnny's most distressing symptoms quickly remitted. Without being explicitly addressed, the urgency to have bandaids on his fingers dwindled over the course of a few months. He became simply a picky eater, and his terror of the fire eyes, who by this time had expanded into a whole variety of beings — not all of them malignant — was much diminished. Though still careful to say that it was much more complicated than this, Johnny became clearer about the fire eyes. They were the reddened and angry appearing eyes of a depressed and angry adult, like those of his grandmother.

A few months after Johnny's fourth birthday his mother told me she was worried about his bowel training. I suggested she talk to Johnny, tell him of her wishes and her motives, which consciously had related to attending nursery school, something which he said he wanted to do. I asked her to let me know how that went and was not surprised when she reported that Johnny had responded in his usual imperious fashion that he would not do it. Against my advice mother tried the technique of making a diaper unavailable for a day, but it became clear that Johnny was willing to go through the same sort of withholding as he had a year before.

The identification of conflict and defense   I told Johnny that I had talked with his mother about using the toilet and said I thought there must be some reason that he would not use it for bowel movements. He glibly said that there was — it felt better to do it in a diaper and described a pleasant, unconflicted feeling of gushy warmth. Not using the toilet was a problem only because he would like to go to nursery school. The lack of manifest conflict perplexed me. I told him I was uncertain about this but wondered whether it felt nicer to think of going in his diaper as a pleasure than to think about worries about using the toilet. He said that things went down the toilet awfully fast and that it made a big noise. It was like a giant that could eat you up. I said that if I thought of a toilet as the mouth of a giant that would gobble up things, I, too, would be frightened to sit on the toilet or put things in it that had just been part of me. He laughed and said I had a "silly imagination" and that everyone knew that toilets weren't giants. His thought went to a picture in one of his books of the cyclops and how frightening it was. I said, "Like a fire eye," and he thoughtfully said, "Maybe."

During the time he was talking to me about the toilet as a giant's mouth he told his mother, without telling me, that he wanted to try sitting on the toilet. He said he wanted to be a big boy. About a week later he greeted me with the proud announcement—he "had pooped in the potty," and his fears about it were all gone. I said I certainly hoped that was true, though I wondered to him if it was less frightening to use the toilet than to think about the fears. He said that he had a nightmare the night before, which was the night after he used the toilet, about "the most horrible fire eyes." He talked about "little children" who are afraid to use the potty—being small they are afraid they might fall in and be flushed away. The noise of a toilet reminds them of a giant's roar. Johnny seemingly used the toilet regularly thereafter but shortly developed a symptom of urinary frequency.

I said to him that maybe he had become afraid that he would lose his penis in the toilet, just as he lost his feces, so he kept running to the bathroom to make sure his penis was still there and working. He told me that if he was worried about his penis he would just hold onto it and, no, it was really that he had to urinate. After a while it became clear that he was again withholding feces and that the urinary frequency was a physical consequence of pressure on his bladder. I said it was a dilemma to want to be a big boy and use the toilet and to be terrified of it. Now he agreed, describing fears that the toilet would flush sucking him into the vortex, swallow him up, and trap him under the floor or in a sewer from which he could never escape. I reminded him that when he came to see me he was afraid of his own chewing up of food and hurting it, and it sounded to me like he now feared the toilet would do the same thing to him. He wondered what it was like to be in a sewer and how you could escape.

Over the course of the analysis I had periodically interpreted to Johnny that the idea that his stories were just from books and not his own ideas protected him from the bad feelings that came when he thought of them as his own. Shortly after the episode about toilet training he referred back to a question I had posed to him several months before. He regularly brought in many more books than he used during the sessions and I had wondered why it was "necessary" to bring all those books in. On a couple of occasions he had "forgotten" some of the books in the waiting room but then grew anxious and insisted we go to get them. Now he came in and announced that he was bringing the books in because "they are not necessary." This seemed an enormous joke to him, one that I did not get.

One day he turned to me in the midst of a story and said that he had been thinking about something. He realized, he said, that his imagination was something that he made. He didn't understand why he made things that scared him so much, maybe I could explain that, but he now felt quite certain that his imagination was his creation. I asked him how he came to that conclusion, and he said that he wasn't sure but he thought that he was less scared of his imagination than he used to be. He was now able to more clearly recount his older ideas about his imagination. When he had first suffered from his fear of fire eyes in the night, his father had attempted to reassure him telling him that the fire eyes were in his imagination. Johnny had taken this to mean that they were in a physical location, a sort of box under his bed, and become even more terrified than before.

Less afraid than he had been, Johnny was able to start a new kind of story at this point, approximately a year and a half into the analysis. These stories were avowedly his own, though he often borrowed characters from the many books he read. In these stories he and Dr. Levy went on exploring adventures together. We would head out into an unknown jungle or forest, confident adventurers together. In each adventure we met a carnivorous animal or giant who invariably ate us. Being trapped in the beast's stomach was dreadful, and we wanted to escape. The two of us became quite expert at tickling, poking, setting fires, and otherwise dislodging ourselves from these creatures' innards so that after several months of this, the threat of being eaten was virtually no threat at all. In fact, the two of us became a rather jaunty and self-assured pair exploring an ever-broadening world. The creatures and monsters we met became increasingly varied in their manner and interests. Some of them were quite friendly, others suffered from fears of being eaten themselves, and some of them were as bloodthirstily carnivorous as ever.

During this period, for the first time, Johnny seemed like a little boy—spontaneous, lively, often humorous. The somber manner, whose utter pervasiveness was only fully apparent retrospectively, disappeared. His parents reported many areas of growth. He was attending nursery school, where several little girls evidently had crushes on him. He played with his father for the first time. Sometimes he engaged father in the same sort of fantasy games he played with me, and sometimes, to his father's great delight, he played catch. But the game of catch could easily become terrifying. He told his father this and explained that if he wanted to have a good time he needed not to throw too hard and to be willing to stop playing. Father said he wished he did not have to be so careful with Johnny but did comply with the boy's wishes.

Johnny next introduced a new series of stories. These were tales of animals who adopted human customs—hippopotamuses that bathed in bathtubs and lizards who used silverware. The animals had seen humans behave in these civilized ways and recognized their superiority, but imitating did not come naturally to them. Much of this play had a strong moralistic quality. The newly civilized animals looked with contempt on those of their species who had not advanced as far as they had. I found myself frequently on the side of impulse, wondering whether the animals didn't miss the old ways—if the hippo didn't miss the lovely feeling of the mud. "Not at all," the hippo responded in a superior tone of voice. "It is so much pleasanter to take a nice clean bath." "On the other hand," the hippo observed, "it is very difficult to find a bathtub large enough for a hippopotamus." Many of the animals had similar problems. They averred that human ways were superior to those of wild animals, but there were all manner of mechanical difficulties in the way of their being fully comfortable in their new ways. Many of them, having learned their human ways from books or by observing people from a distance, were not altogether familiar with how people did things and misinterpreted what they saw. The chimps, for example, could not figure out when to use which utensils for eating. This led to many discussions about how one decides what one really wants and how it is sometimes difficult to understand things that are considered human. I said, eventually, that I thought Johnny felt like the creatures in this story, trying very hard to be an ordinary boy but unsure that was the way he was or how to be a boy. I said he felt a lot of pressure to be more ordinary. He said that there was a lot of pressure: "People don't like weird kids and I want to be liked." In particular he didn't want to stop coming to see me for a very long time because he liked me and we had many adventures. I said that we could continue to see each other as long as he found it useful. And he said no—we should continue to see each other as long as he found it useful and then as long as he found it useless.

I said that I thought useless things were very useful. When we first met, everything was the same—very real, but I thought he had discovered that there was a useless place where things were important but not real. He said that was right and asked how I knew that. I said that maybe we could ask a different question — why he didn't know that when he first came to see me. He said that the people who wrote all the books he read knew it, and that other kids knew it, but he didn't know why he did not know it.

Transference configurations As Johnny grew more at ease with me, he was increasingly direct in the demands he placed upon me. These centered around the telling of stories. Frequently he asked me to anticipate how the story would continue, and I sometimes commented in ways that indicated my understanding of the story. The importance of my understanding accurately was indicated when I misunderstood or inaccurately predicted how the story was to develop, at which point Johnny would frequently dissolve into tearful weeping and felt unbearably pained. It became clear to both of us that part of the terror of his monsters and the fire eyes was the sense of being entirely alone with them and misunderstood. The episode in which father had told him that the fire eyes were "in your imagination" became paradigmatic of the kind of difficulties Johnny experienced at the hands of his parents, especially his father, whom he consciously experienced as meaning well by him. Yet he had the repeated experience of feeling misunderstood or himself misunderstanding things that were intended to be reassuring, which led to a sense of profound despair.

The interpretation that there were things about himself that Johnny feared were so bad that no one could understand them, so that he felt like he must always be alone with his horrible feelings and ideas, led to a new series of stories about monsters. The monsters had a particular problem — the only food they liked was humans. More ordinary food was unacceptable either because it was not a person and therefore not good to eat or, alternatively, because it reminded the monsters of people and so made them feel guilty because they knew they should not eat people.

As the stories unfolded, they became increasingly elaborated. One theme was the benign witch who transformed the carnivorous monsters into beautiful beings. There was also a transformation in the use of the stories to communicate his feelings about me. For example, Johnny began one story describing spooky creatures who do evil and a witch. Thinking the witch was also evil, I made some comment to the effect that both characters were frightening. Immediately Johnny replied that there was a cobra who attacked adults and killed them. I should be careful how I talked to him as he was the cobra. I said that I thought my interpretation and misunderstanding of him had made him exceedingly angry and want to hurt me. At that point he returned to the story, explaining that the witch in the story was a good witch who made everything better, and then he said how he was surprised that I don't seem to get angry at him for being angry at me.

Johnny began to wonder about the origins of his feelings. Although on several occasions I had attempted to place the way he felt in a historical context, he became increasingly curious about these issues himself. For example, he wondered why he had expected me to get angry at him when he was angry at me, since his parents rarely respond angrily to his anger and upset. It is true that sometimes his father got angry with him, but it was his own sense that the intense despair and feeling of being totally rejected by his father at these times was disproportionate to what the father expressed. Within the metaphor of the carnivorous animal stories, I interpreted that Johnny's terror and despair were a response to his own projected hostile feelings. He expected people to be enormously hostile toward him because, feeling bad about his own hostility, he attributed it to the other person and then was terrified and dismayed by the destructiveness that he supposed was directed toward himself. After we had told three or four stories about animals in this predicament, Johnny told me directly that he understood full well that we were talking about him. Since the animals in the story got into trouble because they were so frightened to know what they felt, we should not do the same thing but should talk directly about strong feelings, instead of referring to them indirectly through animal tales.

Drawings and heroes   As Johnny turned five his overall demeanor had markedly changed. He was a lively, engaging little boy who had much to tell me about his world. Part of what he had to talk about was being in love. Janet, a girl his own age in his nursery school class, was "as beautiful as could be." He described her in glowing terms and was especially fond of how he felt when he was near her or saw her. He thought he would marry her when he grew up. He was enormously upset when some of the other boys in the class teased Janet and her friends. He felt furious but unable to come to her aid.

He told me there were things now that he could not talk about with me, and I said that he must see me in some way that made it frightening to talk about some of his thoughts. On several occasions he "forgot" to bring books into the session. On one occasion when he commented on this, I remarked that in the past when this had happened he felt a need to go to the waiting room to get the books. He recalled that as being true but went on to say that I was always reminding him of how he used to be little and scared and that made him feel bad. I asked him if he thought I was trying to make him feel bad. He felt ashamed, he said, because he knew I always tried to help him, but now he often felt like I was trying to make him feel bad and like a little child, and at the same time thought to himself that he must be mistaken.

Johnny began to show a new and quite remarkable capacity. While earlier in the analysis he had never asked to draw, now he did. The drawings were cartoonlike renderings of the characters from the stories he told. They were drawn with great rapidity and deftness, but they were enormously evocative of affect. He once again began telling stories of monsters, the Moym, and the Gump, but this time illustrated by series of drawings that accompanied his narration.

A particularly prominent story that emerged at this time was that the Moym, in great distress over her husband's absences and irresponsible behavior, would come to Johnny's sessions to seek our advice about how to handle her delinquent husband. Johnny, enraged by his misbehavior, recommended that she not "put up with him." But the Moym was firm in her attachment to her wayward husband. Johnny then gave grudgingly supportive reminders that the Gump had always come home in the end and that the Moym would not love him unless he was a good husband. But he confided in me that he liked it better when the Moym was very upset and he could comfort her. He denied that anything like this story occurred in his real life with his parents.

Johnny's mother reported for the first time that there was some mild reluctance on Johnny's part to come to the sessions. He disliked the interruption in his day. I asked Johnny about this, and he said that sometimes the sessions made it impossible for him to go swimming at the pool where he would see Janet. He actually had very little contact with her, but he liked to be there to watch her and to protect her from boys who might give her a hard time by teasing her. He interrupted telling me this by saying that he needed to go to the bathroom, which was very unusual for him. On returning he was at pains to explain the trip to the bathroom as caused by the juice he had drunk before the session. I said that it sounded like he thought he had to make an excuse for going to the bathroom. After protesting that he was allowed to go to the bathroom whenever he wanted, he confided that he sometimes still worried about his "dick." He now knew that the toilet monsters were the result of his own imaginings, but he still sometimes worried that they would come up and get him or get his dick.

With great difficulty he confided in me that he sometimes "got up-dick," especially when he played with his penis; he "knew [this] was all right" because his parents had explicitly told him that it was. It was particularly difficult to tell me what he thought about when he got up-dick because I would think he was silly or I would laugh at him. I told him it was as if he thought that only one of us could be strong, and that I needed to keep him feeling like a little boy so I would be the powerful one. He asked me whether I knew already what he thought about when he masturbated. I said that I did not. He said, "It has nothing to do with you" and then described a recurrent fantasy. In the fantasy one of the "other boys" in his class had captured Janet and tied her up. They made her take off her pants so they could look at her naked, and they were mean to her. Johnny would come on the scene, fight with and beat the other boy, liberate Janet, and treat her with great dignity. He was good to her and kind because he loved her.

This central fantasy recurred in many variations, sometimes involving monsters and other characters but almost always returning to specific fantasies of Janet when Johnny actually masturbated. In class he thought of her as "my girl" and often felt jealous when she expressed an interest in other children of either sex. His direct contact with her, however, was quite limited, and he mostly admired her from afar.

He commented on how difficult it was to talk about his fantasies to me. He sometimes wished he had not thought of them. Spontaneously he observed that there must be "something in him" (a phrase I had used in the past to refer to unconscious motives that could only be inferred from his actions) that made it hard for him to talk about these fantasies because he was well aware that I did not threaten him or act disapprovingly when he reported them. I said I thought the problem was that he also thought of me as one of the people he wanted to beat and conquer. He responded immediately by asking, "How could that be, I love you." I said I thought that was just the problem—that he loved me and at the same time he wanted to beat me. He protested that he only wanted to beat people who did bad things, who hurt his girl. He wanted to be her rescuer. I never did bad things, I helped children and never hurt them, he said. I said that I thought he had created a picture of me that was very nice because he was afraid to think of me in any other way; maybe he needed me to be nice.

At this point he spoke directly for the first time of how frightening he sometimes found his father. His father really was like the Gump, often yelling and screaming at his mother. His father never actually hurt anybody, but he was so big and could yell so loud that it really frightened Johnny. Johnny had the really scary experience of wanting to protect his mother from his father at these times and thinking that if he did, his father would hurt him badly. Sometimes the rough and tumble that had developed over the past year between Johnny and his father would become terrifying when Johnny thought about how easily his father could hurt him and how his father might get mad at him if he knew about Johnny's ideas of beating up his father when he yelled at his mother.

As he repeatedly worked through the topic of competing with men in order to protect women, Johnny's descriptions of his masturbation fantasies became increasingly direct. The descriptions were often accompanied by vivid drawings. The fantasies invariably involved plots in which he rescued a girl from sadistic treatment at someone else's hands. This mistreatment became increasingly intense and overtly sexual, and it was clear that Johnny experienced an uncomfortable excitement as he described evil ones torturing his girl, pulling off her pants, and looking at her genitals. I was surprised when, in response to my observation that the people in his fantasies were either completely good or completely bad, Johnny recalled an interpretation he claimed I had made years before but which I could not remember making. He said that I had told him that the various characters in the Wizard of Oz stood for different parts of Dorothy's picture of herself. He thought that his fantasies were like that too, maybe the characters in the fantasy represented parts of himself. He knew he wanted to be the good hero that he played in the fantasy. But he also thought at times he wanted to be the boy who got to look at girls naked. He admitted that sometimes at the swimming pool he got to see girls undressed, and he liked that very much. (The idea that he also wanted to be the girl in the fantasy was not part of his conscious thinking.) He said that he did not really want to hurt girls. I said, maybe not, but I did think he wanted to have complete control of them, that we knew from some of the ways that he treated his mother and the housekeeper that he very much liked the idea of being in complete charge of women. He thought that was right.

One day he said, "I think I know how I keep from being scared about parts of me that might get me into trouble — I just say they aren't me, they are somebody else." He went on to apply this idea to the masturbation fantasies, as he now could readily own the wish to control the girl and to see her naked. In fact, he reported a change in the masturbation fantasy. Because of the skill with which the "bad kid" had tied up his beloved or because of the "bad kid's" resistance, the character who consciously represented Johnny was increasingly unable to avoid looking at and touching his beloved as she lay naked under the control of his enemy. He found this exciting but, of course, against his will.

The theme of the difficulty of reporting these fantasies to me was recurrent in the analysis. It became progressively clear to Johnny that his fears that I would be angry at him and punish him for his fantasies represented a projection. He was consciously envious and angry about my ability to control the duration of the sessions, to sit in what he regarded as the most comfortable chair in the office, and to buy as many books as I wanted. He came to understand that the idea that I would hurt him arose from a combination of the experience of his loud and threatening father and the projection of his own hostile impulses onto me.

During the time that Johnny was clarifying these issues in the analysis, both he and his parents reported a blossoming in his capacity for play and friendship. He became friendly with two boys his age and played fantasy adventure games with them. He enjoyed playing ball, although sometimes he found it somewhat frightening and was afraid of the ball hitting him. His relationship with his father improved considerably. Retrospectively, the father said that although he had always loved Johnny, he had never before really enjoyed him and had thought of him as something of a disappointment, as a sissy. He had conscious wishes that the young business associate that he had thought of as such a pistol were his son rather than the depressed and frightened youngster that Johnny had been. But now he found Johnny to be quite delightful and found himself fantasying about the boy's genius and creative ability as an artist as well as his athletic prowess.

My own emotional response was somewhat more ambivalent and perfectionistic. Although I fully subscribe to Anna Freud's (1965) idea that the goal of child analysis is the resumption of development—not its completion—I felt uncomfortable with the intensity of Johnny's sadism and thought of that as a possible reason for continuing the analysis longer. Self-analysis revealed not only the expectable continued resistance to the intensity of childhood sexuality and aggression but also a profound sense of loss in anticipation of not being able to watch and participate in Johnny's further development.

Termination phase   About a year before termination seemed appropriate Johnny had begun talking about it. His progress in school and his family's move to a more distant suburb put external pressure on Johnny to finish up the analysis. Johnny talked about not wanting to stop the analysis, or perhaps he could stop when he was forty years old. There would always be things we could talk about and adventures we could have. Coming to the sessions was avowedly the most interesting thing in Johnny's life. As the year went on, the subject occasionally arose in the context of vacations and discussions of the scheduling of school.

After a little over three years of analytic work Johnny felt that he could get along well without the analysis, although he wanted to continue to come to see me. His parents felt that he was doing extremely well—he had two good male friends and a girl whom he mostly admired from afar, and he was a delight with grown-ups, who enjoyed his sharp intelligence and quite remarkable creativity. Although Johnny clearly felt things quite intensely, he was not overwhelmed by his feelings. He remembered his symptoms but was no longer symptomatic. He continued to read a great deal, but his reading ranged more broadly than it had, and there was little of the driven quality that had characterized his earlier involvement with books.

In terms of the internal process of the analysis, too, termination seemed increasingly appropriate. Major areas of conflict had been repeatedly engaged with considerable intensity often within the transference. Characterological defenses had been repeatedly identified and worked through, and the patient had a remarkable functional understanding of his own character. The transference had been intensely engaged on many occasions, but over the last six months the analyst seemed increasingly less centrally significant. Johnny had developed a remarkable capacity to observe himself and to use his own associations as a source of information about his psychological function. He had a truly self-analytic capacity. Most important, Johnny seemed to be moving forward in his development, actively engaging new experience and confident of his capacity to continue development.

By mutual agreement among Johnny, his parents, and me, a termination date was set five months in the future. Johnny was entering first grade, and there was some pressure to not have session interfere with school, but as Johnny said, "Finishing this right is real important."

Johnny's first response to the setting of the termination date was a mild panic. There were things he had to get done before we stopped. He reported that while they were not any where near as terrifying as they had been, he was once again troubled by thoughts of the fire eyes and had a bad dream in which he was running from the fire eyes and then suddenly turned and looked at them head on to discover that they were really eyes.

Johnny referred to my using the phrase "to look at" something to mean that we should explore its psychological meaning. He spontaneously said that this was the most important thing he had learned from me—thinking about and talking about things really changed them. I said, "That's one way to look at the dream." This struck Johnny as extremely funny and he said, "I can look back at the eyes that look at me." The dream initiated an intensive reworking of the fire eyes symptom. Now Johnny was able to give a far more coherent account of the symptom itself and to put it in the context of his life history. Essentially he recognized that the fire eyes were constructed from his own wishes to look at things like "mommy naked," to dominate and control them through being able to see them, and from the anticipation that he retributively would be dominated, controlled, and in this sense injured. Fearing his wish to control and thereby hurt, it had been displaced onto food, which he controlled through tidiness but forbid himself to injure.

These themes seem to have taken on particular intensity in response to the mother's relative emotional unavailablity caused by her father's death. Largely displaced onto the grandmother (and appearing as the witches in the stories Johnny told), the distress and sadness that Johnny saw so clearly in his mother's eyes frightened him and intensified the anxiety associated with his impulses to sadistically control through watching.

It is tempting to speculate that mother's preoccupation with her father's death led to a failure in her self-object functioning. This in turn led to the erotization of Johnny's self-object needs and the emergence of masturbation, voyeurism, and sadism driven by narcissistic rage as well as the use of books and reading as slightly bizarre transitional objects used to provide the solace he was no longer getting from his mother (Kohut 1976). As we worked through this material during the early part of the analysis, however, and as we reworked it again during the termination phase, my idea that Johnny's erotic preoccupations resulted from a threatened fragmentation of the self (as opposed to the idea that these preoccupations threatened as the self was made more vulnerable by the relative lack of support from the child's mother) found little support. The issue did not emerge in the patient's associations or in his theories about himself. Neither did the pathognomonic transferences associated with self pathology emerge in the course of the analysis (Kohut 1976).

What was remarkable in this part of the termination phase was that in the process of again working through this material, Johnny explicitly formulated the story of the genetics and dynamics of his own disturbance with great clarity. He not only found that the further intellectual insight gave him an increased sense of mastery over the material, but he also recognized and

consciously avowed an identification with my analyzing function. He spoke of anticipating a time when we would not be
meeting but still being able to have dialogues with me in fantasy. In fact, he became aware that he did this now, especially
when he found himself in an emotionally difficult situation. He
thought that he also just did not want to stop seeing me and that
having me "in his imagination" would be very nice. This recalled
how confusing and frightening it had been when father spoke
of the fire eyes being in his imagination and how differently he
thought about the world now. While his imagination was not
any longer a concrete place for him, it was not just his imagination in the sense of being unimportant or trivial but rather an
extremely important aspect of his psychology to be treated with
respect, recognized for what it was, and viewed as "a good place
to keep old analysts for when you need them."

Johnny reintroduced the two explorers' stories, now as a consciously thinly disguised way to recount the story of the analysis
itself. This was soon replaced by direct reminiscences of the analytic experience. Sometimes these recollections served to clar-
ify what was going on at the time and to work it through further. Sometimes they seemed to be directed at the shame the
Johnny sometimes felt at the extent of his earlier irrationality
and fear. At other times a competitive theme in which either
Johnny wanted to take all the credit for analytic discoveries or,
alternatively, the analyst won a victory over him by understanding more about Johnny than he understood about himself. A
common sequence was that Johnny would begin to recall something we had done together, characterizing it as the activity of
one or the other of us, and then, as the story continued, it would
emerge that the other party had been an essential contributor to
the experience.

Johnny was puzzled about what he could do for me in return for the analysis. He clearly believed, and I agreed with him,

that the analysis had transformed his life and that without it he would have remained the terrified youngster I first met, incapable of the joy that he now found in himself and in the world. He fantasied giving me things, publicizing my expertise, someday actually taking me traveling, and so forth. During the final week of the analysis he gave me a booklet he had put together, inscribed, "To Dr. Galatzer-Levy, the best psychiatrist in the world." It began with a self-portrait under which was written, "I'll never forget you," followed by pictures of the Moym and the Gump and several other of his fantasy characters with captions like, "And neither will the Gump," and then a group portrait saying, "Because that would be a dumb thing to do." The back cover of the booklet showed a picture of Johnny and me holding hands, under which was written, "Good bye." I said that I would not forget him or all his characters either, but that it was sometimes all too easy to forget some things, especially when they are frightening or that you wish had not been so. He said, very seriously, "I know. That's the most important thing I can remember from you."

CONCLUSION

I hope this condensed description of an analysis that began when a child was very young illustrates the possibility of doing serious psychoanalytic work with young children. Although this patient's intellectual precocity helped him to formulate certain matters conceptually, the basic analytic process did not depend on these intellectual abilities.

The Analysis of a Prelatency Girl with a Visual Handicap

Aimee G. Nover, D.S.W.

Background

Presenting Problem

Mr. and Mrs. L. consulted me about Jenny shortly before her fourth birthday. They were referred by Jenny's pediatrician, who had known them since Jenny's birth and had seen them for the past two years in intermittent parent counseling sessions. The parents' major concerns at our initial meeting were (1) Jenny's negativism and defiance: obstinate and stubborn, she continually challenged authority and became angry and belligerent if she didn't get her way; she could be destructive as well; for example, when sent to her room she might cut an article of clothing or rip a library book; (2) her "poor social skills": Jenny had been attending nursery school two mornings a week since age three; she didn't play with the other children but would interact by trying to provoke or hit them, and, when they wouldn't comply, she withdrew; her teachers described her as a "real loner" who couldn't stand being touched; (3) her frequent clinging to her mother: she resisted separation, yet, at the same time, she showed no fear of strangers and was somewhat socially promiscuous, approaching people in shopping malls; (4) her "manipulativeness" and attempts to get out of things she didn't want to do by offering excuses: "I didn't sleep very well last night so I'm too tired to pick up"; (5) from the age of nine months her mouthing and chewing on foreign objects like plastic tops, toys, play dough, and an eyepatch she wore during part of the day; (6) her bad dreams (for example, a wolf tried to take me away) and fears (for example, fear of dogs). The L.'s wondered why, despite their best parenting efforts and the pediatrician's guidance, Jenny was so persistently unhappy.

Family Background

Mr. and Mrs. L. are college-educated professionals in their early thirties who had been married for five years before Jenny was born. Both are from religious Irish Catholic families and active in church-related activities. Mrs. L. worked until Jenny was born. She remained at home with her for thirteen months, at which time she returned to work two days a week, leaving Jenny at a family day care home. When Jenny was thirty-nine months old, her brother Peter—at the time of writing a robust and engaging three-year-old—was born, and Mrs. L. again stopped work and hasn't returned. Mr. L., an accountant and the family breadwinner, is out of town on business one week out of every six. When he's at home he participates equally with his wife in child care, including giving Jenny baths, and enjoys taking her on special outings. The family appears stable and close-knit, having a large extended family network and many friends.

The L.'s impressed me as intelligent, conscientious, reasonable, and sensitive. They were open in discussing their feelings about Jenny; they felt sad and discouraged because nothing they had tried seemed to help her. They seemed "good enough" parents for the "good enough" child, but Jenny presented unique challenges.

Developmental History

Jenny was a full-term healthy baby (six pounds, seven ounces —
Apgar 9/10) delivered by natural childbirth. Her development
appeared to proceed normally for the first six months: she was
alert, cuddly, playful, and active. She communicated preferences
clearly (for example, wanting to be in an upright position). She
breast-fed, ate and slept well, and had a pleasant disposition,
although she seemed "strong-willed" from the beginning. At
six months of age an organically based, nonprogressive eye defect present since birth was diagnosed by a pediatric ophthalmologist; vision in the left eye was felt to be nonexistent. Jenny
had to have her eyes dilated and was strapped to the examining
table for the diagnostic procedure. In order to prevent blindness
and to maximize vision potential, the ophthalmologist insisted
that she begin wearing a patch over her good right eye for three
hours a day, during which time her vision was severely limited.
Initially, Jenny complied, the only notable behavior change reported being that she began to spit out solid foods. During this
period a conflicted Mrs. L. would play with her daughter for
hours at a time; her favorite activity was "jolly jumper." At nine
months of age she was again forcibly strapped down to have a
tear duct opened. Mrs. L., instructed by the doctor to leave the
office, could hear Jenny's terrified screaming outside. At nine
months of age, when patching was extended to six hours a day,
Jenny protested vehemently. A major struggle ensued for the
next three months, Jenny pulling off the patch up to twenty-five
times a day and Mrs. L., who was told by the ophthalmologist
that Jenny would lose her vision without the patching, putting
it back. Finally the parents resorted to slapping Jenny's hand
each time she removed the patch. After a week of "tear-filled
days" for Jenny and her mother, Jenny left the patch on. While

Mrs. L. agonized over subjecting her baby to this ordeal, she felt compelled to follow the doctor's orders.

About this same time—one year of age—Jenny was weaned easily. When she was thirteen months old, Mrs. L. returned to work, leaving Jenny with one sitter for three weeks, then with a teenager for three weeks, and finally in a family day care home with a few other children, where she went for the next two years. The time of patching from ages nine months to three years varied from two to eight hours a day. For the past two years she has worn the patch for one hour a day, and she protests verbally: "I hate this patch!" Vision in her left eye is 20/200.

Despite her visual impairment—partial blindness alternating with good vision in one eye—and the early trauma of patching, Jenny's cognitive and motor development proceeded well. She crawled at eight months and walked by fourteen months. At fourteen months, Jenny fell and cut herself near her eye and was once again strapped down while five stitches were applied in the emergency room.

Her parents described eighteen months as a turning point. She became obstinate and defiant. She ignored the parental "no" and always struggled to be in control. At eighteen months Jenny also developed severe asthma, with attacks precipitated by upper respiratory infections. She hasn't had any asthma attacks since age three and a half. From twelve to eighteen months Jenny persistently tried to touch hot things. At age two years she became frightened of dogs but would also provoke them to growl or snap. She seemed interested in toilet training at about fifteen months and again at periodic intervals but became very resistant. Mrs. L. did not want to put undue pressure on Jenny, who became trained during a solo weekend stay at her grandmother's house three months before Peter was born.

My first impression of Jenny was of a pretty, engaging little girl whose tough veneer seemed at odds with her delicate features and animated conversation. Her brightness and competence were clearly evident, and she was surprisingly candid about herself and her problems, saying, for example, "I don't do what I'm told."

Psychotherapy was recommended to help Jenny gain insight into the conflicts that seemed to underlie her self-defeating and socially disruptive behaviors. Jenny was also enrolled in a therapeutic camp/nursery program. During the six-month course of twice-a-week psychotherapy with weekly collateral parental sessions, Jenny evidenced a capacity to work therapeutically and to convey concerns and areas of conflict. Drawing was her major activity; she often played school, putting herself in the role of an imperious teacher; she spontaneously sang numerous songs from her vast repertoire, including "Jesus Loves Me," "Just a Spoonful of Sugar," and "Santa Claus Is Coming to Town," and would recount stories, movies, and dreams. Sessions were frequently punctuated by daring gymnastic feats and trips to the bathroom. Twice she openly masturbated (for example, showing me how she put her hands and marbles in her pants) as if to bring this activity to my attention. She invariably had difficulty entering and leaving my office on time. Usually she expressed anger and frustration through action—attempting to throw toys, mark the walls, run away, and, if all else failed, to spit at me.

The following diagnostic picture and main themes emerged: (1) dependency longings and separation fears: she wanted to be able to trust and rely on her parents but, in large part, because they had also been the ones who had repeatedly inflicted pain, she couldn't completely trust them and feared abandonment (for example, Bunny, who was playing alone, got burned by a fire and had to go to the hospital by himself); (2) fear of body damage and castration: she identified with what she felt was done to her and turned the situation around by becoming the aggressor; she was very frightened of being injured and also of her own aggressive feelings (wolves frequently made an appearance in her play, invariably chasing people in order to bite off body appendages); (3) tendency to hurt herself: she would do to herself what she felt others had done to her (for instance, at times she would purposely fall off the chair and comment, "That feels good"); (4) perception of herself as bad: she seemed to connect her "badness" with being defective and actively sought experiences in which she could be bad, thereby offering herself a reason for her perceived deficits (for example, in her stories babies became sick or injured because of something bad they had done, such as eaten poison mushrooms); (5) sexual curiosity: she wanted to learn more about her body and also about how she could effect some restitution (for example, "Forgetful Jones" couldn't remember that he wasn't supposed to look at other kids' bottoms); (6) preoccupation with looking and being looked at versus not looking and not letting herself be seen (she would often play hide-and-seek and turn the lights on and off). This theme became a metaphor for her conflict over "looking at" thoughts and feelings in the therapy.

After five months of psychotherapy, psychoanalysis was recommended because her conflicts appeared to be serious, pervasive, and internalized, while her defenses—identification with the aggressor, denial, avoidance, reversal—seemed relatively inflexible. She also had good ego capacities for proceeding with the work. She could laugh at herself, and she was able to reflect on her actions. Although in our sessions she might become very angry at me, if she happened to see me outside the sessions, she was spontaneously friendly. She indicated that she had some understanding of the nature of our work when she was overheard counseling a classmate in trouble, "You should go talk to Dr. N."

Although analysis was recommended as the treatment of choice, I had questions both familiar to analysis of prelatency children and unique to Jenny. Jenny presented a paradox. On the one hand she had precocious conceptual and reasoning capacities, a rich range of symbolic modalities for self-expression, and age-appropriate phallic and oedipal interests. Yet she was demanding, controlling, prone to action and physical attack. She also had experienced early trauma associated with her permanent physical handicap. Vision, a primary organizer, was only intermittently and, from her perspective, arbitrarily available. An added complication was her experience that those closest to her, her parents, paradoxically were the agents of the deprivation as well as of pain and excitement, forcing her into a passive position and taking away her sight when her own efforts (that is, pulling off the patch) gave her sight.

COURSE OF THE ANALYSIS

One to Eight Months

After a two-week planned interruption, psychoanalysis began in mid-February four times a week, Monday to Thursday, with weekly collateral parental sessions that were reduced to biweekly sessions after three months. The opening phase of the analysis, which Jenny continued to call her work, was characterized by an exploration of my role; she was trying to figure out who I was as she tried to define the nature of our relationship. She assigned me various roles—mother, sister, teacher, friend, distinguishing even between real and pretend friends. Sometimes we both had the same name. She wanted to know if I would visit her—did I know her address and phone number? She brought her crayons from home and "mixed up" hers and mine. In her rendition of "Jesus By My Side" she regarded me as an omniscient savior, intrusive snoop, and ever-present companion. She also tried to ascertain her parents' place in the analysis. For example, she would allude to "my mother's chair," or on days when her parents were coming she would harbor a kind of family secret: "I know something. But I'm not telling. I'd tell if you were in my family." She corrected my pronunciation and my manners, wondering how two adults (her mother and I), both important to her, could have ostensibly different rules. She was also sensitive to my seeing other children and would alternately try to imitate what she imagined they did, ally herself with them (Carol's my best friend), or destroy what she thought was their work.

From the outset themes of looking and seeing, directed both inward and outward, pervaded virtually every aspect of her work. Conflict was expressed through activities that involved looking and seeing. For example, she imposed the most arduous copying tasks on herself to show me her competence in copying numbers, letters, pictures. She had no tolerance for error and would reject countless papers for the slightest deviation from her exacting standards. During this time, for example, only once and then after forty minutes of labor did she allow herself to say, "I'm proud of myself. I got it just right." The repeated experience of dissatisfaction in trying to make exact replications evidenced both her wish to demonstrate her perfection to me and her fear of being seen as defective. In a variation of her expression of this conflict she often became the dictatorial teacher who made harsh and unyielding demands for perfection on me, the kid who after all would be starting kindergarten next fall. To defend against feelings of inadequacy and helplessness she wanted to show off her perceptual acuity. For example, before a long weekend interruption, she turned out the lights in my windowless office, and while we were enveloped in blackness demonstrated that she could write her name and her brother's name perfectly.

Concomitant with her efforts to demonstrate competency was the exposure of herself to me as imperfect and defective. She identified two areas of inadequacy: her genitals and her eyes. The material raises the question: To what extent were fears of body damage and castration concerns accentuated and distorted by her history of impaired vision and repeated patching? She made numerous observations regarding anatomical differences, and through her associations frequently asked the tacit question, "Where is my penis?" (Did it rot like a pumpkin? Was it bitten off by a wolf? Did it fall off like Peter's belly button or fall out like teeth?) She compared herself to her brother, whose lap was different from hers and who looked so much cuter than she in his blue overalls; and to her father, who had accoutrements that she could only aspire to—a big catcher's mitt, a briefcase, and, perhaps most significantly, binoculars through which he could see the stars. She also viewed the possession of guns and swords, agents of both power and destruction, as frightening but desirable for security. Her dilemma was that in wanting a penis, she had to acknowledge that she didn't have one. She associated this lack with her visual defect as the following example illustrates. She drew a spaceship, initially hiding it from me, and then cut off the red tip which she said wasn't needed. She reworked the picture, transforming the spaceship into "a little girl looking through one of those things [binoculars] that help you see better." The doctor gave her the binoculars.

Jenny had mixed feelings about her eye patch, the accoutrement she did have, which unlike her brother's or her father's had caused her pain and severely limited her vision. She was painfully aware of her patch, a badge of defect, which she said she hated and viewed sometimes as an alien appendage to her body and at other times as an integral part of it: "When I take my patch off my eyeball comes out with it. Then I put it back—you know—like contacts." When she was very angry at me she devised the worst possible punishment: "I'm gonna throw this at your eyeball; you'll have to go to the hospital and you'll have to be very brave because they'll take out your eyeball and replace it with another one and put two patches on you." This comment reflects her notion that the visual defect as well as the patching were imposed on her as punishment.

Fear of body damage and castration anxiety were prominent in the material. But if anyone got hurt, it was she who would be the agent of injury: "I don't want that sailfish card. It's long and pointy. I'll kill it. (Pow) Okay. Now I'll have it; he's dead and he can't do anything."

I interpreted her various efforts to compensate for her deficits. She blamed others—animate and inanimate—for her shortcomings. "You made me ruin my picture; it's your fault," she railed at me. The chair which made her fall was a "bad boy," as was the magic marker that got ink on her hands. She repeatedly demonstrated how, in her mind, one sense could substitute for another. For example, she literally showed me how she could see in the dark via touch, hearing, smell, and taste. In her play, she announced, "I can't hear a word you say; I'm deaf you know but keep talking—I can read lips." Gymnastic tricks and upper grade school achievements such as writing in "cursive" or speaking "Spanish" became apparent at times of frustration or self-conscious loss of esteem. She hung upside down to show that she could see "topsy turvy." She engineered melodramatic falls and exaggerated slight injuries in an effort to convince herself and me that she not only didn't mind being hurt but even took some pleasure in it.

Her restitution fantasies involved oral incorporation (containing both aggressive and libidinal aspects) of the feared and desired object. After bemoaning the fact that she had no gun she drew an ice cream cone which she literally licked and chewed. At times she turned me into a phallus, for example, a pickle which she could chew up and swallow. On several occasions she removed her patch and chewed it. After a series of interpretations regarding her wishes to protect herself against separation fears through oral incorporation, Jenny stopped her three-year habit of mouthing and chewing foreign objects. At this time, in the fourth month of the analysis, Jenny's parents reported general symptomatic improvement as well.

As she became engaged in the analytic work, she let me know that we could look on the inside only if she could control where I directed my outward vision, that is, my interpretations. As the analyst I was seen at times as a probing instrument of pain stimulating both wishes to be probed and terror about being intruded upon. She wanted to enter my office on her terms and to surprise me by crawling, hopping, rolling, and so forth. She was to see me before I could see her. She would often caution, "Don't look at what I'm doing" and devised hiding places, squeezing herself behind the file cabinet or crouching under the desk. From these vantage points she could work in privacy and permit me to glimpse her or her work in measured doses only. At times she would turn out the lights as if in charge of recreating the patching of her infancy, letting me know what it feels like to be a helpless baby left to flounder in the dark. I interpreted her attempts to control my looking as an effort to turn passive into active and thereby avoid the feelings of helplessness she associated with being surprised, overwhelmed, and hurt when her parents put on the patch. She subjected me to frequent tests: "Can you tell what I'm making? Can you see from there how many fingers I'm holding up? Let's play Pin the Tail on the Donkey." She became enraged when I didn't comply, like the Jack in the Box who invariably appeared and disappeared according to her direction. On many levels she wanted to look, but she was very afraid of what she might see and perhaps was uncertain whether her ability to see would be taken away from her.

She established rigorous tests to challenge my competence as a loving, protective parent. She played a game in which the child put himself in increasingly greater jeopardy while the mother had to exhaust herself to keep him from getting mowed down by the school bus. She repeatedly darted away and taunted, "Ha, ha, you can't get me!" She entangled herself in the waiting room jungle gym and dared me to extricate her.

As the analysis entered the third month her dependency longings became more prominent. For example, after much deliberation the calf finally relinquished the farmer's pail to nurse at his mother's udder. Jenny herself became a nursing baby and wanted me to be her nurturant mother, instructing me, "Take my patch off, Mama." She triumphantly announced, "I played baby the whole time today." And she was a superb actress, mimicking a baby exactly. At home for the first time ever she began to play with dolls, consistently enjoying the maternal role. In our sessions she also became free enough to express her distress directly: "You can't help me. I'll feel like this for the rest of my life." In one session after a visit to the doctor, her rage gave way to sadness, and she sobbed for a long time, pleading with me, "Stop it, mommy."

In the analysis Jenny had multiple, rapidly changing views of me. She related to me as a bad mother—one who was not only responsible for her defects but who shared a defect. I was punitive and prohibiting. I was probing and intrusive, but also impotent because I couldn't gratify her wishes. As she regressed in the sessions, I also came to be seen as a caring, nurturant mother who could provide the sustenance she needed and who would be good enough to take off her patch. One expression of the conflict represented by these disparate perceptions of me involved her connecting aggression with physical closeness and intimacy. She repeatedly set up threatening situations in which I had to intervene by literally holding her. Or she would try to provoke a fight to stimulate excitement and closeness. These repetitions suggested efforts to reenact the earlier trauma. I wondered whether Jenny saw me as the bad mother in order to defend against wishes for nurturance and closeness, and/or because of loyalty conflict in regard to her actual mother, or whether she saw me as the good mother in order to ward off anxiety generated by angry, aggressive fantasies. At times I seemed to her like her father—I worked every day and went to meetings and on trips. I appeared to have special powers, that is, understanding. Yet I didn't have a penis. She wondered where my wiener was and tried to look for it under my skirt, hoping or dreading that she'd find it. She looked to me, as her father, for protection and security, but there were times when I, like him, wouldn't be available for days at a time. Jenny was exquisitely sensitive to separations. Sessions on Mondays after the three-day weekend and on Thursdays as she anticipated the break were generally more difficult for Jenny. She anticipated separations by denying them ("I don't care if you're not here; I'll just come anyway") or by becoming angry at me or her mother ("Bad mother. I'll just drive myself"). After I returned from my vacation she became a porcupine furiously shooting quills at me. It was crucial for her to control any comings and goings: "I already knew about your vacation before you told me. My vacation will be funner than yours."

I wondered if she used anger and aggression in the service of tolerating the separation. The extent to which she was able to evoke or maintain an image of me was unclear. When I had to delay the start of a session for two minutes after she had seen me walk by, she said, "Where were you? You were never coming back." When she didn't see me over Memorial Day weekend she talked about putting flowers on graves, saying, "You died." Discussing my summer vacation, she asked if I would be playing "Ghosts in the Graveyard." Her regressive defense became apparent as she explained that when she thinks of goodbyes, she likes to suck on things that remind her of a baby bottle.

She worried that she wouldn't be able to get along without me and prepared for interruptions by sucking my blood or turning me into a sweet pickle in a jar with a tight lid or putting scotch tape on my chair just before I sat down.

A number of events made the summer months very difficult for her. She turned five with her attendant expectations of overwhelming challenges, she said goodbye to teachers and classmates and entered a (therapeutic) camp program, she anticipated my vacation, her vacation, the move to my new office, and the beginning of kindergarten. She became extremely provocative, screaming to drown me out if I even mentioned the word "vacation." She attempted to tyrannize me and herself with imperious warnings and challenges, and she created her own reality in which the sky was green and the grass blue. She worried and threatened: "I'm never coming to see you again," and she frequently tried to run out of the office in order to control any leaving. She tried to chew my purse and to put me in jail. During this time, however, she made a positive adjustment to camp and was behaving well at home.

After a three-week interruption Jenny resumed analysis in my new office, one week before beginning kindergarten. During the next three weeks she was very angry. She repeatedly tried to wreck the office, hit me, and spit and threatened, "I'll pour soda in your eyes and it will sting." At times I had to physically restrain her. She wanted the reassurance of physical touch and closeness but demanded physical contact through provocative behavior. She screamed to drown out anything I might say about vacation or school. At least a dozen times each session she called me dummy or stupid.

This period was rough for me as well as for Jenny. I felt like I was containing, confining, restricting. How could I observe with an "analytic eye" or listen with an "analytic ear" when I had to watch for a flying block or guard the lamp? For comfort I turned to Winnicott's definition of analysis, that is, analysis is everything a psychoanalyst does, and for guidance I turned to my supervisor.

I noticed that during this period after the summer interruption, Jenny frequently chose to wear her patch to her "appointments" and appeared to reenact the affective experience of the early patching. For example, invariably on these days she would become panicky, demand her mother as if she couldn't function without her, and then sobbed pitifully; I interpreted the affect as the hitherto unexpressed sadness and longing for the mother of her infancy, whom she couldn't see when her eye was patched. She made herself a bed in my toy cabinet: "You be the Mommy. Say, it's okay, honey, I'll get your doll for you." She fashioned a night light for her teddy bear so he could see in the dark. She even came to imitate herself. She giggled as she wailed, "Wah, wah—I want Mommy."

Despite her efforts to literally keep us in the dark by turning out the lights, she was able to articulate her disappointment that I wasn't magic like a fairy godmother who could make her troubles disappear. She felt that I had left her because I didn't like her, and she feared her anger would hurt me and that she might never see me again. I was stupid because I hadn't made her problems go away, but also she wanted me to be dumb, that is, silent, and not say words which would feel like an assault.

During this period as Jenny was reactivating the early experience in the analysis, she was also using the analyst to displace hostile and aggressive impulses from the current situation with her parents. The displacement allowed her to keep a positive investment in her parents and make a reasonable adjustment to kindergarten; she cooperated with the teacher, followed the routine, and interacted with some other kids.

Nine to Twenty-one Months

Analysis of her identification with the aggressor, that is, the preoedipal mother, and the subsequent reexperiencing in the analysis of the anxiety connected with object loss paved the way for the emergence of oedipal material.

For the next year of analysis the material was more organized and focused. It is likely that Jenny's capacity for greater organization was in part a result of maturation. In addition, my impression was that Jenny had recreated with me the affective experience reminiscent of the early trauma associated with patching. The external circumstances occasioned by my vacation followed by a one-week interruption shortly after we resumed the move to the new office (as well as the experience of beginning kindergarten) served to remind her of the forced and repeated separations and changes she had endured in her infancy. As indicated above, she used the analysis to explore the anxiety with resultant insight and some degree of mastery. Physical assaults and destructive activity diminished markedly in the sessions as Jenny became better able to express her urges and wishes through words and the metaphor of play. She became engaged in sexual research. She made innumerable observations about male/female differences invariably coveting what boys have—special privileges, velcro boots, balls for soccer, baseball, and football. She admired their skills—making paper jet planes and building teepees; she identified their preferences— dinosaurs, trucks, and the colors black and brown—as distinct from her own. She would embellish herself with such adornments as a tall hat, a bow tie, an extra long tongue, an elephant trunk. Yet, at the same time, she indicated conflict about acknowledging anatomical differences. She brought her toy Butterbear—two animals in one—a girl butterfly and a boy bear; she emphasized that boys lose their front teeth just like girls do. Despite the presence of udders, she couldn't tell the mother cow from the father cow. She informed me that it's better to be in the dark because you can see things in the light that might scare you. And she projected her avoidance onto me: "Don't look at the giraffe. You won't want to see that his leg is missing. I hurt my finger. Don't look, it's disgusting."

Repeatedly, she presented herself as castrated, lacking essential equipment as a result of having been maimed. She would speak of her fantasied bloody wounds, protecting me from the sight of the yucky injuries to her fingers or knees because she was sure I would find them offensive. She frequently identified with a lady pig, the epitome of everything dirty, messy, and foul. The wounds were disabling in that they prevented her from being fully competent (for example, she couldn't draw rabbit ears or Christmas trees; she couldn't read or make perfect copies). She made more direct connections between her wounds and her patching. For example, she might remove her patch and then "hurt" herself by falling off her chair. Yet at the same time the injuries gave her a sense of entitlement. After a storm scene during which she would hurt herself or become extremely frustrated because she couldn't get her picture just right, she would order me around, demanding and imperious.

Jenny used the analysis to find an explanation for what she believed to be her castration. At times she expressed the fantasy that she really had a hidden phallus (that is, she stole the ancient crystal—the most precious possession in the universe and older than Jesus—and secured it in a cabinet safe even from God). She perceived her mother as the castrator and railed against her for repeatedly causing Jenny to hurt herself or for depriving her of what she wanted (for example, Mommy wouldn't get me a sun visor; Mommy made me bump into the wall; Mommy bought me the wrong size underwear). Jenny's mother also made frequent use of cutting implements—it was she who cut out Jenny's chicken pox, cut off her hair, and cut down the "burning bush" in their yard because it had prickers. Mothers, she revealed, were castrators as well as castrated, as she chanted the riddle, "Your mother punched my mother right in the nose / What color was the blood? R-E-D spells red—Oh yuck!" She viewed me as both castrated—a pig, like Jenny—as well as the maternal castrator. Her vociferous complaints were like a refrain: "Look what you made me do—I messed up . . . you made me hurt myself—you pinched my finger in the door . . . I can't get this right because you're talking."

She sought vengeance on the castrating mother/analyst. When she was frustrated after I made her "mess-up," she tried to mess me up by writing on my walls or on me. Her April Fool's joke was "Your pants are on fire." After I had disappointed her by declining an invitation, she fashioned a paper snake to put in her pants and then cut it in half because it bit her.

In her view, castration was a punishment occasioned by fantasied sins related to her sexual impulses. For example, in one version the lady pig's snout was cut off because she had uncontrollable sensual appetites—she had devoured her cake and everyone else's. More specifically, Jenny connected genital castration to her visual impairment as punishment for her own voracious appetite for knowledge, that is, her sexual curiosity. She began one session with a riddle: "There's a place in France where naked ladies dance / There's a hole in the wall where the boys can see it all." After I noted the boys' curiosity, she showed me a picture in her book of a boy with no feet. As she proceeded to trace the picture, she sang of the three blind mice, whose tails were severed with a carving knife. She followed the song with an eye-witness account of a squirrel shooting: its eyeball was shot out, leaving a bloody hole. I said that it seemed like the boys were so interested in seeing the ladies' bodies, but they were worried that if they looked, they might wish to see even more and then someone would punish them for their wishes by hurting them—cutting off part of their body or even making them blind so they wouldn't see anymore.

That interpretation led to a subsequent riddle: "I like candy 'cause it's sweet / I'll take my socks off and smell my feet / If you say I don't care, I'll pull down your underwear." With this more direct approach, she let me know that she was ready for me to take the next step in interpreting her own sexual curiosity and wishes toward me, and through the link to the previous riddle, also her concomitant fear of punishment: "Like those curious boys, you might be curious to see what's under my underwear, but maybe you're worried that if you have those wishes something might happen to you like it did to them." Jenny's positive oedipal strivings were increasingly evident. She reported exciting outings with her Dad—"just the two of us," she emphasized, "not Mommy and not Peter." She began telling me secrets. Devising a clever solution for a difficult dilemma—how to have Daddy to herself and not incur mother's anger—she told of numerous occasions when she and Daddy would go on secret shopping trips to get surprise presents for Mommy.

Jenny attempted to entice me like her Dad by treating the sessions as intimate trysts. Wiggling her hips, she would perform seductive dances and on occasion offered me candy that Daddy had made. On Valentine's Day she made me an elaborate card. She began to tell about her mother's bad deeds and described how Snow White was poisoned by the jealous stepmother. She exchanged play clothes for her best dress and issued invitations to me for special school or family events. When I didn't respond to her overtures she felt rebuffed and sought vengeance. For example, when I declined an invitation to her school fair she demanded my home address so that she could go to my house over the weekend and shoot my husband.

At the same time she was ready to seize on any sign of gratification, which would then burden her with guilt. For example, when I got new markers shortly after she had remarked the old ones were worn out, she felt flattered, satisfied, and worried that I wouldn't have enough money to buy food. "I hate the word 'guilty'," she said, as if forbidden libidinal wishes had been fulfilled.

During this second year of the analysis Jenny redoubled her assiduous efforts at copying, an activity which I had interpreted in the early months of the analysis as an expression of her attempt to master the sense of inadequacy connected with her visual impairment. Now, in the context of the oedipal material, the copying took on an expanded meaning as she revealed how her oedipal conflicts were influenced by the preoedipal fixation on her imperfection. Laboriously she would trace pictures or sentences from waiting room magazines. She brought her rubber stamp set to make exact duplications. She tried to make freehand copies. She was experimenting with various methods of reproduction. She subjected the finished products to a vigorous test—did they look exactly like the original? Mothers, she decided, were not very good at reproducing (the mother butterfly laid disgusting, slimy eggs; the mother had too many eggs to sit on; her mother had babies before they were ready to come out). She longed for a "copy machine" like the one Daddy had; it was perfect. I had one, too. Being the chosen spouse of her father/analyst, she felt, would empower her to make exact replications.

Jenny's research efforts yielded a compromise solution. If she was displeased with the product of her labors, she could make a revised edition. In the fashion of a corrective surgeon, the father/analyst, Mr. Fix-It, who could make all kinds of repairs, she altered and adjusted her copies. Tracing her doll, also named Jenny, she commented, "If I don't like the way her braid comes out, I can cut it off and tape it on again." And she did. She would also alter her features, slanting her eyes, squishing her cheeks, or assuming a foreign accent to take on a new genetic heritage: "I vas born in Chermany."

She struggled with guilt occasioned by the expression of her sexual wishes and masturbatory fantasies in the analysis. After telling me a secret (for example, "Sometimes I take off my jammies in bed"), she conjured up Jesus hanging on a cross in the upstairs hall. When she became excited in telling me how Daddy gave her a shampoo in the bathtub, she did penance by recalling how Jesus had to carry the cross up the hill only to be crucified. When she displayed and labeled her muscles during a gymnastics performance she chastised herself with a rendition of "You've Got to Have Heart" called "You've Got to Have Self-Control."

Jenny's expression of positive oedipal strivings in the analysis evidenced the interference with resolution of earlier phase conflict, that is, separation-individuation, and was characterized by sadomasochistic tendencies. The following examples illustrate the extent and intensity of her regression. When I turned down her invitations she would become verbally provocative, making demands that I draw for her and threatening to write on the walls if I didn't. She would at times demand physical contact to stop her destructive behavior. She continued to be extremely sensitive to separations, however brief. When she anticipated an interruption she would regress to the position of a demanding, insistent toddler who would yank on my telephone wire, spit, and throw markers at the wall. Underlying this behavior was the anxiety that she wouldn't be safe without me; she needed me in order to resist impulses and wishes. After a period during which we would work closely together and she gained insight, she would behave in a similar way, as though the understanding created an intimacy that she needed to defend against.

Technical Considerations

My technique in the analysis was influenced by Jenny's age and level of ego development. During the early phase, for example, when impulsive action prevailed over words, one aspect of my interventions was directed toward identifying the affect. This helped her to discern specific feelings from the inchoate mass of affect, for example, to discriminate between anger and anxiety, and thus become better equipped to utilize words as a symbolic alternative to action. When destructive impulses broke through, I needed to restrain her physically, emphasizing my role as an auxiliary ego. For example, mediating between drive and super-ego: "You're so angry you want to kick me but you also feel very uncomfortable when you do that. You're letting me know now you need my help." As her frustration tolerance increased, so did her capacity for sustained verbal interaction. She offered opportunity for interpretation in the displacement through her role play, drawings, and spontaneous singing, but she would invariably go a step further and personalize the interpretation as she did in the example cited above, moving from the riddle about the boys and the naked ladies to her own wishes to see me without my underwear. In another session she related the story of Peter Rabbit. After my interpretation about Peter Rabbit's guilt and punishment for disobeying his mother, Jenny removed her patch, which her mother, in my presence, had instructed her to leave on. Interpretation in the displacement led to a here-and-now interaction that demanded direct interpretation: "When

Mommy tells you not to do something—take off your patch—maybe you decided to do it here in front of me to see what I would do, if I would punish you like Mrs. Rabbit punished Peter."

Interpretations were made in incremental steps over time, but the following example, in a brief interlude, illustrates a typical pattern from affect to defense to underlying anxiety and is paralleled by movement from action to words. In a session just before an interruption, Jenny noted that two pictures she had made the session before to decorate my office walls were still in her basket. She began to pull on my necklace, kick at me, and spit. She wasn't able to verbalize any feelings. I told her I thought she felt angry at me for not putting up her pictures—that she was afraid I might not remember her or even think of her if the pictures weren't there to remind me, and while her kicking and spitting showed that she was angry, it was also a way of being close: "But I wanted you to have them to take them to your house."

Reconstructions were possible and most meaningful with Jenny supplying the data. For example, during one session Jenny, wearing her patch, had wrapped up some plastic straws and then cut off the tips through the wrapping, claiming that it was an accident because she couldn't see. I wondered if she did things like that—had accidents—when she couldn't see so well, like the times when she was wearing her patch, because she felt then maybe she wouldn't have to take responsibility. She proceeded to remove her patch, noting, "It's so big." I commented on how it might have looked very big to her when she was a little baby. "When I was a baby I hated that patch. I kept pulling it off but my Mommy spanked me every time." She then hit her hand and smacked herself in the face. "Sometimes I had to wear it all day and night."

I struggled over how to conduct the analysis in accordance with my understanding of child psychoanalytic technique. Initially, the most difficult aspect was her understanding of my role in her life. The analyst as analyst is a rarefied being in the life of a four-year-old—there is no model. Jenny experienced significant deprivation; in the hours I worked very closely with her four days per week, yet I didn't often compliment her, give her presents, do things for her, or attend family functions. In the beginning of our work her wish for gratification was uppermost. Adaptation, on my part, was necessary to sustain the alliance. For example, when impulses gave way to destructive activity I did restrain her physically by holding her, and I occasionally carried her back to my office from the waiting room. Because of her sensitivity to separations and because she did not have a reliable sense of time or place, when I went away I decided to tell her where I was going, (to a meeting, on a trip to Maine), and I sent her post-cards. When I moved to my new office I showed her pictures of what she could expect. I wrote out the dates of canceled sessions and dates we would resume.

The deepening transference was vulnerable to myriad events in her life: family trips, birthdays, the start of school, losing a tooth. She turned to me to fill developmental needs. For example, when her mother was on vacation, she looked to me as a substitute. On one occasion out of exasperation she defined my role: "You're not a mother or a brother or a teacher—you're just nobody!"

At the same time, aided by her growing capacity for conceptualization, abstraction, reality testing, and her understanding of causality, Jenny developed an increasingly sophisticated and precocious self-observing function which also both grew out of and assisted the analytic work. For example, after I called her attention to her singing "How Do You Solve A Problem Like Maria?" ("How do you make her stay / And listen to what you say . . . How do you hold a moonbeam in your hand?"), she wondered if she was the problem or if I was, thereby giving evidence of her psychological curiosity as well as her understanding of metaphor. In an effort to convince me to go to her Mom's show, she made what was from her perspective a logical suggestion: "You could go on a different night so then you wouldn't see me," indicating her assessment that extra-analytic contact, at least on one level, isn't desirable. She differentiated between fantasy and reality: "Some things you know I make up and some are true." She became an increasingly accurate reporter of events outside the analysis and let me know in advance about sessions she would miss and schedule changes. She assumed a sense of responsibility for her sessions, thereby conveying the importance the analysis had in her life.

She revealed an appreciation for the richness of language and for sophisticated symbolic capacity. On the session before a holiday she scornfully called me "Mrs." When I commented that "Mrs." had the word "miss" in it she reflected, "You could walk around the block one way and I would go another and we could walk right past each other and miss; you could miss a plane like at the airport; you could miss a ball like when Daddy plays softball. Mrs. — that's a lady too."

She explained to me that a coat which wasn't in the room could still be "in your brain — just think of it." When she was angry because I had canceled a session she fumed, "And don't even have a picture of me in your mind," suggesting an awareness of her capacity to sustain an internalized image of the object. Concomitant with this development, she began to make use of an additional, higher level form of resistance: long periods of silence. She also became a coach in analytic technique. "Are you writing something down? Wait until after I leave." After several minutes of silence when her back was turned, she asked, "Are you asleep back there?" Or after a lengthy interpretation she would complain, "You've said enough now!"

When Jenny began analysis both Mr. and Mrs. L. wanted to

continue weekly sessions. Both parents were psychologically un-sophisticated (neither had been in treatment), and they wanted to make sure about the person to whom they entrusted their child four times a week in this intensified treatment. The L.'s used the session to report on Jenny's and their own behavior and to seek my reactions, insights, and advice. Unburdening them-selves was a relief. As they came to feel less guilty and more confi-dent in their parenting, they discovered their own psychological mindedness, a factor which enabled them to feel less helpless. Mr. L., for example, observed, "Now that I'm describing Santa Claus and Jesus, it's as if she thinks of them as CIA agents." I did not actively give advice or make recommendations, although in-evitably my attitudes were often communicated, and I remained an important presence in the family. For the work of the analy-sis the parent sessions were essential to ensure parent support, to continue the unfolding of the developmental history, and to give a picture of what was going on in Jenny's life.

As both the L.'s and Jenny became increasingly invested in the analysis and Jenny in addition became a more accurate re-porter, we reduced the parent sessions first to twice a month and after the end of the first year to once every three to four weeks. Jenny's deepening transference increasingly made events exter-nal to the analysis less relevant, as she provided the material for the analysis of her intrapsychic conflicts in the sessions. The col-lateral work continued to be useful to me to see the extent to which symptoms were contained in the analysis.

Jenny had a successful school year, and her behavior at home was consistently better except for periods of regression which inevitably occurred around major transitions. Her analysis con-tinues.

Discussion of Nover Presentation

Katharine Rees, Ph.D.

I would first like to express my appreciation to Dr. Nover for presenting us with such a fascinating case, one in which there has obviously been such careful work and thought given to the treatment. I will raise some diagnostic questions, discuss some general issues regarding technique with this age group, discuss the particular problems of self-knowing for this little girl, and look at specific examples of kinds of therapeutic interventions which seemed most helpful in her treatment.

The first question concerns the effect of the visual handicap on this child's early experiences. Through personal communication with Dr. Nover I gather that the handicap involved some damage to the optic nerve and also affected the eye musculature. The result was poor peripheral vision and depth perception, and generally very blurred vision in that eye, which persists in her present 20/200 sight in this eye. She has been able to compensate, however, to the extent that "her early cognitive and motor development proceeded well," and I gather she is now an excellent reader, acrobat, and skater.

From ophthalmology colleagues, I learned that with most children the patching process, while initially disturbing, is usually then accepted and does not lead to such widespread, long-term behavioral and relational problems. One question is whether there may have been other neurophysiological problems that might have shown up on testing and contributed to the child's developmental difficulties. Also, I wonder whether the early parent-child interactions may have been more disturbed than is indicated, that is, the difficulties the mother may have had in comforting this child, being more sensitive to premature separations, providing enough libidinal security and ego support to contain the anxiety and aggression, her fear of the child's aggression and tendency to get into sadomasochistic fights. There are also suggestions of father's overstimulation contrasting with his absences.

One is left with many questions as to how the visual deficit specifically affected this little girl's perception of her world and relationships to self and other as infant and toddler in addition to the particular experience of the patching. We know from psychoanalytic studies of blind children the pervasive effect of the lack of vision on the inner construction of self and object, on object constancy, and on virtually all areas of ego functioning and relatedness. Jenny suffered no such total blackness, but intermittent extreme blurredness for several hours at a time when her good eye was patched. Since we do not have detailed observations of that time, we can only speculate on the confusion as well as unpredictability and deprivation she may have experienced. Nevertheless, her motor and cognitive functions seemed less disturbed than her relationships to self and others, and her ego functioning within relationships. In addition to the visual deficit there is the history of many changes of objects, traumatic medical procedures, and premature day care experience which must have put a severe strain on her development during the second year of life, when processes of integration, internalization of the object, control of drives, and relationships to objects and self become structured. The aggressivized relationship to others could be seen as adaptive and even a strength, as her way of maintaining contact with her objects, as opposed to the other extreme of overly passive submission and excessive withdrawal.

But it also puts severe stress on the development of her external relationships and internalized world.

This brings me to another issue—that of a differential diagnosis. Despite her basic capacity for libidinal attachment and some remarkable cognitive and verbal abilities, I think one is struck by the degree of more primitive aggressive fantasies, intensity of separation anxieties, provocation of fighting relationships, libidinization of aggression, and an unusual kind of self-stimulation by auto-aggression. She uses many primitive defenses such as projection and identification with the aggressor, and there is an ego deficit in the integration of positive and negative aspects of relationships and self. Aggressive affect and excitement predominate over greater trust, comfort, and range in her relationships. For a four-year-old, she is still very involved in intense exclusive relationships and essentially preoedipal issues of control and need of the object for narcissistic purposes, rather than the more stable and deeply elaborated affects of the oedipal drama. There is a severe problem in the internalization of the good object, and this does not allow her a confident sense of self and other. The superego is internally harsh and pregenital or is reexternalized.

All of these considerations lead one toward the diagnosis of developmental disorder particularly in the area of ego and object relations. Many authors have, of course, emphasized the complex intertwining of developmental disorders and conflict.

The diagnostic issue is inevitably important in one's decision as to technical approaches, my next main topic. Broadly speaking, one must decide how much one is going to be giving developmental help in structure building, in contrast with the more classical analysis one can do with a child who has basically good object relationship, ego and superego development, and neurotic compromise solutions and symptoms. Many young children referred have somewhat similar pathologies to Jenny's and pose similar questions.

So my next point has to do with how the young child can change and grow emotionally through treatment. What is the process by which she comes to know more about herself and others and to integrate this knowledge in a useful way?

There has been increasing interest throughout psychoanalysis as to what really goes on in the process of treatment: how does the patient experience the analyst's interpretations? how does she come to know the workings of her own mind better? how far does this go on nonverbally and preconsciously, as opposed to more consciously through processes of insight and control? As regards the child's response to interpretations there is much to be learned from Piaget's approach, as I have suggested in a previous paper (Rees 1978). Piaget believed the child's verbal responses may not in themselves give us a clear enough indication of the processes of thought that go on as the child absorbs our interventions; I think this is the truly fascinating challenge in our own cases and in studying this report. Piaget, of course, also stresses the young child's difficulties with abstract concepts, and the child's need to learn via actual experiences.

Hansi Kennedy and Anna Freud have shown the difficulties that even the "good-enough neurotic" prelatency children have in making use of interpretations. Such use involves complex cognitive capacities but also requires a trust of the object, a beginning sense of differentiated self and other, a predominance of libido over aggression, ego control over action, capacity to symbolize rather than only enact, and to tolerate disappointments and frustration. Even then self observation and insight are very difficult.

We can see how a child like Jenny has very few of these capacities. Although very verbal and alert to her surroundings, she cannot really use these to help in self-integration. Such children feel constantly endangered, on the verge of panic, and unprotected. But their constant projections make objects untrustworthy, to be blamed, coerced, hated for not bringing immediate relief. Words and interpretations can seem like attacks, triggering more anxiety, fear, and primitive defenses. Feelings of helpless badness make them demand constant narcissistic supplies. They defend against vulnerability via omnipotence, grandiosity, and sadistic attacks in identification with the perceived aggressor. In the midst of all this, the child can achieve little sense of continuity of his experience, cannot bear to look into himself, or see himself as responsible for his own emotions and actions so that many interpretations are experienced as criticisms. The analyst feels helpless and devalued, and interventions, whether "holding" or verbal, seem like attacks, and countertransference reactions are powerful.

At this point the concept of the analyst as "a therapeutic object" is, I believe, a very helpful one (Grunes 1984). In this view, the child analyst is not merely offering a corrective object relationship, as opposed to exploring fantasies and defenses and acting as interpreter: "The relationship is the core of the psychoanalytic process but also is organically interrelated to transference and interpretation." The therapeutic object relationship seeks to mobilize early levels of attachment and aggression and is based on a sound knowledge of archaic ego states, urgent object needs as well as primitive drive impulses, and of the ways in which early and later levels of conflict form special kinds of condensation.

With these patients, the past and the present, the transference and the actualities of the analyst's real presence are interpenetrated. They make intense, distorted demands on the analytic relationship, but this very relationship can then be engaged in a maturational process: "Conscious management of the milieu by the analyst's verbal and nonverbal behavior goes hand in hand with interpretation of primitive defenses and fantasies which have distorted development." For a while, the child analyst has often to provide a different experience prior to, and concurrently with, interpreting the distorted expectations, and contrasting these with the new experiences in the here and now (A-M. Sandler 1985). The working through of these basic issues then leads to more stable and differentiated libidinal attachments, resulting in new structure formation and elaborated relationships (Loewald 1960). Pine (1985) has emphasized the receiving of an interpretation as in itself a psychic act having multiple functions, with drive, ego, superego, object relationship, and self-esteem meanings. So, especially with a child like Jenny, one listens to hear which meanings are received.

As the child patient becomes able, often for the first time, to experience a safety in relationships, he can begin to give up omnipotent coercions, accept increasing disillusionment and separation, become aware of other realities besides his own, move from enacting distorted object relations toward capacity for symbolic expression, and "play" within the analytic relationship, including a new self-observation. Once this more stable self-object relationship has become established, it becomes possible for the child to accept interpretations which imply ownership of his own drives and concern for the other.

It seems to me that the examples of effective interpretations that Dr. Nover gives in her discussion all concern the immediate therapeutic object relationship, and that other examples given of "insight" are less convincing.

Jenny begins treatment by showing the intensity of her demands on the relationship with her analyst, her problems in dealing with frustration and exerting ego controls, her omnipotent defenses, wishes to be perfect, and sense of narcissistic inferiority expressed in her feelings of damage, penis envy, and so forth.

I think that a good deal of ego support and reality explanations went on at this time, although they are not specifically described. The interpretation that then seems to have been very effective was addressed to the therapeutic object relationship, that is, her oral incorporative wishes defending against her intense fears of separation from her analyst. This interpretation was very close to her immediate experience in the session. It could be heard by her and seems to have helped her turn the corner toward improvement. It is also later repeated by Jenny herself when she explained that "when she thinks about goodbyes, she likes to suck on things that remind her of a baby bottle." Although there are many conscious and unconscious fantasies easily discernible in the material, from fantasies about her visual deficit to primal scene curiosities, it would seem important to focus on the separation implications first.

Jenny attempts to set up a relationship revolving around pain and rescue. The analyst shows her this pattern, but also has to establish herself as actually protective to Jenny. The analyst also shows Jenny how she often confuses aggression with affection and clarifies this as a defense against positive longings and need for sympathy over the patching. Jenny can perhaps for the first time allow herself to experience this from her analyst.

Jenny does continue to show intense anxiety over actual present separations, and this is enacted with the analyst rather than only being symbolized via play. Again the analyst has to show her attunement to Jenny's anxiety and distress as well as to assist her ego functioning. But the analyst must also interpret Jenny's fears of herself as bad, that is, her own superego anxiety, and help her recognize the contrast between expectations of retaliation by the analyst and the reality which she experiences in the here-and-now relationship. I believe the present experience was more important to her even than talking about the past. This work seems to have led to her improved object relationships at school.

The second phase of the treatment is conceptualized as dealing with a more oedipal level of development. But I believe most of the work still needed centers around the two-person relationship and the remaining self-object distortions.

There is much material that can be understood in terms of penis envy and castration anxiety. Our questions often revolve around the importance of interpreting these unconscious fantasy formations and their derivatives, or seeing this material as symbolizing narcissistic issues which require different interpretations, or even ego support to enhance the feelings of self-worth. Grossman and Stewart (1976) have described how neurotic patients make use of this metaphor in a very different way from non-neurotics. I believe all these interventions have their place, but it is important to be careful about their timing and to ascertain which kinds of intervention the child is really responding to.

With Jenny, we are aware that the early experiences of pain and hurt in her relationships must have become woven into later fantasies of other pains and hurts. There is surprisingly little material about her envy of and aggression toward her brother. But the penis envy complaints may also need interpretation as to their many defensive functions, as a masochistic defense or as defense against positive feelings which need to be reexperienced and underlined. This may be the approach to the potential for masochistic perversion (Novick and Novick 1987).

Such complaints can also defend against envy of the preoedipal and oedipal mother and analyst, whose power the little girl wants but feels inadequate in relation to, and she fears the witch mother who may keep her deprived. The effect of such interpretations can enhance identification with the mother and thereby improve ego functioning. Some of the material interpreted within the positive oedipal framework might also be seen as relating to positive feelings toward the analyst and thereby more directly used in object relationship building.

The continuing intensity of Jenny's reaction to separation from the analyst, including her excited sexualization and provocations, suggest how precarious her object relations still were despite more adaptive behavior at school. As Dr. Nover notes, Jenny still could not feel safe without the actual object present and could easily feel deserted, destructive, and helpless.

In summary, from the material so far presented I believe the "therapeutic object relationship" as defined above was the crucial medium for change, although this was not the explicit formulation. Most analysts now focus on the vital role for psychic growth of the two-person, here-and-now experience occurring at the moment of the interpretation. While this is important with all patients, I believe it is even more so in the treatment of the very young child. Self-knowing and change must be slow and cumulative, but it is of great interest to look at the inner processes of thinking whereby interventions are absorbed and integrated. Alas, even the psychoanalytic method cannot reveal all we would like to know about this mystery.

Rachel: The Analysis of a Prelatency Child after Urinary Tract Surgery

Alicia S. Gavalya, M.D.

Rachel, age three years, six months, was referred while under-going surgical evaluation for ureteral reimplantation. One year earlier she had suffered several urinary tract infections which led to the diagnosis of a congenital urinary tract defect. She had al-ready undergone two urethral catheterizations with cystoscopy and an intravenous pyleogram. Since then her behavior alter-nated between being very compliant and so difficult that her par-ents, especially her mother, felt at a loss as to how to handle her. This was in stark contrast with the previously cuddly child very much enjoyed by everyone.

Rachel had never achieved full urinary control, and in the pre-ceding five months there had been occasional episodes of fecal retention and soiling. Sometimes she displayed anger over not being the same age as her sister, who was two years older, while at other times she reverted to baby talk. She exhibited increasingly controlling behavior and often burst out into temper tantrums, which greatly embarrassed the family.

Rachel's observant Jewish family environment provided her with warmth and consistent care. Her father, a successful young professional, clearly loved his children, although he was not as available as sometimes necessary because of Rachel's demands. He was very supportive of his wife, an educator and gifted art-ist who was taking time off from her career to care full time for her family. Rachel's mother was the younger of two sisters and had a good relationship with both her parents, with little or no conflict or turmoil even during her adolescence. This made it difficult for her to comprehend her child's behavior, and she felt increasingly hurt by Rachel's oppositionalism.

EVALUATION

Rachel was a beautiful, blond, verbal child who was shy at first but soon became confident and self-possessed as I became familiar to her. She was seen in a clinical setting with the initial idea of helping her to utilize and reinforce her defenses in order to understand and master what was happening to her body. My thinking was that the invasive procedures and threat of the unknown overwhelmed her resources, to which she responded with regression, anxiety, and anger. As I learned more about Rachel, I began to think analysis might be required, a conclusion I reached shortly after the operation.

Rachel's psychoanalytically oriented therapy consisted of nine months of weekly sessions prior to the surgery and four months of biweekly sessions postoperatively. Analysis began after a six-week recess from the psychotherapy and lasted sixteen months.

Preanalytic Psychotherapy

Rachel showed her good intellectual capacity by throwing herself into learning about the anatomical and surgical details of her condition. She typically denied feeling vulnerable by bragging about going through the intrusive procedures with no fear. She demonstrated her ability to trust by putting herself in the hands of her doctors and showing great respect and admiration for the surgeon and affection for her pediatrician. It was also clear that sometimes she became overwhelmed and would then regress to baby talk, demanding behavior, overcontrolling, and temper tantrums.

Although uneven, her development had proceeded normally. Her concerns with anal issues were played out through her interest in play dough, and she showed much excitement with the noise making which accompanied such play. She was overly concerned about making a mess. Her sexual curiosity, heightened and burdened by the intrusions and manipulation of her genital area, was expressed in her obsessive search and exploration of apertures and orifices of available toys. She demonstrated her good capacity to free associate while exploring the different holes of a toy ambulance: recalling "a hundred years ago" when she had entered the bathroom while her father was urinating, she intimated that she had purposely gone in without knocking. She also confessed that she actively indulged in looking at her little boyfriend while he went to the bathroom. I understood her castration fears to be evident in her insistence that everything we made had to be just right, pointing out the damaged or broken pieces of toys and in making sure we did not violate the laws of her religion. She was fearful that she had caused damage to herself, but as a way of denying the responsibility she blamed her mother. As Rachel put it later on when she had another episode of cystitis, "My mother always goes away at the wrong time." She demeaned her mother and conveyed the feeling that she did not trust her as much as she did her powerful father, whom she would choose to be at her side on the way to the operating room.

In Rachel's mind, mother's role was to be the keeper of rules and to make sure that Rachel did not break the dietary laws. Prior to the operation, Rachel engaged in a ritual activity of sneaking out of my office, by-passing the waiting room where her mother sat, going to the clinic cafeteria, and purchasing food from a vending machine. She liked to pretend that she was buying the food behind mother's back, although she knew that her mother had given specific permission for her to eat before dinner. Sometimes Rachel would become unsure and preoccupied with doubt as to whether a particular item was kosher. On these occasions it became imperative that we ask her mother. This vignette is representative of the initial stages of Rachel's relationship with me; she carried me along in her forbidden excursions. I was there when she dared to get the food, but I was unable to keep her from violating the law because I did not know the law myself. Since I was just as powerless as she, she still needed her mother; but as mother was unaware of Rachel's wishes to do what was forbidden and was not always there to keep her from breaking the rules, there was still danger. Mother herself was not seen as being as powerful as Rachel's father.

However, Rachel fought her wish to return to a more infantile relationship with her mother by rejecting her and becoming overly controlling. She was also aggressive and intrusive with her sister and other children, with the result that they stayed away from her, leaving her feeling even more lonely. She told me an incident in which her sister locked herself away with her friends, saying Rachel was too young to play with them, whereupon Rachel had a "big fit." In this context I said it was too bad her sister didn't know how sad and lonely she felt; unfortunately she had been able to express her feelings only through angry words. Following this, there was a considerable diminution of the temper tantrums.

Prior to the surgery and as the time for it approached, Rachel became very aggressive toward me, blaming me for anything she did which she considered wrong. She played a game with the dictaphone in which we would take turns pretending to speak on the radio, but she insisted on holding the mouthpiece for me so that she had control of the switch, which she sadistically turned on and off so that I could not tell my story. At times I felt her wish actually to hurt me physically was so strong that I had to reassure her that I would not permit it. In this context I empathized with her helplessness and interpreted that she was doing to me what she felt was being done to her with regard to the impending surgery. With her characteristic defenses of intellectualization and reaction formation, Rachel made good use of the information she got from her surgeon and the hospital team. She learned about the anatomy and physiology of the urinary system and about the surgical procedure that eventually took place. She made innumerable drawings while explaining it to me, and she bragged about not being afraid while reassuring herself that her doctors knew best. Nine months after our initial session, Rachel went through the surgery with flying colors. Her hospital course was uneventful, and she came home a few days later to experience a two-week moratorium during which there was no soiling or wetting and her relationship with her family was wonderful.

To everyone's dismay her symptomatology returned in an even more dramatic form two weeks after the surgery. The soiling worsened, she sustained a painful rash, and she became afraid of moving her bowels, leading her to express her annoyance at me by saying, "Dr. Gavalya is not doing her job." At the same time, Rachel was better able on occasion to accept responsibility for her bodily functions. Once she asked her mother if she knew why her "duty" would not come out. When her mother asked her why, she said, "I won't let it." In reporting the conversation to me, Rachel associated to the hospitalization, during which a nurse gave her permission to move her bowels in the diaper-like sheet she was wearing in bed. I interpreted her association as her having received permission to be like a baby again, and if the stools were in the diaper she then knew they were not lost. About this time, Rachel was particularly nasty and rejecting toward her mother; she conveyed her abandonment fantasy when she reproachfully told that she remembered waking up in her crib when she was a baby and being all alone in the house. Yet her treatment alliance with me continued to develop, allowing her to confine her hostility to the play situation. She engaged me in helping her work through the trauma of the surgery, which she did by turning passive into active. On one occasion, after she lovingly touched my hair and had a little bird whisper some unintelligible message in my ear, she angrily threw marbles on the floor. I suggested that she was angry because I did not understand the bird's message. She responded by going around me, sliding over my shoulder, and, after landing on my lap, undoing her shoelaces. Once the laces were undone, she directed the tip of one of them toward my nose. At first I thought she wanted to tickle me, but then I realized that she intended to introduce it into my nostril. I then interpreted that she was trying to do to me what had been done to her, with the result that she spoke at length of her feelings about the different procedures she had undergone. Still, she relied mainly on denial, externalization, and reaction formation to avoid the affects associated with those traumas.

In subsequent sessions Rachel became interested in making things out of cloth. She did not know how to sew and ambivalently accepted my help. When I began to teach her she protested, "I am sewing myself" and made every effort to stick the needle in my finger, expressing great delight when she succeeded. When we cut out a pattern for the dress of a favorite doll, she associated to the surgery and said, "My legs could be cut off" and proceeded to show me cuts and scratches, biting off and eating a piece of skin from her finger. She became intensely involved in making a purse, which metaphorically became the bag which holds the urine and where she had had the operation. After spending several hours working on the opening, she announced that when the bag was completed she would take it home and requested that I make a strap for it.

Three months after the surgery, Rachel's behavior had improved in that the temper tantrums were less frequent. At school she was shy and had a peculiar habit of tightening her lips whenever she spoke, as if to keep her words from coming out. Most of the time she played with an old childhood friend, though if invited she would interact with other children. At home she continued to be very demanding, intruding when her sister's friends came to visit; the relationship with her mother was much more strained. Rachel's mother told me she had just about lost hope, as so much mean and rejecting behavior hurt her deeply. For instance, while at a restaurant Rachel had refused mother's offer of help, turning immediately toward her aunt and sweetly requesting assistance. A representative vignette which gave us insight into the way Rachel experienced her mother as intrusive occurred in my waiting room. As I greeted them, mother said, in explaining that Rachel had almost fallen asleep on the way over, "We almost fell asleep." To this ostensibly benign comment, Rachel responded with a huge temper tantrum, leaving her mother in shock. Rachel felt understood when I interpreted that she wanted to speak for herself and about her own sleep, but her mother could not overcome the hurt at the thought that Rachel needed to keep her away, even though she understood that Rachel was irrationally angry at her.

As already mentioned, Rachel's character structure and defensive constellation, as they became evident in the psychotherapy, suggested that she might need long-term treatment. Soon after the operation, I expressed to the parents my conviction that Rachel required more intensive treatment, probably psychoanalysis. They had hoped that once the stress of the surgery had passed the symptoms would go away. They supported the recommendation because of their fear that the relationship between Rachel and her mother was becoming irreparably damaged. Since both parents were committed to helping their daughter, they were able to trust me and not interfere in the relationship she formed with me even though our ethnic and religious backgrounds were so different. When Rachel learned of the plan to meet four times per week, she embraced the idea enthusiastically and told me we should meet every day. At home she halfheartedly complained to her mother about the planned frequency of the sessions.

In preparation for the analysis the following steps were taken. First, I decided to have an interruption of the treatment, taking advantage of my summer vacation. Second, I decided to transfer her treatment to my private office, located in the basement of my house. This move was necessary to achieve a proper analytic setting, which had been very difficult to obtain at the clinic where she had been seen up to then. The last session of her therapy took place at the new location. She was very pleased and announced that she was glad to have transferred because the other office was for babies. She also expressed satisfaction with the new toys and said we could leave the others behind. I let her know that I expected that we would continue to work on both, the baby and the more grown-up parts, the present and the past, and I offered to bring any toys that she wished from the other office. She requested toys that she had used to express her aggression, such as Max the dinosaur, on whom she had "operated" by sticking a pencil down its throat, the Incredible Hulk, which she had not yet used, and the purse she had made which awaited a shoulder strap.

The Analysis

Rachel started her first analytic session by talking about the recent English royal wedding. She had been fascinated by it and expressed her identification with the bride when she requested we make a princess costume. We improvised a bridal train with which she solemnly paraded about the office. At the end of this session she quickly rolled her costume into a ball and before I could say anything she darted out of the office hiding her "veil" under her jacket, barely making a motion for her mother to follow her. I was impressed by the air of secrecy during the hour and at its end, Rachel's behaving like a robber, bent over and avoiding the gaze of my next patient in the waiting room. This was the first of many forbidden games that we were to play during her analysis. The play had a romantic cast, and I came to understand it as a flight away from her troubled pregenital past.

The first few months of analysis brought about an intensification of her positive feelings for me and the consolidation of our working alliance. During this time she requested endless gifts from me in the forming of asking to be taught how to make various craft items. She threw herself into her projects, staying very close to me, describing in detail accounts of school activities, conversation with her friends, nasty private jokes, and in particular sharing with me what she was learning of her Jewish tradition. She knew our ethnic backgrounds differed, but she knew I was safe, I did not abandon her, and I could tolerate her aggression; she feared no retaliation from me, and she could confide in me her sexual excursions. Above all, I was expendable as a vehicle for disavowed aspects of herself. For example, wishing to make me acceptable, she brought me a miniature Torah and suggested that I attend a dinner at her house with the rabbi. On the other hand, she fed me forbidden foods. For a long time we played restaurant; she was the cook and waitress and I was instructed to sit at a table, carefully read a menu, and choose an entire meal. If I asked for something she did not want me to have she flatly told me, "Tough, you have to have" such and such. So I ate dozens of pepperoni pizzas, ham, and dishes prepared with pork. She stood in front of me watching until I finished my meal and then either gave me more or cleaned the kitchen. She not only projected onto me her sense of being unclean, but also made me do all the things she wished to do but feared doing. I understood this game to be an expression in the transference of her need to deal with those parts of herself which were not acceptable to her parents. As the analytic process became deeper and involved all of her fantasy life, Rachel typically worked on several projects at once, so that at some points our room looked chaotic, though the sessions never felt out of control. When her projects began to extend into the part of the office used for adults, she became concerned that other patients would see her work. To protect her privacy and to keep all the projects well contained, we built a tent which she called the store. She built a communications system with a tower in the center which kept us in touch whenever either of us was outside the store.

Approximately six months into the analysis Rachel's parents reported that her relationship with her mother had improved dramatically. The soiling had stopped, the wetting had diminished, and although she was still demanding, she had no more temper tantrums. At the same time as this peaceful period at home, she found the opportunity to begin expressing her ambivalence in the office. Just before a brief separation which required missing one session and rearranging another, she decided to make fake matches, for which she cut chips of wood from fireplace logs in my office and placed them into several boxes. At the end of the session she became very anxious, insisting she must take the boxes home; I was unable to persuade her not to and being pressed for time I consented to it. On her return, she did bring back the boxes and alluded to the issues having to do with urination and defecation by explaining that if she had left them in the office, everything that was yellow or gold would have caught fire. While she made a kosher magic potion which required magic words that only she knew, she explained that the words were protective so that whatever was gold or yellow did not catch on fire. As she mixed the ingredients, the potion turned very dark and she said, "If you do not put in black waterproofing like the color of your couch, it will catch fire, things will explode." I acknowledged that I understood why she was so worried if she feared I was not safe. She replied, "Your house and my house are safe." She continued, saying that she was the only one who knew the words and even if she forgot she could make new ones. As we were putting the boxes away she noticed the ring I was wearing, a fire opal which under the light has an intense red color. She said, "I have that part of the magic in the ring and it could come out if we pull the stone out. But if you break it, and then you look at it, your eyes will become fire and you will not be able to see." She then told me that she has a ring with diamonds and rubies and if they are crushed the same thing would happen to us. I wondered how long it has been since she has known the words, to which she replied, "Since I have known you. Before, I was just a baby, a child and it was not necessary." I told her at this point that when she was a baby her mother protected her from doing things she thought were bad, but later if she makes fires and explosions, like when she gets angry and says, "I am really fired up," then she cannot be sure that it will be safe. I wondered if she was afraid that if she left her fire and explosive feelings here, I would not be safe. She responded by picking up a plastic bag and placing paper clips in it, saying, "You will have to clean this up, otherwise the magic will be lost. You will have to clean forever, and you cannot be messy, and I can help you straighten out right now." I declared at this point how difficult it would be to keep from being even a little messy, while she continued straightening out and finally said, "It is clean enough." I told her that she reminded me of the movie "Raiders of the Lost Ark," in which people looked at something they were not supposed to see. She knew about it and said though her parents said it was not a movie for small children, her friends told her all about it. Returning to her fantasy, she said she has a fairy godmother and that she, Rachel, is the only one who can hear and see her. With the appearance of the fairy godmother, Rachel took over the powers previously assigned to me, the analyst.

In the next period of treatment, the trauma of the surgery re-appeared, associated with her concerns over castration, her confusion and guilt over sexual curiosity, and her religious identity.

Rachel performed an elaborate operation on some wooden dolls. There were six of them: one Jewish, one Christian, one both, and three of unknown religion. An operation on the mystery dolls was necessary to determine from an examination of their bodies into which category they should be placed. I was instructed to keep notes on the procedure. Vials of anesthetic were given with the result that all of them threw up. Then Rachel placed them on the "operating table" and while sticking them with the "fork," she instructed me to "take the knife and cut." Responding to my asking, "Where?" she lifted her blouse and, pointing to the lower abdomen, showed me her scar, saying, "Like where I got cut." Returning to the play, she found that the vial of anesthetic had altered the Jewish man and the Christian woman's blood in such a way that no one would ever be able to tell what sex they were. Then a confusing and disastrous scene occurred: the doll we thought was Jewish received too much medicine and died. She checked the others and, finding out that their blood had turned blue also, declared that now for sure we will never find out what they were. We had almost reached the end of her session, and I only made a comment indicating that next time we would continue to try to solve the mystery while we put the "instruments" away. The following session when I showed interest to get back to the mystery, she abruptly said, "We already figured it out; four of them are dead and the other two are something, and that's all we care." I pointed out how she must have been afraid to die when she was operated on; but my efforts to return to the play by saying that she had lots of feelings and ideas about the surgery, and that there seemed to be a lot of confusion about being Jewish, Christian, and about being a boy or a girl, were unsuccessful.

From this point Rachel's castration fantasies and the surgical trauma became the main themes of her treatment. She engaged in two major activities. The first was the building and rebuilding of both a house and a stage through which she elaborated these concerns. She placed enormous emphasis on the details of the structure, making shutters and arranging the windows and doors to fit exactly. Particular care was taken that the shutters cover the opening of the windows. The second activity was creating a script for a play with an oedipal theme. The major characters of the play were two girls named Rach and Danya, the Incredible Hulk, three musketeers, and three dolls which were "old and dying." The girls showed great love and sweetness toward their father and tended to him, whereas they talked back to their mother and usually ignored her. The two girls competed for the father, but it was Rach who at some point grew up into a woman and as a woman was supposed to get married. Just at the time the wedding was to take place, the Incredible Hulk barged in and disrupted everything. In working on the script, she made different versions. In one, Rach is discussing with her sister how many children she was going to have. When she pretended that Rach had a baby in her arms, she looked under the doll's dress and asked, "Is this a boy or a girl?" She answered herself, "She is a boy; no, she is a girl." Then she became silly and aggressive by teasing me and demanding that I show her my underwear even to the point that she tried to lift my skirt. I suggested that perhaps she was trying to see if I had a penis or a scar. Rachel labored hard to work through her sense of being damaged and defective, frequently expressing metaphorically in her focus on not having a penis. At the time of the circumcision of her best friend's brother, while explaining the ceremony to which she had been invited, she suddenly said with a dreamlike expression that her teacher told the class that the cord that attaches a baby to the mother is cut and that it is from there that the penis grows!

When I wondered about this, she insisted on the accuracy of her story, firmly stating that her Hebrew teacher knew better than I. I suggested that she draw an illustration of what she thought. As she did, she suddenly looked up and exclaimed, "That's the belly button!" I agreed and said, "You are right, the penis is placed lower, and only boys have it. Although many girls wish they had it, it is only boys who are born with it." She laughed at her having insisted just a few minutes earlier on the accuracy of her story.

In subsequent sessions, her wish to have a penis, her castration fantasies, mother as the castrating agent, and the surgery as the castrating procedure reappeared in the following way:

While explaining the origins of some scratches on her face, she told me her mother decided the cat had to be declawed. I said I thought that it must hurt the cat, but she nonchalantly replied that the cat will still be able to go out. She associated to the fact that she was again taking medicine because of "urine burning" and explained how useful it was to have a tube inside while she was in the hospital so she didn't have to worry about wetting her pants. Then she went back to the issue of the cat's claws, now with a little more feeling, saying, "It must hurt a lot because once I had an ingrown toenail and it was awful," and, "A boy in my class has very short fingernails. His father cut them that way because he chews on them." By describing to her the trend of her associations step by step, I could show her how her thought went from scratches on her face, to the scratcher who is being punished by having something cut off, and then to her own being in the hospital with a tube inside, sticking out of her maybe like a penis, and then again to the thoughts of the boy's nails being cut off. She was immensely pleased to find out "how my mind works."

On another occasion, after several weeks of stating that she was very hungry and demanding food, I noticed that she covered her mouth when she chewed. She also insisted that dry cereal be in a paper bag instead of a plastic one. When I inquired about it she argued that it was only for the sake of good manners since she did not want me to look inside when she opened it. I interpreted that she thought I wanted to look in like all the people in the hospital. She adamantly denied it and said, "Doctors are allowed because they are used to it and only members of my family are allowed to look at me when I eat." I told her I was a doctor also and she may still be worried that if I looked inside of her I might see that she only had a belly button and not a penis. Two sessions later she decided that she did not require the paper bag; she had thought about it and decided I could look, that I really was a member of her family because, "After all, we all come from Adam and Eve."

Termination Phase

In the twelfth month of the analysis, during the disruptions of camp and summer vacations, Rachel's mother told her social worker that Rachel was complaining about not having enough time to play with friends and attend other activities, particularly not having time for music lessons. Mother confessed that she herself could not understand why Rachel had to continue, given the fact that things were going so well. Rachel was doing wonderfully at school, and at home their relationship could not have been better. I suggested that mother tell Rachel to bring her concern to me. Using her growing writing skills, Rachel promptly wrote, "I am doing very well. I do not want to come every day." It happened that the following session Rachel's mother was in a great rush for an appointment, so she needed to drop her very promptly and run. Rachel had been playing with a friend, was tired, and had given her mother a hard time by moving very slowly. When she had to go out of the car under her mother's pressure, she panicked, began to cry, and clung to her mother, who then brought her into the office feeling very upset herself. She explained what had happened, and I suggested that it had been hard for Rachel to leave her friend, particularly at this time when she wished not to come so often. I said that when Mommy was in such a rush it may have seemed to Rachel that she would be abandoned here. With this explanation both mother and child relaxed. Once her mother left, I told Rachel I agreed she was coming close to terminating her treatment, but from what we had just observed together it seemed clear that she still had several worries and she was afraid of telling me she wanted to leave me. I told her she was angry at having to come to see me but, since she also loved me, she did not want to face those feelings, especially the ones that might set my house on fire. Lastly, I said the more she would let herself express her feelings, the more she would be able to understand about her worries and the faster she would be done. She responded with her characteristic "let's get to it" manner, decided it was time to organize her projects, and began the process of selecting what she wanted to pick out, what needed to be thrown away, and what needed to be finished. Ultimately she literally folded up her tent.

About two weeks later, while emptying a box filled with crayons and old drawings, she suddenly decided to paint a picture of me. She said it had to be very exact, "including the pimple on the right side of your face and the line on the left side of your nose." Then she decided she should make an extra one plus two self-portraits for each of us. I said, "This way we can remember each other." "Yes, you can remember me, after I fire you," she shot back. When I asked if she had to fire me, she gave a lengthy explanation about leaving things for other children to use and also for her use when she came back. I said she was angry when she said she was going to fire me, but now she was being so good about leaving things for other children that she made me think perhaps she feared if she were not nice, she wouldn't be allowed back. I added that even though she wanted to end her sessions soon, she may be feeling herself fired by me, since I agreed that she would be terminating at some point soon. She replied, "Of course I am going to see you all the time. I will be able to see you in the crystal ball that belongs to my fairy godmother." I said, "Too bad I do not have a crystal ball, since you are the only one with a fairy godmother." She then assured me, "But from now on you will have the magic words because I will leave them to you. So from now on every time I see you in my crystal ball you will have the words whispered in your ear."

An example of the resolution of Rachel's oedipal conflicts and the reconciliation between her loving and angry feelings is portrayed in the following material: In addition to making our portraits she decided to make duplicates of many of the meaningful objects in the office. We copied Rach the doll and Incredible Hulk, and she assembled them on a sheet of paper, carefully arranging them so that they would be holding hands. I commented about the angry one being together with the sweet one and humorously added, the beauty and the beast. She laughed and said, "Particularly if you remember what Incredible Hulk did at Rach's wedding." It also reminded her of her father telling her and her sister that he was already married to their mother when they said they wanted to marry him. The resolution of Rachel's ambivalence toward her mother was foreshadowed in the transference when, in asking me to teach her to knit, she sat on my lap, had me hold her hands, and teach her step by step, stating, "You know better." For several months at home she had been teaching herself to play the piano. Finally she convinced her parents to let her take a couple of music lessons just prior to the summer vacation, and she requested a change in the analytic schedule so that she could do it. In the fall when regular lessons started, she decided to pick the cello as her instrument, and, most touchingly, she began studying a method that required her mother to play the piano along with her.

Another vignette, which I observed by chance, occurred outside her analytic session when Rachel's mother was late picking her up. I accidentally looked out the window and saw that she had gone out from the waiting room and was hiding behind some bushes. Thinking that she was in distress, I went out to find she was hiding from some boys walking in her direction. I decided to stay with her for a few minutes as we both admired the roses in the path. She expressed her admiration for one of them, and I plucked it and gave it to her just as her mother arrived. Rachel lifted the flower to show it to her mother and her mother, assuming it was being offered to her, exclaimed, "For me?" After an instant of hesitation, Rachel answered, "For us," and gave it to her mother as she looked at me knowingly.

Thirteen months after the start of the analysis we established a termination date for five months later; she wished to end on her birthday. Her mother suggested a follow-up session three months afterward. Promptly Rachel became bossy, giving us the opportunity to talk about the intense need for control in the past. Patiently she listened to my interpretations. I playacted for her the scenes in the car and at home when she would have temper tantrums if mother acknowledged her as Rachel instead of a make-believe character. To this she responded with great delight, laughing away and saying, "I can hardly believe it, I can hardly believe it, but I remember, it is true!" The issue of ambivalence toward her mother actually provoked her to wet herself a bit in the office, which led us to discuss the fact that her feelings get expressed through her body. She then said she had used "body talk."

Three months before termination and shortly before Yom Kippur, Rachel announced she was going to fast, explaining to me that this was something one should do in case one had done something bad. As I inquired what she thought she had done, she responded by telling me that for her it had been optional because of her age; she said her mother believed she was only going to try for a few hours, but she intended to fast the whole day because she thought she was old enough. A few minutes later, to my great surprise, she casually said, "My mother said you are divorced and you have two children." Recovering from my surprise, I said, "Hum, maybe you think I ought to fast because of being divorced? Or perhaps because I ate the pepperoni pizza?" She responded that if I were Jewish I would have to fast also, and then proceeded to tell me what I would have to do to keep kosher. About a week after this session, she came in feeling very uncomfortable and confided that she had soiled herself at school that day, but had been unable to tell her teacher or to clean herself well. I took her to the bathroom and helped her, for which she was very grateful. Something in Rachel's sudden reaction made me aware that there had been a certain distance between us which I had not noticed, and that a shift in our relationship had occurred. I experienced her as a very separate person. She seemed now again to acknowledge me as a separate person, not kosher but still valued as helpful to her. After she found out I was divorced she became extremely critical of me for a while. Not only was everything I did wrong, but I was made wrong: my legs, my nose, the color of my skin, my hair, my dresses were ugly. She stated, "Everything is wrong except your ring," as she pulled on my finger to take the ring off. I felt that in discovering I was divorced, meaning to her, unclean, she was not able to idealize me anymore and that her efforts to correct her own sense of defectiveness in the transference by making me right could not be indulged in the same way anymore.

At the beginning of treatment Rachel had noticed that I took some notes during the session; she just naturally made entries in the same notebook, so my notebook became our notebook. When she decided to review all the projects, review of the notebook was of course included, so she not only saw her drawing but my own notes and some of the comments I had made on the material. She was amazed at the fact that she had had such intense concerns about sexuality and not having a penis. She could hardly believe her own eyes when she saw that just as she was learning to draw the letters of the alphabet, she had talked about making love by saying F was for fucking in the toilet, and H for hair between the legs. She exclaimed in disbelief, "You mean I knew that much when I was so little?" She laughed at herself for having insisted that a penis would grow from the umbilical cord. She delighted in remembering our first meetings and the old building in which we held our sessions, laughingly remembering the song I sang while squeezing the play dough. Rachel noticed how her memory of those times was beginning to fade, since she could not remember how long we met at the old building. She wanted me to remind her of what she was wearing the first time we met, and when I recalled for her the clown dream she had spoken about during her first session, she revised it by saying that the clown was chasing after her, pretending it wanted to kiss her. In the original version of the dream it was going to bite her. I had interpreted her dream as having to do with her visits to the doctor and the hospital. I said that when you go to the hospital everyone smiles at you, and then they stick a needle into you, put a tube inside of you, and even cut your abdomen. She replied, "Yes, of course the doctor is going to help you, but it is weird that first they smile, and then they hurt you." I said, maybe your clown was the smiling doctor and you were afraid he was going to bite something off you. Maybe that is why later on you thought you did not have a penis. She replied, "No wonder so many people are afraid of doctors."

Rachel advanced quite far in the development of latency. Her academic and religious education progressed by leaps and bounds, no doubt spurred on by a most remarkable family environment in which the teaching of tradition seemed to take place with every breath. We talked extensively about her reliance on her family and her religion, how it was important that she belonged to a Jewish family, and how there was a time when she felt very bad that she was the only one with blond hair in her family. She responded by saying that it was true, and also that she did not like being the only one who did not wear glasses, although her doctor has now said that she will need them at some point. She added, "My eyes are not so bad yet." I said, "So you will have to keep on seeing doctors," to which she responded she knew that although her bladder was fixed, she had to continue to take the medicine and the doctor will keep track of her for a couple of years. She shared with me much of what she was learning, patiently recounting the biblical stories and explaining the meaning of the holidays. She also requested that I tell her the Spanish words for her Hebrew vocabulary. There was so much of this that her mother told the social worker that Rachel would be speaking Spanish by the time the treatment was over. Rachel was learning so fast that her sister seemed to be threatened and had said, "Rachel is learning too fast."

Once she had finished reviewing "the book," Rachel moved to play more board games and became very intensely involved in learning to play chess, which brought us back to the times when she could not stand not winning and she had to cheat. This time she demonstrated her ability to include cheating as a possible approach to winning without acting on it. She took great pride in having a history in the area of her personal relationships. She was delighted to have a friend that she had known "since I was born." She felt regretful that she had rejected him when she had wanted to be as old as her sister. She felt he was like a brother and that they would take care of each other at school if any bully were to bother either one of them. She confessed her apprehension that the class bully might turn on her, but then decided that instead of running she would turn around and "pull his pants down" to humiliate him. I said, "So just because he has a penis does not mean that he is stronger than you or just because you don't have a penis you don't have to feel bad about yourself."

While playing checkers a month before termination, Rachel casually noted my ring, apparently not remembering that she had asked about it in the past. "What is the stone in your ring?" I told her it was a fire opal, to which she suddenly responded with a shout, "That is my birthday stone!" As I reminded her that we had talked about it before when we made matches and she was afraid that my house would catch fire, she pulled the ring from my finger and slipped it on hers, put her hand under the light, and said, "I can feel the fire." I said, "You are not afraid of the fire anymore." "No," she responded as she gave back the ring and resumed the checker game. Two weeks before termination she instructed me to write a list: wood chunks, red tissue paper, and a match box. She then made a picture of the fire and the box of matches. Without pausing, she made a picture of a rose and instructed me to write a four-item list: petals, stem, sun, rain. She drew a rose with a long stem, raindrops, and a shining sun. At the bottom of the picture she wrote, "a grown up rose," "very, very nice," "mixed with chicken soup with rice." I said, "You are the grown-up rose, there is rain like tears because it is sad to end, the sun is shining because there is happiness at the same time." She responded by writing "the end."

Two days before termination Rachel again turned to magic. While she was talking about Hanukkah, I pointed out that I would not see her on that day, to which she responded, "You will not see me after my birthday, I am going to fairyland on

Hanukkah. I am going to be a fairy. It is only for Jewish people."
"I guess I will never go there," I said. "Yes, I will get you a pass,
but you will have to wait for me to take you next holiday, maybe
Passover. You may get to go only one time." I said, "Maybe you
can think about me this time." She replied, "No, because when
you get there you lose your memory, and when you come back to
earth you recover your earth memory." I answered, "So when you
come back you will remember me since I will be in that memory." "No," she said, "what happens is that you put your memory
in a box and you buy it back when you are ready to leave. I will
remember you if I am on earth." "That's good enough for me,"
I said, as she moved to play a game of checkers. During the last
session I gave her a Hanukkah present, a small box with different
animals, and a pin with planets on it which prompted her to talk
about her fairyland fantasy. It had changed in character and was
described with much less passion. She said she would give me
the password when she saw me the next time, since her mother
had reminded her of the follow-up session. Although she had
carefully separated and set aside all the drawings and mementos
she had wanted to take home on this final time, at the last moment when her mother came to pick her up, she made no move
to take them. Her mother was in tears. When she inquired about
the follow-up session, I said that Rachel and I had talked about
it and she could give me a call in three months. Rachel promptly
said, "That's March, okay for Passover." Mother moved over
and kissed me good-bye, while Rachel went away with just a
wave of her hand.

Summary

Rachel had been born with congenital misplacement of both
ureters, discovered after repeated episodes of urinary tract infection. The diagnostic procedures which began when this child

was two years and eight months of age, and before she attained full control of her bladder, required manipulation of the genital area by mother and by medical personnel. Intrusive procedures such as urethral catheterization and intravenous pyleograms caused further invasion of her body integrity. She had reimplantation of her ureters when she was just a little over four years old, during her preanalytic psychotherapy. Her symptomatology included enuresis, fecal soiling and retention, antagonistic behavior, particularly toward her mother, baby talk alternating with insistence that she was older, and temper tantrums. Rachel had a gratifying early relationship with a mother whose need for perfection and tendency to deny aggression made it very difficult to accept rebelliousness and misbehavior in her child. This, in addition to the fact that Rachel blamed her mother for her defectiveness, lowered her mother's self-esteem and set the stage for a disruption of the mother-child relationship. Her parents' religious duties made them in her eyes the agents of God. In addition, the trauma caused by the hospitalizations and surgery accentuated her view of herself as helpless and her caretakers as omnipotent. She came to feel that she had many forbidden thoughts and feelings not acceptable to her parents and to God. This was manifested in her preoccupation with not breaking the dietary laws and in her emphasis on cleanliness. Because of the anger at her parents she was unable to identify with their helpful qualities; rather, she took on the aggressive aspects of her image of them. In reaction to her helplessness she took the position of being omnipotent and became controlling and punishing, particularly with her mother. She turned her fears into the opposite, becoming very brave and denying her need to cry. As this was strongly reinforced by her parents' attitudes, it became a central defensive constellation, but she came to treatment because in fact she could not achieve the necessary control and mastery and was frightened and angry that her mother had not been able to protect her.

The goals of her analysis included the mastery of superego conflicts and the mastery of her traumatic experience. This involved the ability to bring coherence to an experience of overwhelming chaos by allowing her unconscious and preconscious fantasies of bodily damage to come to awareness through play. Another analytic goal was to diminish her use of denial of helplessness and the externalization of her sense of defectiveness onto her mother, with the consequent damaging effects to that relationship. I became a nonomnipotent companion who also did not know all the rules, but who was willing to share her uncertainty. This was an alliance with a protective person who was neither the representative of the rules nor a seducer from them. Rachel transferred to me her sense of being bad. She made me bad by making me eat all the forbidden foods. At the same time she idealized me and assigned to me powers which she wished to take for herself. After becoming disappointed in me, she maintained her working alliance by turning herself into the authorized person who could help her analyst learn the rich tradition of her culture and religion. She bravely took on the power-angry, evil power that at one point threatened to become unleashed if she left it unattended.

Rachel embraced latency with passion, virtually every minute presenting a new opportunity for mastery. In the course of analysis she resumed her relationship with her mother as a strong separate individual, able now to accept from her the knowledge and affection she had earlier been fearful of accepting lest she regress to a helpless state. She had come to better accept her mother as well as herself. In the termination phase she was able to integrate at a different cognitive level the split between her aggressive and her loving sides as well as the polarity between her own sense of defectiveness with respect to her overly idealized parents.

Although the plan had been that they would contact me for follow-up, I have not heard from the family in four and a half years, though their pediatrician reports that Rachel is doing very well.

Discussion of Gavalya Presentation

Samuel Ritvo, M.D.

The analysis of Rachel is instructive for what it permits us to learn about the effects on the child's psyche and the relationship to the mother when the integrity of the body is threatened by malformation, illness, and inevitable surgical intervention. The long duration of the treatment from three years, six months to six years permits us to see how the preoedipal, oedipal, and beginning latency girl copes with the trauma, that is, in the context of the transference and the actual relationship to an alternative maternal figure.

At two years, six months, Rachel underwent a personality change when she suffered several urinary tract infections and was subjected to invasive diagnostic and therapeutic procedures. Her reactions were of a bodily nature, that is, incomplete urinary control, fecal retention, and soiling, as well as behavioral and affective, becoming very compliant or very controlling and given to angry outbursts and temper tantrums. The marked personality change can be viewed as a reaction to the rage, fear, and helplessness at the invasion of her body, a reaction directed at the parents (primarily the mother), who were unable to remove the danger. At the core of her difficulties was her own heightened ambivalence toward the mother, who she felt had failed her and whom she held responsible for whatever was wrong with her body, which in the course of development came to include her castration.

In the beginning of the treatment Rachel experienced the

analyst as someone who was both a partner in misdeeds against the mother's rules, as well as a tempting rival to the mother who entices her to break the mother's rules and to be fed by her. In these fantasies and activities, she projects or transfers onto the analyst her own conflicts over the negative wishes and feelings toward the mother, providing an opportunity to analyze the conflicts and the defenses involved.

These aspects of the transference had origins also in the mother's conflict over turning Rachel over to the analyst for help. The mother wanted Rachel to have the help she needed. At the same time, she was deeply wounded by Rachel's anger toward her and resented her attachment to the analyst. There are indications that the mother struggled with these feelings throughout the treatment, and they probably had a role in Rachel's not returning after the end of the treatment as she had said she would. In this same connection, the Orthodox Jewish rules which the family observed served a number of functions for Rachel and her mother in relation to the analyst. As the mother is the keeper of the home and the enforcer of the rules in the home, the Orthodox rules keep the child basically loyal to her. By the same token, Rachel could use her adherence to the rules in the service of her ambivalence toward the mother—expressing loyalty and devotion to the mother by joining her in the observances and displacing the negative side onto the analyst as the nonbeliever or outsider.

This device, projecting her own aggression and feelings of wrongdoing onto the analyst and attacking it in her, was part of her effort to control her aggression and the threat it posed to the tie to her mother. Here we can see the superego in statu nascendi before it is internalized and structuralized. With the attacks on the analyst, she also tries to reverse her helplessness in the surgery by being the attacker instead of the victim. At the same time, having the analyst to blame helps to preserve the positive tie to the mother.

With the start of the analysis at six, Rachel's use of the transference in her struggle with drive expression and control in the oedipal period becomes much more visible. All unclean (non-Kosher) motives and behavior are projected onto the analyst. In this way Rachel is in the psychologically advantageous position of both participating in them and condemning them. She keeps the projects with the analyst secret, not to be shared with anyone else. The analyst becomes a partner in the expression of the drive derivatives, but a partner who helps the ego to observe and understand and to exercise selective controls. Under these circumstances she improved very much at home. She invoked the religious traditions of her parents to gain control over her destructive wishes and fantasies. Kosher potions and magic words give her mastery over fire.

In the play with the six dolls, Rachel goes back to reworking the surgical trauma, this time in the setting of oedipal and primal scene fantasies. But the outpouring of aggressive and mutilating fantasies makes her recoil, almost in horror. She then returns to the castration and trauma themes in a subtler, more disguised fashion: building a special place with windows, doors, and shutters carefully fitted to hide and cover. She elaborates complex fantasies about castration and childbirth, in which the penis would somehow come from the mother via the umbilical cord. The repeated working through of the conflict over her own aggression in the context of the mother as the castrator and the surgery as the castrating procedure culminates in the triumph of cognition and reality testing—with the recognition that only boys have the phallus.

When the analyst shows her the train of her association from the masturbatory scratching to castration as punishment, first in the boy she knows and then to herself in the surgical situation, she is pleased to find out how her mind works, as perceptive an understanding of the psychoanalytic endeavor as many adults have. A short time later when she insisted that her food be in a paper bag instead of clear plastic so that the analyst could not see what was inside, the analyst offered the view that Rachel did not want her to see that she did not have a penis. It seems likely that the behavior also represents a resistance against being aware of and revealing something in her thoughts and feelings. In such a resistance, the opaque bag could be a metaphor for the mind, which, as Lewin (1971) pointed out, is represented as an enclosed space. This view is corroborated when, a few days later, she says the analyst can look because she is after all really a member of Rachel's family because they are all descended from Adam and Eve, indicating that she had been using the old religious exclusion as a form of resistance.

Having seen how her mind works, that is, having seen how she went from being scratched to being the scratcher who had to fear something being cut off—that is, from her own aggressive wishes and feelings to fears of being attacked and castrated— after a period of further defensive resistance with the paper bag, she is able to accept the reality of her body and to give the whole matter a Shakespearean ending, welcoming the analyst into the family of man. She is aided in this by the greater cognitive capacity that comes with latency.

In the termination phase Rachel is intensely involved with the oedipal conflict. Again she displaces it to the transference, facilitated by her having learned, presumably from her mother, that the analyst is divorced, leaving the father-husband available. Although this is a pejorative in the mother's eyes, it is an exciting prospect for Rachel and her sisters, who have been asking their father why he cannot marry them.

Again, the analyst is available for the projection of the guilt-generating strivings, and Rachel can once more be on the righteous side in condemning the impulse by being critical of the analyst.

The termination had some features of a mourning process. Rachel reviewed and revived memories of experiences with the analyst. Particularly interesting was her surprise at encountering her repressed infantile beliefs and fantasies, which, having lost their intense cathexis, appeared quaint and silly from the vantage point of latency.

Rachel demonstrated how memory is used in conjunction with object constancy in anticipation of the separation and the loss of the analyst — she will go back to fairyland, that is, back to her own fantasy world and back to her family, since fairyland is only for Jewish people, and she will have access to her memory (of the analyst) if she needs it. But not before she has tried other ways of identifying and uniting with the analyst — the ring, the birthday stone, and learning Spanish so rapidly, to the consternation of her mother.

At the final parting, her intention to come back is expressed in her leaving her things behind. But her mother, tearfully grateful to the analyst for restoring her child to her, has no intention of coming back and turning her daughter over once more to this alien woman. But all three principals, Rachel, her mother, and the analyst, could take comfort that this seriously traumatized child had been greatly aided by the analysis in coping with the trauma and its potential pathogenic effect on her development.

The Case of an Angry
Two-and-a-Half-Year-Old Child

Alan Sugarman, Ph.D.

A. was a mildly plump two-and-a-half-year-old, the youngest of three children, when her parents sought consultation for her unusually intense "terrible two's." They were unable to control her temper tantrums or to get her to comply with their demands and expectations. A. simply refused to sit in her car seat, hold her mother's hand when walking in the street, or accompany her parents into any store which failed to interest her. She was so difficult to manage that they avoided taking her out in public whenever possible. In addition, A. was refusing to use the potty, ate only a few foods, usually sweets, and was reluctant to go to sleep at night or to allow her mother to leave for the office in the morning.

A.'s parents' inability to delineate clear expectations and implement firm discipline was apparent. A. was allowed to stay awake at night until 10:30 P.M. because she "did not seem tired." She was encouraged to watch videotapes in the den next to her parents' bedroom whenever she awoke in the middle of the night. Complaints of "I scared" had begun to accompany her frequent awakenings during the two months prior to the consultation. A. was still being allowed to drink her morning cocoa in a bottle and was placed in a playpen whenever she was upstairs with her mother.

Toilet training had been initiated two months prior to the consultation. Because of their difficulty in training their two older children and A.'s temperament, her parents expected a difficult time. Although A. did initially reject the potty chair, she had urinated in it for the first time just prior to the evaluation. No attempt had been made to remove the nighttime diapers.

A. was conceived when her parents were in their early forties. Her siblings were seven and fourteen at the time. Mr. B. candidly admitted his reservations about having another child at his age but acceded to his wife's wishes rather than exacerbate their chronic marital discord. Pregnancy, labor, and delivery were all uneventful. Breast-feeding was discontinued after chronic gastrointestinal upset began at one week of age. Constant diarrhea began at three weeks of age and continued for several months until it was finally brought under control by a change of formula. Uncontrollable crying of several hours' duration continued until A. was almost ten months old. Her mother returned to work on a part-time basis when A. was three months of age, entrusting A.'s care to a live-in housekeeper who spoke broken English.

A., who slept in her room from birth, began to awaken regularly between 12:00 and 2:00 A.M. at one year of age. Her mother would then give her a bottle, place her in the portable crib, and put on a videotape until A. drifted back to sleep. A. was still using a pacifier at the time of the evaluation, but her ability to leave it behind without discomfort or anxiety suggested that it was not a true transitional object. At the time of the evaluation A.'s use of language was limited and immature for her age. Motor development, by comparison, was advanced.

Negativism became intense and pervasive by eighteen months of age. Discipline involved halfhearted limit setting and occasional "time-outs." Mother wanted to protect A. from what she perceived to be father's bullheadedness and excessive control issues. The parents made little effort to reason with A. or to explain rules because they assumed that her comprehension of language paralleled her verbal output. Thus, the playpen was used to protect A. from falling down the steps without attempting to educate her about the danger involved. Except for nursery school, A. had little contact with other children. Her teachers described her play as immature and lacking in rudimentary mutuality.

Although A.'s multiple problems and conflicts over aggression, control, and separation indicated a need for analysis, the discord between the parents over all aspects of parenting and decision making precluded the acceptance of such a recommendation. In fact, A.'s mother was so angry at her husband over the length of his own analysis (fifteen years at that point) that she threatened to divorce him if he insisted on the same treatment for their daughter. Therefore, a recommendation for parental guidance was made, and weekly meetings with A.'s mother were begun. Only the mother was seen because her resentment toward her husband and fear that I would ally myself with Mr. B. against her was so intense that it undermined her alliance with me. She would not consider seeking treatment for herself.

During these sessions, which lasted six months, we explored aspects of parenting, particularly limit setting; the result was an increase in A.'s ability to control her behavior. As mother set clearer limits, A.'s tantrums subsided. She responded to verbal limits and used the toilet routinely for urination, episodically for defecation.

These weekly meetings clarified the severity of the B.'s marital problems. Mrs. B. felt that her husband and his analyst had ganged up on her and criticized her parenting. Consequently she reacted to her husband with icy rage that contrasted with his outbursts of temper. They also argued over Mrs. B.'s interest in her older daughter's athletic endeavors. She frequently took A.'s sister to competitive meets that required their absence from the home for seven to ten days at a time. Mr. B. resented this time and financial drain.

In the midst of this parental discord A. began to withhold her stools. Two significant events precipitated this behavior. First, mother went on a week-long trip with A.'s sister without preparing A. for the separation in advance. In her typical preoccupied way Mrs. B. simply said goodbye to A. one day and returned one week later. Second, this event coincided with A.'s third birthday and her seeming conflict over the wish to be a "big girl" and move ahead developmentally at the same time that she was experiencing increased separation anxiety. A. became distracted and preoccupied and withheld her feces as though all her attention had become focused on her bowel sensations and attempts to prevent the passage of stool. She contorted herself and arched her body backward to take pressure off the anal sphincter. When laxatives failed to alleviate the problem over a month's time Mrs. B. resignedly agreed to allow A. to begin an analysis, but clearly experienced her decision as a capitulation in the face of what she perceived to be her husband's refusal to cooperate with medical treatment. Thus, I saw A. on a four-time-weekly basis and Mrs. B. weekly for a parental meeting. Mr. B.'s eager support of analysis during the initial evaluation made parental sessions with him unnecessary, while his wife's animosity made them undesirable. Phone contacts with him were made whenever necessary during the analysis.

A. began the analysis by refusing to accompany me into the office without her mother. It took some months of analytic work before A. was able to leave her parents in the waiting room. During that first session she had the stuffed animals hug and kiss each other, explaining that one was the mother and one was the baby. My puppet commented on how much the mommy and baby loved each other when they kissed, but otherwise I was silent as A. played by herself or with her mother. A. remained silent and emotionally inhibited during the early portion of the analysis. In subsequent sessions A.'s problems with separation anxiety became clearer as she had a monster alternate between cuddling her puppet and beating it. Then A. hid behind her mother. Soon A. routinely retreated behind her mother whenever she became excited and engrossed in the play. Such retreats seemed independent of the particular drive impulse being expressed, suggesting a general fearfulness of any strong emotion or impulse. Consequently the mother was allowed to remain in the playroom during the early sessions of the analysis, an arrangement that also helped A.'s mother to support the analysis.

It was A.'s aggressive conflicts that were elaborated more fully in early sessions. In one interchange the baby knocked the "mommy" out the window of the dollhouse. Then the baby and the mother fought. A policeman came and took the baby to jail. I said that the baby was being put in jail in order to help it be the boss of its fighting feelings. In another sequence wherein a doggie behaved provocatively I interpreted that the doggie wanted help with being the boss of its "knocking down" feelings so that it could feel like a good doggie. This intervention on the side of A.'s defenses was based on the assumption that A.'s provocativeness involved the externalization of her superego conflicts. The alternation between material about aggression and punishment with separation issues—for instance, A. frequently had the mother figure save the baby from a monster who wanted to take it away—was taken to mean that A.'s separation fears involved her anger with her mother. Similar conflicts appeared in the transference. For example, A. shot me and then ran to her mother for protection.

A.'s behavior at home did not improve during this initial stage. Tantrums were frequent, and the parents used laxatives recommended by the pediatric gastroenterologist in the face of

A. withholding her stool. The laxatives became a source of contention between the parents because mother reduced the dose every time A. became regular. A. was willing to sit on the toilet seat to urinate but insisted on getting off before defecating. During this period she told the family housekeeper that she did not want to go poopy because her mommy got mad when she did. Her family drawing made at home during this time portrayed everyone but me as being "mad" at A.

Prior to the nineteenth session and in consultation with my supervisor, I introduced a potty into the playroom. My supervisor and I believed such a technique could be helpful, although we agreed to be sensitive to possible boundary conflicts precipitated by it. A. walked into the room and looked at the potty silently. She began good guy–bad guy play and finally asked me what the potty was. I said that I thought that she knew what it was and then explained that it was a potty for her to go pee and poop in. At that point A. asked her father, who had brought her to the session, to take her home. I commented that her feelings about pooping and peeing scared her so much that she wanted to leave. A. retorted, "Don't talk, you bad guy! You don't know!"

Nonetheless A. seemed to use the potty as a stimulus to bring her concerns about pooping more directly into the analysis. She began a subsequent session by commenting on her mother's sadness. (And, indeed, the mother was on the verge of tears that day because of her unhappiness with her marriage.) A. then had the baby make pooping sounds. I said that it sounded like the baby was pooping. A. responded by having the mommy change the baby's diaper and then said that the mommy was mad. "Are you worried that your mother is mad at you?" I asked. A. nodded and had the mommy change the baby's diaper again. I then asked if A. worried that her mother was sad because of her poops. This time the baby in the play got scared and bawled for its mommy.

These themes continued into subsequent sessions as A. had

the baby poop on top of the fire station only to have its mommy clean its diaper. I said that the mommy wanted the baby to stay clean. Soon thereafter, the play about pooping expanded to the transference as A. created huge messes in the office. Probably in reaction to the countertransference that she sensed in me and her own anxiety about messing, A. asked her mother to take her home after creating one of her gigantic messes. An interpretation that A. wanted to leave in order not to feel her "messing feelings" allowed her to happily resume the messing play. I explored my own discomfort in supervision and remained alert to needing to interpret her anxiety about displeasing me with her messes. But self-analysis resolved my own reaction formations and allowed A. to expand her material.

By the third month of the analysis A. used the potty regularly as a prop in her play. In one sequence she put the policeman in the potty and had "Suzy" save him. Then A. requested her "Ni Ni" (pacifier) and her "bommy" (blanket) from her mother. This play seemed to be an expression of regressive longings to remain a baby and not to use the potty. In another sequence A. stuffed family members from the dollhouse into the potty. Then she began to fill it with puzzle pieces. I said that A. seemed to want to fill up the potty so that there would be no room left for her poopies. She ordered me to eat everything that was in the potty and say that it was yucky. A.'s apprehensive glance at her mother led me to comment that she appeared to be worried that her mother thought that her poop was yucky. At that point A.'s mother added to her conflict by explaining that A. could get sick if she ate her poops. A. reacted by putting the play poops in the refrigerator.

The link between A.'s stool retention and her fear of her anal sadism seemed to become clearer during the fourth month of the analysis. Torturing became a regular feature of the play. GI Joe would beat up the puppet and then A. would stick it into the potty in order to torture it herself. Marbles, which A. called poopies, were then dumped on the puppet's head. This seemingly anal sadistic torture expanded into the transference as A. dumped messes from the potty bowl onto my head or shook up the messes in the potty bowl before scattering the "poopies" around the room only to order me to pick them up. My comment on her delight in making me clean up her mess led A. to torture the policeman figure, suggesting that she heard the interpretation as a superego injunction.

As A.'s anal sadism came into the transference she began to object strenuously to coming to sessions, complaining that the potty in the playroom was dangerous. A. demanded to be carried into the session by her parent. After her fear of her wishes to mess on me were interpreted, she attempted to throw marbles at me but readily accepted the suggestion that she throw them at the puppets instead. Soon she requested that her father throw the marbles at the puppet instead of herself. More direct aggressive themes followed my interpretation that if her daddy threw the marbles A. would not feel that she was bad for doing so.

In a subsequent session A. threw a toy telephone at my head and hit me. I told A. that I thought that she was testing to see if I would be the boss of her throwing feelings. I reassured her that I would not allow her to hurt herself or me. When A. immediately tried to throw a marble I told her to stop, that I would be the boss of these throwing feelings.

In the fourth month of analysis I suggested to A. that her parents remain in the waiting room, reminding her that we had known each other for some time and had played together many times. Father, who was with her that day, interjected before A. could respond that he and she had already discussed the idea, adding that she had told him that she did not want him to leave. Then he suggested that she "try it now" and rose as if to leave. I suggested that he stay because A. and I needed more time to discuss the idea before it happened. A. would not respond directly to the suggestion that session.

She ignored my proposal the next session as well. Instead she started to play in the potty. Soon A. said that she wanted to pee in it and did so. Then A. wanted to poop. I asked if she wanted to use the potty. A. said, "No." Instead she went behind a chair and had a bowel movement in her pants. I said that she seemed to still want to be the boss of her poops and where they went, for now she wanted them to go in her pants. This attempt to interpret her control struggles allowed A. to use the potty and to pass a stool. When she finished, we discussed what to do with it. A. wanted to watch while I emptied the potty into the toilet. She played at hitting me when we returned from the bathroom. I asked if she was angry because she had pooped in the potty. Instead of responding verbally A. played at having kidnappers take a baby and return it, seemingly showing me that her encopresis involved separation fears, exacerbated, perhaps, by my suggestion that she leave her parents in the waiting room.

A. again expressed the wish to poop the next session. My puppet asked whether she was going to poop in her pants or in the potty. A. replied matter-of-factly, "My pants." After pooping she asked to be taken to the bathroom to wash her hands. Such reaction formations also occurred at home during this period as A. pooped more regularly in the bathtub while bathing and requested clean pants after soiling. She also sat on the potty at home and allowed stools that she had already passed in her pants to fall into the potty.

After several sessions I pointed out that A. had not brought up the idea of leaving her mommy and daddy in the waiting room while she came into the office alone. I said that she seemed not to want to talk about it. A. played, while ignoring this interpretation of defense. She began the next session by playfully hiding after she entered the office. I said that she was leaving me all alone; perhaps she was thinking about what it would be like to be alone with me while her mother or father were in the waiting room. A. responded by having the alligator throw marbles at her father. Then she ordered him to go behind the chair. I interpreted this command as another attempt to see what it would be like to be in the office without a parent.

Themes of separation continued to crop up in sessions over the next few weeks as A. worked through the anticipated change. She continued to elaborate anal sadistic themes as work on the separation issues continued. One session I interpreted that she was particularly angry at me that day because I wanted her to come into the playroom without either of her parents. A. responded by stating that she wanted to poop in her diaper.

In another session she made a huge mess, lay on her belly, and wallowed in it. A. then said that it smelled like somebody had poop on their hands in the office and denied that it was she. She took the puppet and stuffed it in the potty, gleefully explaining that she was "putting it in with poopies." The time seemed opportune for interpreting the impulse side of her conflict. Consequently, my puppet exclaimed, "Good, I like the way the poopies smell and the way they feel all warm and gushy." Then I said that I thought this was also the reason that A. pooped in her pants—because she liked the way it smelled and felt good. A. protested that she did not like to poop in her pants. "Yes," I agreed, "sometimes you like being like your mommy, daddy, sisters, and brother and pooping in the potty, wiping yourself, and being clean. But other times you like to poop in your pants and to smell and feel your poopies."

No sustained elaboration of other themes occurred over the next several sessions as A.'s resistive stance seemed focused on the impending separation from her parents during our sessions. A. began the first session under the new plan by crawling toward the playroom door. Then she entered the office, stood up, and said, "I wanted to poop." The link between her separation anxiety and her letting go of her stool seemed clear. A. explained that she wanted to poop in her pants, which provided me with another opportunity to interpret her ambivalence about independence and separation. "Sometimes you want to be a big girl, to be in the office with me, have your mommy wait in the waiting room, and to poop in the potty," I said. A. agreed. "But sometimes, like now, you still want to be a baby and to poop in your pants because it feels good on your tushy," I added. A. agreed but reminded me to say "bottom, not tushy."

Passive was turned into active during the next session as A. played at leaving me with her mommy in the waiting room. At one point A. went to the waiting room and returned with her pacifier. "Your Ni Ni helps you not to miss your mommy so much," I said. Another reaction to leaving her parents in the waiting room was A.'s angry refrain of "Go away" when I appeared at the waiting room door. When her wish not to leave her mother or father was interpreted she would usually accompany me into the office, frequently returning to the waiting room to check on her parents' presence. Often this return would be in the context of her being Dorothy while I was assigned the role of Toto. "Dorothy was taken away from her family by a tornado. Maybe you're worrying that your mommy will be taken away, too, so you check on her in the waiting room," I said.

Gradually, anal sadistic impulses in the play alternated with reaction formations and/or superego reactions, such as A.'s complaints that the Gloppy Molasses Monster on the Candy Land game looked "gross." On other occasions she instructed the play characters to "stop throwing."

Sadistic impulses became more elaborated as A. cast me in the role of a witch who killed babies. She first sided with this expression of impulse and decided that she, too, would kill babies. But such open expression of sadism seemed to stir anxiety as she punished me for being bad. Siding with the sadistic impulses that were precipitating the superego reaction, I protested that I (as Toto) liked to be bad. A. told me to be a dog who pooped in the potty. When Toto protested, stating that it felt and smelled so good to poop in his pants, A. replied that he had to go on the potty, just like she did.

Over subsequent sessions A. wanted to take off her clothes in the office. At this stage of the analysis, her motives for this wish seemed to alternate between engaging me in her toilet training and reaction formations in which she did not want her clothes to be soiled. Only later did her wishes to strip off her clothes take on predominantly exhibitionistic and oedipal overtones. Thus, A. engaged me routinely in her symptoms by saving her poops for each session. Such regular pooping during sessions coincided with increased anger and control struggles in the sessions. A.'s routine protests that she did not want to stop the sessions were taken to indicate that she was angry at not having more contact with me.

As the first year of analysis drew to a close, A.'s mother, at my suggestion, requested that she wipe herself. This new developmental demand led to increasing anger both at her mother and at me. A.'s angry feelings were elaborated further in a developing maternal transference. She became regularly angry with her mother at the beginning of each session. When I wondered about this, A. replied that she had wanted her mother to stay home and not work. Increasing anger at my failure to gratify her wishes paralleled A.'s anger at her mother. I pointed out that she seemed equally angry when I did not do what she wanted as she was when her mother did not do so. A. agreed and confirmed this transference interpretation behaviorally by ordering me out of the office. She exclaimed that I was bad and a "mean lady." I suggested that she might also feel that her mommy was mean when she did not do what A. wanted. She responded by ordering me to touch the poopies. I said, "This is like when you want your mommy to touch the poop on your bottom when she wipes you." A. seemed to confirm this interpretation by ordering me to bathe in "dirty poopy water." Then she reversed roles, having the mommy trap the baby in the "dirty poopy water" as her anxiety over her anal sadistic impulses led her to project it onto the maternal representation.

As her anal sadistic conflicts were worked through, A. asked her mother to take her into the bathroom during sessions to help her clean herself. But she continued to insist that her mother do the wiping, thereby expressing her sadism by making her mother touch her poop. By the halfway point of her two-and-a-half-year analysis, A. regularly discussed her poop in detail, whether she wanted to hold it in or let it out, whether it was mushy or hard, whether it was warm or cold, and so on. Her greater comfort with expressing her anal conflicts led to a dramatic increase in elaborate fantasy material during sessions.

This fantasy play evolved to a greater focus on her father and dawning oedipal issues. During one session A. asked me to build her a "body gun" that got "bigger and bigger," explaining that her father had such a gun and that she used to have one when she was little; she used to shoot everybody with it until it got old. Castration themes continued to evolve when a son cried for his father, worrying that "something terrible" had happened to the daddy. The father took off his hat, and the son took off his own hair. Then the father became angry and ordered the boy to replace his hair. Soon the son complained as A. pulled off his legs. A. instructed me to have the boy call her a poopy (recently she had called her father a "little shit" at home). The boy was then punished for his audacity.

The transition to oedipal issues occurred gradually, intermingling with anal issues as A. approached the end of her second year of analysis. Cinderella play themes in which the mean stepsister mistreated Cinderella emerged. A. alternated between both roles. She became more sensitive to separations from me and more curious about my life away from her as these themes emerged. After one three-day weekend break A. wanted to play Legos, saying it had been *so long* since she had played with me. My reflection that A. felt it had been a long time since she had seen me led her to make a garbled statement about kissing a book. Her proclamation that she loved me led me to say that it sounded like she wanted to kiss me. A. denied this, saying that she loved Scooter, not me. Regressions to pooping in her pants often followed such oedipal play.

A. soon began repetitive play in which she ordered me to be a mean, devaluing stepsister. Her intense affect and frequent repetition made me wonder about unconscious beating fantasies. In one session A. called me a "sum of a bitch" and ordered me to spank her. Then she stopped the play, saying, "It's too scary!" A. went on to say that her mother said that it was okay to call me dumb. Then she complained that her mother sometimes called her dumb. At that point A. became Cinderella again, "the prettiest in the world!" A rapid regression to anal themes of wiping bottoms followed.

Soon this vulnerability to regression was worked through, and A.'s themes became consistently oedipal. Wishes to take me, as an oedipal partner, home with her were expressed directly and indirectly along with anger at my failure to gratify these longings. I was also assigned the role of the angry, punitive oedipal mother. During one play sequence the baby wanted to go to its mother's office and then to see Dr. Sugarman. The housekeeper took the baby to Dr. Sugarman's office, where Dr. Sugarman spanked the baby's "butt" and called it a "sum of a bitch." A. then had the baby dislike Dr. Sugarman and instructed me to "spank the baby hard." A. then picked up a toy baby accessory and called it a "bottom-in," her term for the anal suppositories administered by her father before the beginning of the analysis. I said, "I remember! Your daddy used to put those in your bottom!" A. said, No. Mommy put them in "to make poop come out." I thought that this distortion indicated either an exaggeration of her mother's complicity to defend oedipal guilt and/or an avoidance of the erotic excitement and anxiety about being penetrated by her father.

A.'s play during this stage also suggested that she was angry with me for having a penis like father and for depriving her of one like mother. During one session she said that I would have the boy ponies and that she would have the girl ones. My question about how to differentiate them led to a vague statement that it had to do with the way they looked. I said that horses seemed different from people in that boys had penises and girls had vaginas. A. asked, "What's a bagina?" I reminded her that she had one, it was where her pee came from. A. then asked, "What's a penis?" I explained that it was what boys peed from, surely she had seen her brother's or her father's. A. insisted that they did not have penises, although her attempt to steal marbles at the end of the session suggested a wish to steal my penis. Play during a subsequent session wherein a father and brother were sent to jail for stealing ladies' purses suggested a defensive reversal and/or an unconscious fantasy that her penis had been stolen.

More obvious oedipal material emerged in another session when A. asked me if I thought she was pretty. Before I could answer, she instructed me to say that she was "ugly, gross" and other "mean things" to her. Then she asked if I loved her. I wondered if she wanted me to love her, to which A. responded, "I hate that word, it's gross! Do you love me?"

During another scenario I was Cinderella while A. was the stepsister. Cinderella had to say that she was glad that she was beautiful and her stepsister was ugly. Then Cinderella danced with the prince before they departed on their honeymoon.

Themes of punishment surfaced as A. became the bad baby who was banished from the house.

Soon A. said that she wanted to be the only girl whom I saw. I asked, "What would you want us to do together?" A. explained, "Drive me to school." The next session she interrupted some play to ask, "Aren't I cute?" After a Christmas break she asked if I had missed her. I wondered if she wanted to feel that I loved her. A. said that she hated "that word." Then she went on to say, "Okay, okay. I love you! No I don't love you." I commented that she seemed not to want to love me, to which A. responded, "I like daddy and mommy." I chose to address the superego facet of A.'s loyalty conflict and said that she felt that she was bad if she loved me instead of her parents.

A. developed age-appropriate modesty about being observed on the potty as her oedipal wishes deepened. Consequently I removed the potty from the playroom, saying that she was now big enough to use the bathroom in my suite. Reluctance to wipe herself resurfaced around A.'s fifth birthday. Castration conflicts seemed implicated in her failure to wipe her vagina after urinating. My questions about this led her to claim that she did not have a "bagina," she had a "plain." She then asked, "Boys have a penis, right? It's that long thing, right?" I agreed, adding, "And girls had vaginas." A. disagreed but added, "The bottom is next to the bagina, right?" She went on to say, "Boys poop from their butts, it's gross" and then said, "Boys sometimes have baginas." I suggested that A. sometimes wished that she had a penis. That interpretation was ignored; in a subsequent session, however, A. related that she had wiped her penis. The relationship between her penis envy and her rekindled bathroom concerns was illuminated when she became afraid that a boy would come in the bathroom if I did not remain with her. I refused to do so while exploring her fear. Theories about fecal babies developed as her bowel anxieties took on oedipal overtones. Questions like

"Do babies come out your bottom?" alternated with vehement denials that they came out the vagina. Working through these oedipal concerns allowed A. to become more accepting of her impulses to be a big, pretty, beloved girl.

After A. was symptom-free for some time, her mother agitated for termination. More than two years after the start of analysis, A.'s developmental momentum was on track, and she was comfortably traversing the oedipal stage. Her inhibitions in speech and problems modulating affect seemed resolved. A. now enjoyed symbolic fantasy, showing a genuine creative potential that suggested a capacity for sublimation. Peer relations were good, and she was considered a model kindergarten student. More time to work through her oedipal issues would have been preferable, but the risk of a loyalty crisis for A. argued for compliance with her mother's wishes. In fact, her mother even brought termination up with A. before the mother and I discussed a termination date. Considering A.'s age and her earlier difficulties with separation, a plan to reduce the frequency of sessions over the next four months was negotiated with mother and patient.

A. became tearful and irritable both at home and in her sessions after I broached termination. Protests against stopping occurred at the end of each session. Finally I told A. that I thought she did not want to stop seeing me and so was protesting. She angrily ordered me to be quiet. I said that she did not like to think about those feelings because they felt so bad. Eventually A. wondered if she could see me after she stopped coming and asked why I planned to stop seeing her. Efforts to explore her fantasies met obstinate silence. Consequently I emphasized her mastery of her worries about pooping and not needing to use her "bommy" and her "Ni Ni." A. said proudly, "I don't use my Ni Ni anymore!"

Brief regressions occurred during the termination phase as

many of her conflicts were worked through one more time. For example, A. wanted me to accompany her once again into the bathroom, saying that she had diarrhea. I interpreted her wish to feel like a baby with poop problems again in order to keep seeing me. Such regressions responded readily to interpretation. Temper outbursts occurred sporadically at home and at school but always diminished after interpretation of her displaced anger at me. Nighttime awakening cropped up and was interpreted as a fear of being alone and separated from me. Despite these episodic regressions A.'s play remained primarily oedipal.

A. talked directly about termination as it drew closer and speculated that I lived near her house. I interpreted her wish to remain close together with me. Her questions about people in the waiting room were interpreted as curiosity about who would replace her. Near the end of the analysis A. said that she had cried the night before because she had to stop seeing me. During the last session we acknowledged that we would miss each other. I added that I also felt happy for A. because she had worked so hard to get rid of her worries about pooping. A. agreed proudly that she felt good also about that work, and then asked for a birthday present when she turned six.

Daytime Encopresis and Enuresis in a Prelatency Girl

Psychoanalysis and Oedipal Development

Diane Hoye Campbell, M.D.

In 1967, Morton Shane published "Encopresis in a Latency Boy." In it he wrote, "The paucity of material on encopresis in the psychoanalytic literature has been the stimulus to report the psychoanalysis of a latency boy who suffered from this symptom." Some twenty years later, I would say that the continuing paucity of literature describing in detail the psychoanalytic treatment specifically of girls with this symptom prompts me to write the case of Mary Lou.

Pertinent literature on childhood encopresis dates to Lehman (1944), whose clinical work led him to stress the importance of mother's love in establishing bowel control. In 1957, Anthony reviewed seventy-six cases of encopresis. He delineated a number of subtypes and recommended that children who had never been trained needed not the benefits of analytic treatment, but the benefits of being trained. Anna Freud's description in 1963 of the developmental line "from wetting and soiling to bladder and bowel control" presents her thoughts on the child's progressive control and the regressive loss of control when the child experiences profound disappointment in mother.

A number of other clinical papers in addition to Shane's describe the treatment of children with significant constipation (Glenn 1977), psychogenic megacolon (Garrard and Richmond 1952), or ego/superego pathology of a severity not approached by the child I write about here. Most of these articles refer to boys, which is not surprising given that this troublesome symptom occurs far more often in boys than in girls. Those few clinical articles on encopretic girls (for example, K. Novick 1974) tend to describe girls who are severely constipated during the day and then soil and wet in their beds at night.

The clinical literature on enuresis includes more articles on girls, many of whom wet primarily during sleep; the child in this paper was dry every night. Melitta Sperling (1965) seemed the author most familiar with girls who used their control of the bladder as my patient did. Sperling described girls with "sudden outbursts of temper equivalent to the sudden letting go of the bladder. The underlying character trait usually appears to be repressed aggression, which may come out as timidity accompanied by hostile, destructive behavior." Sperling's thoughts, together with Greenacre's "Urination and Weeping" (1945) and K. Novick's (1974) description of an enuretic and constipated preschool girl who feared an inevitable link between her autonomous strivings and the destruction of her bond with the mother, all provide a rich historical matrix of clinical writings useful in thinking about this particular very young analysand.

Central to the interpretive work with this child has been my concern that she was significantly at risk for failure to develop pleasure in her femininity. A series of authors who followed Freud (1931; 1933) have developed the ideas on female development from the early emphasis on castration anxiety and penis envy to current formulations of a positive developmental sequence in the formation of feminine identity. By the time Robert Stoller was writing his key papers on core gender identity and related issues, the ideas of object relations theorists, self-psychologists, and others contributed to his position (1976) that the development of femininity in women is of two orders: one which is "conflict-free and mostly ego-syntonic" and another which "results from conflict and envy in the oedipal situation. It brings a new desire and danger to affection, erotism, awareness of anatomical differences between the sexes, and to wishes for children. And it gives depth and richness, via the fantasy systems the girl creates to manage these problems, to those behaviors we label feminine. This form of femininity is made from conflict and its resolution, and simply cannot appear without such creative tension."

Because this little girl's analysis took place from 1987 to 1990, the thinking about her and the formulation of interpretive statements found enrichment not only from the decades of clinical and theoretical writers summarized above, but very specifically from current views which offer both expanding and unifying ideas on such matters as the steps involved in the development of the tripartite psychic structure, the types and roles of affects, drives, defenses, and conflicts in the first several years of life, what is required to become an oedipal child (Parens and Pollock 1976; Van Dam 1980; R. and P. Tyson 1982, 1990; P. Tyson, 1989a, 1990b), and what is required to form a nurturing superego (Sandler 1960; Shafer 1960; R. and P. Tyson 1982; P. Tyson, 1988).

Mary Lou began analysis at age three years, ten months. She lived with her parents and her high-achieving eight-year-old sister. Her parents brought her for analysis because of extreme separation anxiety, severe tantrums, and daytime enuresis and encopresis. Nursery school had excluded her after she smeared stool on the floors there and because they were so concerned about the intensity of her separation struggles, which persisted a few months into the school year.

Mary Lou was physically healthy at birth, but there was a sense of developmental vulnerability in her almost from the start. She was difficult to settle, easy to unsettle. She had colic until three months and was awake screaming for hours during the night. Both parents experienced her as easily frustrated and overwhelmed; while learning to crawl, she would flop down on the carpet and wail. The parents had difficulty in finding ways to help her with her frustrations, and they described difficulty in feeling affectively in tune with her. When not frustrated she was a happy and engaging baby who laughed and played. She met her milestones easily on time. She was weaned from the breast at about ten months after she had gradually "lost interest" in nursing, as mother described it. She continued with a daytime bottle that she dragged around with her "like an elephant trunk" hanging the nipple from her mouth. Mother continued to offer a bottle during her frequent awakenings at night. But by twenty months she was a defiant, demanding toddler by day and an anxious, frequently waking one at night. Mother was sleep-deprived, furious, and at her wit's end. One night when Mary Lou was twenty months old, mother let her daughter shriek until the toddler fell back to sleep exhausted; beginning the next night Mary Lou slept through.

As a toddler, Mary Lou did not confront her mother directly with her aggression by saying, "No." Instead, she used action in manipulative and provocative ways which the mother found maddening. Mary Lou would begin to climb to the kitchen countertop, mother would tell her to get down, and Mary Lou would continue to climb without so much as a glance or a moment of hesitation. Mother would lift the child down and tell her to stay down. Mary Lou, without looking at mother's face, would set her jaw and resume climbing. Removing her from the scene led to huge tantrums which never seemed followed by remorse or by cuddling. By that time, Mary Lou had invented an imaginary companion named Bossy. Bossy was a little girl responsible for all the "bad" things Mary Lou did. Mother would insist that Mary Lou instruct Bossy in how to behave, but Mary

Lou shrugged her shoulders in a look of feigned helplessness. Bossy, she said, was on her own and could not be controlled.

In the midst of all this, toilet training was initially a surprisingly easy matter. Mary Lou was dry at night before she was dry during the day, and she achieved both by the time she was two years and six months. But she had not gone on to the more subtle aspects of toilet training. She never said when she had to go to the bathroom. Mother continued to check and ask if she needed to go. At first, Mary Lou would respond to mother's question and go if needed. But by age three and a half she would verbally ignore mother's question or assert she didn't have to, and soon thereafter she would wet or soil her pants. She continued to be dry, however, throughout the night and occasionally to independently use the bathroom during the day.

This basic difficulty in the forward progression of toilet training seemed to reflect the ongoing difficulty in object relations development and to be paving the way for drive regression, for the use of her body to express aggression at the parents and at herself, for a self-punitive superego, and for a basic sense of being defective.

Not surprisingly, the history revealed no major strivings of a clearly triadic nature. Father seemed to be experienced as an extension of mother and as a source of criticism and punishment instead of pride. "Don't tell Daddy," Mary Lou would sadly beg her mother after wetting her pants. This little girl, so caught in an increasingly complex rapprochement struggle, was clearly experiencing herself as defective. "I'm ugly," she frequently whimpered at home. As I listened to the parents sadly tell me about Mary Lou, I wondered how she herself or they could possibly be taking any pride in her or any joy in her developing femininity.

The parents and I agreed I would meet Mary Lou and evaluate her for psychoanalytic treatment. When I first met Mary Lou, she quietly insisted that mother come in and remain with her in the office. She was a slender, shy-appearing child with wispy hair and gazing eyes. She sat in mother's lap for ten minutes, then slid down and sat in a little chair. She showed me a book she had brought with her and said plaintively, "I can't even read." Mother began a detailed explanation of how she doesn't have to read now; she'll go to school when she's older and learn to read. Mary Lou just looked at me again plaintively and said, "Four is still little . . . I'm three." She then engaged me in an elaborate game of peek-a-boo, followed by coloring on paper with crayons. She made wide sweeps of bright colors, saying, "This is your whole office!" Then she made what she said was a picture of me, telling me I am happy and have a smile and "pretty ears." I wondered if the pretty ears could be Mary Lou's way of telling me that being listened to was very important to her and that she had high hopes for me in that regard.

At her second evaluation appointment, Mary Lou left her mother in the waiting room and shut the door behind her as she stepped tentatively into my office. She took out a few preschoolers' games and asked me to teach her each one, which I did. She played each game easily. At one point I reminded her I am a worry doctor for children and that we could talk about her worries if she wanted to. She countered immediately with an extraneous question about a toy. When there was a second similar exchange I let her know that I had noticed the sequence and that she did not have to answer any questions I might have or talk about anything she did not want to. She looked at me in silence, with a very interested, gazing expression on her face.

By the end of that appointment it was clear to me that psychoanalysis was the treatment of choice for this child. She certainly had problems severe enough to warrant such intensive treatment, and I could not imagine that any less intensive work could begin to lift her out of the preoedipal sadomasochistic struggles she was caught in. I thought she was at severe risk to never engage the oedipal conflict in any significant way. But in my meetings with her I had discovered a child who interacted eagerly, had a strong intellect, fluent language development, and the capacity for fantasy. So I discussed my thinking with the parents, and we began the analysis four times weekly.

In the early months of analysis, she elaborated her presenting problems via a maternal transference to me and offered many opportunities to interpret those developing feelings and her resistance to them. At times she did her best to provoke me by wetting and soiling in the office and by having huge tantrums. She then listened wide-eyed as I helped her begin to understand the multiple meanings of these symptoms. I talked with her about her regressive pull to "baby" times and "baby" feelings, about her wish to dominate the mother, her insistence on using her body to gain and express power but also to yield to regressive impulses. She began to show me her confusion about soiling and wetting, how angry she was with herself, what a shameful and defective view she had of herself, how she punished herself with a wet and sore bottom and with the provocation of the mother, and how she experienced a secret pleasure in all this distress.

For the first several hours of analysis, Mary Lou stayed dry during her time with me, though the parents let me know she continued her frequent wettings and soilings every day at home. We often made one or two trips to the ladies' room down the hall, where Mary Lou used the toilet in private and with apparent ease. We played multiple games of Candy Land with emphasis on the "poopy pond," as she called it, and huge elaborations on the experience of being "stuck." It was often that game plus puppet shows she put on with a "big bad wolf" that provided the multiple opportunities for interpretations.

Then in the seventh analytic hour she was encopretic during the session. As soon as I noticed the smell, I told her that I knew what had just happened. She rolled around on the floor, making sure I could see the stain on her shorts. At her request, she and her mother went to the bathroom to clean her up and change her shorts. When she returned, she said to me ashamedly, "I still smell just a little bit." That sequence gave me an opportunity to interpret the timing of this event in the analysis, how I thought she was feeling safe with my response to the "poopy pond" game, but she wasn't sure how I would respond to the real poop in her pants. I spoke to her about her fear of her own aggression, her confusion and shame, and her hope that I will help with all this.

After several episodes of Mary Lou wetting and soiling in the office during the next few weeks, I realized I had a practical problem. Mary Lou was not easily going to give up her wetting and soiling, my office needed some protection from being made soiled and smelly, and the ladies' room was down the hall and not entirely private. To avoid a likely struggle between us involving a reenactment of the rapprochement crisis in the transference and to create instead a developmentally appropriate environment that would facilitate the interpretive process, I decided to buy a potty chair for Mary Lou. I would keep it in a storage area and bring it out just before the start of her hour, placing it in the more private area of my L-shaped office, where it was easily accessible to her but not out in the middle of our space.

I brought it out one day and told Mary Lou that this potty would be just for her and that having it in the office for her would help us to understand her worries. She immediately pulled her pants down, sat on the potty, and urinated into it with evident delight. She used the toilet paper I had put next to the potty, pulled her pants back on, and announced that she and I would take the potty to the ladies' room to empty and clean it. We did that, and she repeated the entire sequence twenty minutes later.

She began to save urine and stool to put in the potty during her hours. At first this activity brought her evident pride and pleasure, but she still managed to wet or soil at other times during the hours. This was done sometimes as an intended provocation of me, sometimes as an expression of a regressive impulse, and sometimes because she had retained these bodily contents too long and suddenly couldn't "make it" across the room to the potty. The timing of these events in the hours let me see and begin to interpret multiple meanings of her symptoms. These included her fear of my power in the transference to me as the controlling preoedipal mother, the regressive wish to be my baby, and simultaneously the desire to have me help her develop an ease within her own body and a mastery over her bodily products.

Much to my relief, she began also to use a baby doll as we worked on these issues together. She would alternately nurture and abruptly abandon this baby. She gave it to me for diapering while she scorned it for its babyish and smelly soiling and wetting. As I linked her experience with the doll to her experience with herself, her play became more and more expressive, leading to her creation of two imaginary characters central to our analytic work: Big Kitty and Little Kitty.

Mary Lou almost always played Big Kitty, the bossy and depreciating big sister who managed always to get her own way with adults, to win all the coloring contests, and to force Little Kitty to grovel, to clean up all the messes Big Kitty deliberately made, and to suffer verbal humiliations and banishment to prison for the tiniest offenses.

I was almost always told to play Little Kitty, and then I was instructed how to play each detail of the role. Every time Little Kitty asserted herself developmentally, she was struck down by the powerful tyrant Big Kitty. I interpreted the developing themes of sibling rivalry, the mother-child sadomasochistic struggle, and most fruitfully the intrapsychic struggle with her own beginning structuralization of a punitive superego and her powerful attachment to me as a maternal transference object.

With these repeated interpretations, Big and Little Kitty began to take on an oedipal configuration. About ten months into the analysis, Big Kitty became a bride. She and I fashioned wedding dresses out of white paper and scotch tape. Little Kitty stood jealously by as I was turned into both the preacher and the groom, and Big Kitty got married. We elaborated these weddings for a few months with interpretation of Mary Lou's evident delight and her refusal ever to play the role of the forlorn Little Kitty—a role she was all too familiar with within her intrapsychic world, but which she defended against so powerfully with her arrogant Big Kitty stance. I was able to interpret Mary Lou's anxious regressions when the role-playing felt too real and she feared that her mean and bossy Big Kitty feelings would invite retaliation from me, from her mother, and from her own superego.

As Mary Lou settled into being Big Kitty the bride, Cinderella appeared in her fantasy play at home and in the hours. While Big Kitty was the bride beset with preoedipal struggles, Cinderella was more clearly oedipal. Mary Lou played Cinderella over and over, always winning the prince. And at home, father no longer seemed to be experienced merely as an extension of mother. Mary Lou began to flirt with him and to announce grandly that she would marry him when she grew up. Oedipal fantasy filled her days; she constantly dressed up as Cinderella or a bride. Mother found her in the kitchen one day scrubbing happily at a wet and soapy floor, insisting that this was important fun for her because she was Cinderella. Early another morning she came majestically down the staircase dressed in a white "gown" and carrying a pretend wedding cake.

During these months of significant developmental transition, Mary Lou turned to me constantly to interpret her fears of success and retaliation and to help her understand both her sadness at seeing her baby feelings recede and her confusion when she felt the regressive pulls to reestablish the old and the familiar.

Her harsh superego was poignantly evident to me and to her parents during these transitional months. When she had tantrums at home during this period it was usually in response to feeling she had failed to live up to some high standard she set for herself, coupled with an expectation that mother could be disapproving and constraining of her. In my choices of how to interpret her inner world to Mary Lou, I had always to consider her lingering rapprochement concerns and those harsh superego pressures which had to yield in order to form a nurturing superego that could protect her from narcissistic pathology, including self-degrading introjects, unreachable ego-ideal standards, and disturbed ideal-object representations.

As she became more clearly oedipal, Mary Lou became worried that her developmental gains would lead to the loss of me. I was on a two-week vacation about one year into her analysis. While I was away, a neighbor remarked to the mother within the child's earshot that Mary Lou had stopped soiling and wetting, so why was the mother still taking her to analysis? The child did not wait to hear her mother's response. She fled into her house and left a wet and soiled trail up the stairs for all to see, shrieking, "I'm going to pee and poop in my pants until I'm fifteen years old so I can keep Dr. Campbell!" The mother hugged her close and reassured her that she did not have to wet and soil in order to keep me. Mary Lou calmed down and returned to being dry.

Back in my office after vacation, I told Mary Lou it was not just the neighbor's words that kindled her fears of losing me. She was afraid I might only like babies and that I might abandon her because she was no longer a baby. She felt caught between enjoying the fun of being big and her fear that in her bigness she might lose me because she could no longer please me as a baby.

As we moved into the second year of her analysis, it was clear to the parents and to me that Mary Lou would be ready to begin kindergarten with her peers. Her intensity and distress were largely confined to the analytic hours, in which she worked well within the transference. At home, her symptoms were minimal and she was a much easier and more enjoyable child to parent. She was enjoying friends and preschool. She had moved beyond her earlier avoidance of cognitive learning and was now happily playing with letters and numbers and getting quite adept at preschool computer games.

Mary Lou was five years and three months old when she started kindergarten, and we were well into her second year of analysis. One day she again soiled her pants in the office. We had just been talking about her mean, mad feelings at herself. "Bad poopies," she informed me when I told her I noticed the soiling. I told her that she claims it is her poopies that are bad, but really she thinks it is her mean, mad feelings that are so bad—mean mad feelings at herself for sometimes wanting to be such a big girl and for sometimes wanting to be mama's baby again, and my baby, too. She feels these wishes are forbidden, and so she punishes herself for them by putting messy poopies in her pants. But then she feels like a bad girl for doing that—(Mary Lou giggled.) I wondered if she might be pretending that her poopies are her mean, mad feelings and that she could push them out of her into her pants. Every time she makes more mean, mad feelings she could just push them out again with newly made poopies. (Mary Lou giggled again.)

It was not always so easy for Mary Lou to hear me interpret her experience. Sometimes her feelings were hurt, and she would tell me to shut up, or she'd get out the scotch tape to tape my mouth shut so she could be in control of when I would get to speak.

I had to remember her narcissistic vulnerability to misinterpret my every action. When I took a Monday off for a holiday, Mary Lou came in the next day and had an enormous tantrum in her mother's arms, lasting almost the entire hour—when I told her our time was almost up for today, she shrieked at her mother, "Rewind the clock! I want my time with Dr. Campbell!" After she and her mother left, I realized I had misinterpreted her fury at me by stating it simply in terms of my absence from her, and her fury in my not taking her with me. But she was experiencing the holiday as my personal insult to her. She was afraid I had taken a holiday because I needed a respite from her powerful terrible feelings and wishes. I offered that interpretation the next day and was rewarded with an abundance of confirming talk and play.

Over the next few months, she easily became well established in kindergarten. But in her analysis, we saw ever more intensely her harsh and bossy superego embodied in the character of Big Kitty. "Little Kitty!" she spat out. "Did you put your dolls on the bookcase? Look at this mess! Is this any way to behave?" She tossed dolls and furniture furiously out of the dollhouse as she continued her tirade. "If you're not going to do it right, I'll just have to put all your stuff over here. YUCK!" She continued to rant and rave, and I told her that Little Kitty had really been enjoying how she'd arranged her dolls, but now Big Kitty was making her feel just awful. Mary Lou told me tentatively that her mother and her sister behaved a little like Big Kitty "but not really that bad." So I offered her the idea that we were playing about her big and bossy feelings at herself. (Mary Lou giggled.) Something she then did in the play invited me to say, "Oh, I know one thing that you do to make you have Big Bossy Kitty feelings at yourself." Mary Lou looked interested. "You pee and poop in your pants. You make yourself feel wet and yucky. Then *you* get mad at *you*." I explained that when she enjoys doing big girl things she gets afraid her mother and sister will retaliate, but she is most afraid of her own Big Bossy Kitty feelings that yell and scream at her for enjoying being a big girl. She wants my help to be a big girl without having Big Bossy Kitty feelings that punish her for such enjoyment.

Over the next few days, Mary Lou developed her play into a new scene. Big Kitty became quite snobbish because she was going to become a mother. Little Kitty was once again feeling so envious and so left out. She would phone Big Kitty at work just to talk with her, and Big Kitty would loudly hang up the phone. I told Mary Lou that she so much wants to grow up and marry and have babies like mama and me, but she is scared to tell us that, fearful that we will mock her and make her feel awful for daring to have such a dream. Sometimes it seems to her that I am the all-powerful Big Kitty, getting to do anything I want to do. "You do," said Mary Lou, so softly and longingly. "I'm going to pee in my pants forever so I can keep seeing you." I talked with her about her persisting conviction that she had to continue as a wet and needy little baby in order to keep me; she was so afraid that I would punish her via abandonment for her competitive oedipal strivings and that she would have to live with the pain of her own Big Bossy Kitty feelings.

In the context of this interpretive work, the triadic nature of Mary Lou's oedipal experience blossomed. She competed with mother for father and began to identify with more subtle and complex aspects of mother.

The perceived threat of retaliation for oedipal strivings and the regressive pull to preoedipal organization were strong and persistent in this child and required ongoing interpretation for her oedipal progression to continue and to become dominant. By now, any episodes of enuresis or encopresis were confined to the home or my office and were specifically timed in response to feeling the power of her oedipal wishes. She feared retaliation for these strivings and in one action simultaneously punished herself, regressed to a "safer," preoedipal state, and felt defective.

Continuing interpretation of this complex state led to forward developmental progression. Two years into analysis, a few months before her fifth birthday, Mary Lou finally relinquished her potty in the office. She'd given up the one at home many months earlier but saved this one for occasional use yet mostly as a beloved object so symbolic of the babyhood she had outgrown and of the complex path she and I had traversed together. She entered into a time of quiet collaboration with me, as we considered the question, "What shall we do with this potty?" She gradually decided I could save it for another child to use, a child littler than she is now, a child who would need my help to achieve the gains she had made.

As Mary Lou adopted this big-sisterly attitude toward some unknown child yet to appear in my office, she added a new character to her Big Kitty and Little Kitty projective play. Big Kitty developed into Big Big Kitty, Little Kitty grew and became known now as Big Kitty, and the family got a new baby, new Little Kitty. An abundance of opportunities for interpretation arose: Mr. and Mrs. Kitty had made this new baby together, and for quite awhile Mary Lou was interested in but resisted learning how conception occurs. Finally, she asked her mother, who explained to her the basic facts of intercourse and conception. Mary Lou came to her next hour telling me that this activity was "gross" and that it was hard to imagine adults thinking it was so wonderful. Gradually, she conceded that sex was only one of many things so puzzling about adults. Work, quiet time, beer, and spicy foods were added to the list of puzzling things adults like. Meanwhile, Mr. and Mrs. Kitty continued to live lovingly and quietly together in my office, and the primary action was among the two oldest Kitty girls and their new baby sister.

As sibling rivalry was interpreted and the obvious links made between the play and her real family life and as I continued to interpret the superego pressures and Mary Lou's identification with the angry maternal introject, the Big Kitty character really began to mellow and to develop some nurturing qualities. Occasionally, Mary Lou would say softly to me as she played, "You *do* know this is about me, huh!"

Mary Lou completed kindergarten and entered first grade with gusto. Now about two and half years into analysis, this little girl who had once shrieked that she would pee and poop in her pants until she was fifteen so she could keep me was finding that after-school activities with friends might be more enticing than four trips per week to see me. For a while, the intensity of her transference was dissipating, and I thought we were approaching the completion of her analysis.

But we had one more major hurdle to clear. Mary Lou's sense of entitlement began to take center stage in the transference. She would boss me around, noisily at times, loftily and grandly at others. "Go get scotch tape," she would intone with a queenly look on her face and a dismissing sort of gesture with one hand. If I followed this command she would follow with a string of others and an obvious sinking into the deep pleasures of being queenly. When I interpreted this blatant sequence of events, she belittled me with a sniffy, "That's totally ridiculous."

Sometimes I sat quietly and explained that her commands feel very real to her, and I'm not following them. I have feelings, too, just like her parents and her sister and her friends and her. None of us like being really bossed around. She got furious and screamed at me, "Can't you do me a simple favor? What's the *matter* with you anyway?" Her shrieks of how despicable I had become culminated with, "You're no *use* to me at all! You're only *useful* to me if you do me favors!" I was quite taken aback by the newfound power of her entitled stance. I had paid attention to it as a theme running through the analysis, as a hostile maternal introject. But now it seemed to me that this new power in the introject spoke of the intensity with which this child felt caught between two loyalties—loyalty to the internal representation of mother with whose own sense of entitlement the child had powerfully identified, and her loyalty to her internal representation of me, her analyst, who was always interpreting such a narcissistic stance as defensive against the fear of loss and the fear of discovering she was basically a defective, puny creature after all.

It seemed to me that the narcissistic entitlement could be best worked with in the context of giving me up. It appeared that in the other major spheres of her functioning, Mary Lou was ready to begin termination of her analysis. Her oedipal gains were solidly established, her superego was much less of a problem for her and indeed was demonstrating a nurturing quality, life at home as well as with friends and in school showed basically age-appropriate object relations, with an enhanced capacity for affective expression and modulation. Her very strong cognitive endowment was bringing her pleasure via learning and creative activities.

So I opened the topic of termination and thus unleashed the power of Mary Lou's hostile entitlement. She who had taken such pleasure in long-term freedom from soiling and wetting now returned to these symptoms occasionally at home or in her analytic hours—never at school or with friends. She insisted she could do this or anything else she wanted, and no one could stop her. I interpreted her soiling now as shooting out bombs, bombs of fury at me for having the nerve to be the one who brought up the subject of finishing analysis. She looked stunned at my talk of poopy bombs; then she giggled in the way of a child discovered. She played for weeks in arrogant, haughty ways, soaking up interpretations not only for their content but for the power and the pleasure of playing in ways that could command such responses from me. She turned Big Kitty into Biggest Kitty, enormously powerful. I interpreted her defense against a feared helplessness and vulnerability, and she responded by turning the tables on me. She taunted me with tales of all the wonderful things she would do when she would no longer "have to" come to see me, and she sneered that I could do nothing to stop all this. I would be helpless and missing her. She would be out having fun.

The fear that without me she needed to be haughty in order to protect herself from feared defectiveness and helplessness and from the power of others, including the mother, gradually yielded during several months of a termination phase. Little by little she began to show me her pride in what she had accomplished for herself in analysis, and she began to tell me with obvious affection that she would miss me.

I began in the final weeks of our work together to see the beginnings of early latency. Her stream of talk and play was less magical and less driven by triadic competitive strivings. She was looking more like the school-age latency child with an ego resilient enough to explore the world available to her, well supported by a sufficiently nurturing superego and by sufficiently well modulated drives. Her basic vulnerabilities seemed to be some lingering narcissistic entitlement, and (if sufficiently stressed) some regression in superego functioning.

As we completed our work together, her development appeared restored to its normal progression; the goals of treatment were met for this child, who began analysis shortly before her fourth birthday as a child caught in the rapprochement crisis, and completed her analysis three years later as a girl who had consolidated her oedipal gains and was beginning to move into latency.

The analysis of Mary Lou demonstrates the possibility of intervening psychoanalytically when the forward developmental progression of a young child is so severely compromised that a highly endowed child may well become a devastatingly insecure, needy, and demanding adult suffering from multiple symptoms and failing to find pleasure in her feminine identity.

The psychoanalytic process appears to have made possible her progression from the rapprochement crisis through the oedipal situation to its consolidation and the beginning of latency.

Eighteen months of intermittent follow-up with this family show that Mary Lou is now well established in latency. Times of crisis bring brief symptomatic regressions but so far have been significant opportunities to consolidate her development gains and reorganize them in the service of further intrapsychic development.

I hope that continuing contact with the family at intervals will afford ongoing opportunity to evaluate the interplay between her lingering vulnerabilities and her significant developmental strengths.

Discussion of "The Case of an Angry Two-and-a-Half-Year Old Girl," by Alan Sugarman, Ph.D., and "Daytime Encopresis and Enuresis in a Prelatency Girl: Psychoanalysis and Oedipal Development," by Diane Hoye Campbell, M.D.

Martin A. Silverman, M.D.

These two cases are similar enough to lend themselves well to joint consideration. The presenting problems that brought the children for treatment were quite comparable. So too were the core developmental conflicts that appeared to underlie the surface symptoms. There were some differences between the two children, of course, in temperament, defensive style, and other ego characteristics, as well as differences between the families of which they were a part; and they were not quite the same age or at exactly the same point in their development. Nevertheless, the technical challenges confronting the two analysts were quite similar. Therefore, I shall address the two cases together in my discussion.

Mary Lou began her analysis with Dr. Campbell at the age of three years, ten months. She came for treatment because of intense separation anxiety, severe temper tantrums, encopresis, and diurnal enuresis. There had been problems from the very beginning. Her first three months after birth had been marked by colic, during which she lay awake screaming for hours every night. Her parents experienced her as easily frustrated and easily unsettled. They found it difficult to tune in to her ups and downs and did not know how to soothe her and settle her down. Her mother, "sleep-deprived, furious, at her wit's end," bribed Mary Lou with bottles at night to leave her alone and allowed her to dangle a bottle from her mouth during the day, "like an elephant trunk." When Mary Lou was twenty months old, her mother, apparently succumbing to exhaustion, frustration, and anger, let her shriek at night until, worn out, emotionally depleted, and admitting defeat, the child collapsed into an exhausted sleep. From then on she slept through the night. During the day, however, a pattern developed in which she repeatedly challenged her mother in provocative ways that her mother found "maddening." She would climb up to a kitchen countertop and continue to climb, heedless of her mother's injunction to get down. When her mother lifted her down and told her to stay there, she "set her jaw" and climbed right up again. When her mother then removed her from the kitchen, she erupted into a monstrous tantrum.

Toilet training was instituted in the midst of this monumental mother-daughter struggle. Although she achieved bladder control, day and night, by the age of two and a half, a subtle nonverbal interaction developed in which she never indicated to her mother when she needed to use the bathroom during the day, and her mother continued to check with her periodically as to whether she needed to do so. By three and a half, she would ignore her mother's request or answer in the negative and soon thereafter soil her pants. A pattern of diurnal encopresis and enuresis had emerged, and she appeared to be caught up in an intense, ambivalent, insoluble rapprochement struggle that made her mother feel helpless and inadequate and made Mary Lou feel "defective" and "ugly."

A., who came to Dr. Sugarman at two and a half years of

age, arrived with quite similar presenting symptoms. There was separation anxiety directed toward her mother, uncontrollable temper tantrums, negativism, and refusal to accept parental authority. She would not sit in her car seat, hold her mother's hand in the street, or go where her parents wanted to go. She had experienced extremely uncomfortable gastrointestinal distress during her first ten months in the form of nonstop diarrhea, accompanied by hours and hours of crying which could not be relieved. She was still using a pacifier and a morning bottle, and her mother, in order to protect her own sleep, encouraged A. to turn to videotapes during her frequent nighttime awakenings. Toilet training had recently been initiated, but A. refused to use the potty during the day and was still in a diaper at night. In the midst of parental discord and struggle, including disagreements over her behavior (among other things), A. began withholding her stool. Like Mary Lou's mother, A.'s mother felt helpless, beleaguered, and unable to deal with her.

Another similarity between the two children was that each was the youngest child in the family and each had been born well after the next older child. Mary Lou had a sister eight years older, and A.'s siblings were seven and fourteen years older.

In both cases, then, there were developmental struggles and conflicts centered on ambivalence and its impact upon the process of separation-individuation. Each child appeared to be caught up in a love-hate struggle with her mother. This interfered with the taming of aggressive impulses and with their mobilization in the service of self-assertion and self-empowerment. It also interfered with pursuit of mother as a love object and as an object of identificatory union. Each child had been born late to a mother who apparently was tired of struggling with the exigencies of raising a demanding infant and toddler. And each had problems (colic in one instance and gastrointestinal distress from the wrong formula in the other) that made her more uncomfortable, unhappy, and difficult to console than the average child. Each child's mother felt overburdened, exhausted, and helpless to relieve the burden. Each responded to the demands placed upon her with frustration, anger, and a degree of abandonment. This situation led either to the use of force (in the case of Mary Lou) or to such fear of anger that (A.'s) parents could not impose effective limits or appropriate discipline. The outcome in each instance was a power struggle characterized by passive-aggressive refusal to comply with parental demands, especially with regard to cleanliness and toilet training, and a negativistic style of self-assertion that hindered developmental advance rather than facilitating it.

How did the two analysts approach these issues? They both were quickly drawn into an adult-child power struggle that centered on the issue of toilet training. But there was an important difference. Following the very first evaluation session—in which Dr. Campbell sensitively read an interchange between parent and child involving the asking and answering of questions as reflecting Mary Lou's need to be assured that compliance would not be forced upon her—Mary Lou elected to leave her mother out of her analytic sessions. A., on the other hand, needed to have a parent present in her sessions for several months. It may also have been that her parents felt the need to be present. Dr. Sugarman, therefore, did not at first have a child as a patient, but rather a child-with-parent. Whereas Mary Lou plaintively announced that she was little and weak and welcomed help from Dr. Campbell in becoming big and strong, A. shrank from Dr. Sugarman and retreated to her parents for protection. Mary Lou could split her ambivalent feelings between her mother as the mother she had to struggle against and her female analyst as the mother from whom she could accept assistance. It was just the opposite with A. She had to struggle against Dr. Sugarman, who had the misfortune of being both a "psychoanalyst-doctor" and a man, the very pair of personae toward whom A.'s mother felt so angry and against whom she was so defensive.

Both analysts introduced a potty chair into the room, but with what a difference! When Mary Lou brought her oppositionalism into the interaction between her and her analyst, in the form of provocative wetting, soiling, and huge tantrums, she welcomed Dr. Campbell's offers to talk about the ambivalence conflicts underlying the behavior. For reasons of pragmatic exigency, she bought a potty chair to keep in the room. She placed it unobtrusively in a corner and told Mary Lou that it would be "just for her" and that it could help them to understand Mary Lou's worries. Mary Lou, who was in a state of positive transference, readily accepted its introduction.

Dr. Sugarman's introduction of a potty chair took place in a very different transferential atmosphere. His child-with-parent patient, who was in a state of predominantly negative transference, arrived one day to find something in the room that stood for the efforts by A.'s mother to impose her will upon the child. Dr. Sugarman, who had decided in consultation with his supervisor (both analyses were supervised training cases with different supervisors) to introduce a potty chair in order to bring the "concerns about pooping more directly into the analysis," one day brought a potty chair into the room. He did so without commenting to A. on its arrival upon the scene. A. seemingly ignored it at first, but after a while asked what it was. Dr. Sugarman replied, "I think you know what it is; it's for you to go pee and poop in." She immediately asked her father to take her home. The predominantly negative transference situation and the lack as yet of an analytic working alliance with A., we can conclude, had not been sufficiently taken into account by Dr. Sugarman and his supervisor. Despite this apparent error, however, A. did bring her toilet training conflicts into the analysis, although for a long time she used the potty chair as a plaything rather than for its intended purpose. This is a testament to the power of the wish to get well, even in very young patients. It also serves as a testimonial to the regularly observed truism that mistakes are inevitable in analysis, but they are less important than sincerity, good technique in general, and the ability to bounce back from errors.

Mary Lou settled into prolonged fantasy play in which she expressed her preoedipal "mother-child masochistic" struggles, her nascent oedipal conflicts, her complex oscillation between oedipal and preoedipal longings, and her struggles with the harsh, sadomasochistically organized superego she was building in the course of wrestling with these conflicts. Dr. Campbell wisely permitted Mary Lou to take command of the fantasy play. She deftly not only oriented her interventions toward the defensive activity in which Mary Lou was engaged, allowing Mary Lou to take charge of her own struggles rather than intrusively taking control, but also helped her build the strength she needed to win her inner battles. She allowed Mary Lou to direct the play. She accepted regularly being accorded the role of Little Kitty, who was weak and powerless and had to grovel before Big Kitty and clean up all the messes, while Mary Lou dominated her and lorded over her in the role of Big Kitty or Cinderella.

Dr. Campbell intervened largely in connection with what she perceived as Mary Lou's need for assistance in recognizing the excessive harshness of her budding superego. Otherwise, she respected Mary Lou's need to build her ego strengths, strengthen her (appropriate) defensive tools, and try out her own capacities, as Kestenberg (1969) has emphasized for prelatency children. It was not until well into the second year of the analysis, when Mary Lou was five years, three months old, that Dr. Camp-

bell addressed the encopretic and enuretic symptoms interpreta-
tively. She did so in terms of Mary Lou's harshly punitive superego attacks upon herself for peeing and pooping in her pants.

Mary Lou eventually gave up the potty chair in the office and
relegated it to the use of another, "littler" child to use. She grew
Little Kitty into Big Kitty, grew Big Kitty into Big Big Kitty,
and added a new baby, a new Little Kitty, into the fantasy play.
Oedipal configurations expanded, and preoedipal strivings significantly receded. Developmental advance was taking place. It
became possible to address oedipal rivalrous feelings more directly in interpretive work in the analysis, although this was done
largely in terms of the intrusion of preoedipal, sadomasochistic
power struggle conflicts and the extent to which they contami-
nated the structure and functioning of her superego. It wasn't
until the unfolding of the termination phase that references to
drive derivatives appeared in the interpretive interventions made
to Mary Lou.

A.'s analysis followed another course. Beginning in a state
of predominantly negative transference, A. threw herself into
play themes of attack, sadism, and torture. When Dr. Sugarman
made an early id interpretation, commenting on her delight in
making him clean up her mess, she responded by torturing the
policeman figure. The eruption of her anal sadism, without sufficient defensive control, prompted A. to "object strenuously to
coming to sessions" and to complain that "the potty in the playroom was dangerous." When Dr. Sugarman verbalized her fear
of her wishes to mess on him, she threw marbles at him. Now
realizing her need for defensive restraint, he offered her assistance in the form of a suggestion that the defense of displacement might be useful to her. She gratefully accepted his suggestion that she throw the marbles at the puppets instead of at him.
She went even further, in fact: she asked her father to throw
them at the puppets. When this was then interpreted to her as

an effort to not feel bad for being aggressive, again too close to the id wish, A. responded with "more aggressive themes." She forced Dr. Sugarman to take control—to become "the boss of her throwing feelings"—by hitting him in the head with a toy telephone!

When Dr. Sugarman, in the fourth month of the analysis, urged A. to leave her (protective) parents in the waiting room and in essence become a big girl, she and her father jointly responded in the negative. Instead, she peed in the potty chair, apparently in deference to the threat of parental abandonment she apparently perceived in Dr. Sugarman's pressuring request. But she indicated clearly that she could and would retain the power to refuse to poop in the potty chair. When he acknowledged (that is, accepted) her wish to be the "boss of her poops" rather than pressing her to use the potty chair, she was able to use it to defecate.

Dr. Sugarman, apparently in conjunction with his supervisor, continued to try drive interpretations (for example, "The time seemed opportune for interpreting the impulse side of her conflict"). A. responded by being "resistive," a response that aptly illustrates the way in which prelatency children will defend against the analyst, perceived as allied with the dangerous id impulses, when they do not perceive the analyst as allied with their ego in wrestling with those impulses. The need of prelatency children to be assisted in building their ego strength vis-à-vis their impulses requires respectful consideration.

"Siding with the sadistic impulses that were precipitating the superego reaction" of punishing her analyst for being a "witch who killed babies," Dr. Sugarman protested that, like Toto in the play, he "liked to be bad" and then that he preferred to poop in his pants because it "felt and smelled so good." A. reacted to what she perceived as encouragement of drive expression by wanting to take off her clothes in the sessions, another illustration of her not having yet developed enough ego strength to be able to deal with id-oriented interpretations. Nevertheless, the analysis proceeded and succeeded. At first, A. required her parents' insistence that she continue, but with time Dr. Sugarman's decency, sincerity, genuine devotion to helping her thrive and be happy, and persistence in battling the forces that were creating unhappiness carried the analysis toward a successful conclusion. A. gained full bowel and bladder control, wrestled analytically with her sadomasochistic conflicts, developed positive transference feelings, and proceeded into oedipal configurations, which she was able to bring into the analysis. Two years of analysis brought her back on track developmentally. I have a question, however, about the phase of the analysis in which oedipal conflicts were addressed. The interpretation that was made of A.'s play fantasy in which a father and brother were sent to jail for stealing ladies' purses seems incomplete to me. The wish for a penis impresses me as only part of the story. It seems to me that A. was also expressing fear of damage to her prized female genitals. And telling her that her vagina is "where her pee came from" strikes me as inaccurate and misleading. But, again, this did not stop the analysis from progressing toward a favorable outcome. Every analysis is imperfect, and a good analysis, if one is lucky, will weather the imperfections.

Developmental Considerations in Prelatency Analysis

Melvin A. Scharfman, M.D.

When Dr. Robert Tyson initially asked me to act as overall discussant of a series of prelatency analytic cases with a particular view toward emphasizing the developmental implications, the full degree of complexity of the task did not quite hit home. Several months later when I received the cases that were to be discussed, it didn't take me long to realize that this was an enormous challenge, something perhaps not even possible in the sense of doing full justice to the variety of cases presented. I will not discuss much of the specifics of any of the interesting cases presented but rather attempt to extract some general considerations concerning the developmental issues involved in the analysis of prelatency children.

One could immediately note that it is most unusual to have so many analyses of prelatency children presented at one time. Certainly I have never had that experience. I'm not sure that it represents an increase in the number of prelatency children taken into analysis since it probably reflects a significant proportion of the total number of such children in analysis in the entire country. Dr. Tyson mentioned some thoughts about why there might not be more prelatency children in analysis. I would like to amplify on his remarks, considering separately factors that may operate within the analyst and those involving the nature of prelatency analysis.

Analytic training in this country has traditionally started with adult analysis. Child training does not begin until the third or fourth year of analytic training or often not until after adult training is complete. During analytic training most candidates are appropriately concerned about learning to maintain an analytic stance and learning the techniques of adult analysis. Much of that training is not completely applicable to doing child or adolescent analysis, but even less so to doing prelatency analysis. During that time, the analyst in training gradually constructs in his or her mind a model of what psychoanalysis is or should be. That model contains elements familiar to all of us. To mention just a few of those, we come to think of analysis as related to someone suffering from some inner distress, as coming to seek treatment voluntarily and agreeing to the basic structure of the analytic situation, that is, the use of a couch, free association, a restriction on nonverbal expression and the relative abstinence of the analyst, particularly in terms of the absence of visual contact or physical contact. That is, all the elements that presumably contribute to a controlled regression in which the patient focuses more and more on the intrapsychic and gradually develops an intensifying transference, ultimately developing a transference neurosis. This comes about through making the patient more aware of patterns in their thoughts and behaviors and by interpreting defenses as they appear with the resultant increasing intensity and clarification of drive derivatives. These ultimately become organized around the person of the analyst, and through interpretation of those past object relationships now repeated with the analyst, a resolution of the transference neurosis occurs. Again, ideally, that resolution is the primary indication for the termination of the analysis. All of these varying elements, without elaborating them further, constitute the core of what we call an analytic process in which patient and analyst share the joint task of increasing awareness of unconscious conflicts with the understanding this will allow for possibly better integrated and more adaptive solutions to earlier conflict situations.

I know I do not need to belabor the point of the distance of this model from child analysis, particularly prelatency analysis, but what I'm trying to point out is the difficulty the analyst has in giving up this model. Indeed, the attempt to compare it to adult analysis has plagued child analysts for many years. Obviously, here I am doing to some extent the same thing. Child analysis is not adult analysis. The developmental level of the child dictates what is possible. The child cannot verbally free associate. What we use as a substitute for this is the combination of that degree of verbalization of which the child is capable along with a setting in which conflicts can be expressed in play. Play is, of course, one of the normal modes of expression of the child. We observe the child's play from varying perspectives. In order to do this, we assume that the play contains elements of symbolic representation of conflicts, of earlier experiences, of trauma in the child's life, of wishes, prohibitions, and so forth. Prelatency children tend to externalize in play, and part of what they externalize contains varying aspects of their psychic organization. Just as wishes may be attributable to an object used in play, so too can superego precursors be expressed in play. The play will contain elements of psychic conflict, elements of early memories, and elements of the varying components of the psychic apparatus. It is not really the equivalent of free association, but it is the material that we have to work with in treating the child.

The limitations of play come from varying directions. One has to do with the fact that play within the analytic situation may be relatively free, but the physical expression of certain libidinal or, more often, aggressive impulses in the relationship with the analyst has to be limited. We cannot let the child do anything that might hurt him, seriously destroy property, hurt the analyst, or, for that matter, directly express such sexual wishes as wanting to explore the analyst's body. Of course we try to set these limits in an appropriate way, but the limitations do mean that the play cannot be completely free. We sometimes are able later in the analysis to analyze these interventions in terms of what they mean to the child, but by no means is this always possible.

The play of the prelatency child offers several seductions to the analyst. First, play is fun, and the analyst may enjoy it to such an extent that it sometimes interferes with the functioning of his or her observing ego. The child analyst needs to be able to be both participant and observer at the same time in this context. Second, the play can be seductive because it seems to present so openly some of the child's conflicts. This is in part because the child has the capacity to symbolize, but a relatively limited repertoire of symbols. One of the attractions for the analyst of treating a prelatency child is that there seem to be transparent representations of the unconscious, representations that in adult analysis sometimes take a long time to appear. On the other hand, this brings with it the temptation to interpret symbolic content directly, sometimes prematurely, and before appropriate work has been done on defenses. The analyst, particularly the young analyst, may be threatened by such seduction and the regressive pull of the young child's manifest drive derivatives. This can be expressed by hesitation in recommending analysis as a treatment of choice with such rationalizations as "This child is too young for analysis," or "Let's give it time and it will clear up by itself" or "He will grow out of it."

Analysts also take care not to interfere with the evolving capacities to symbolize, as can happen when direct interpretation is premature. This can interfere with the child's normal need to play. Play is used not only to express conflicts but also to experiment with mastering them in the play. The role of play for the child, both in normal development and in analysis, requires much study. In the material presented here there are examples of children playing out earlier traumas. This is a normal means used by the child to deal with trauma or other frightening external events, that is, to turn a passive experience into an active one, and a number of questions can be asked. For example, do we always need to interpret the content of the play? or is the child working through a conflict in his own way, striving to master some impediment to development in a manner that may be quite sufficient without interpretation? This is a complex issue, one that again touches upon the analyst's role. Interpretation needs to be modified in relation to a child's age just as the relative amount of reconstruction can vary considerably. Does our adult analytic orientation incline us to overweigh the need for verbal interpretation, verbal elaborations or corroborations of our interpretation, or, ultimately, verbal reconstruction?

Motor discharge in play occurs all the time and often directly involves the analyst. The analyst cannot be abstinent to the same degree as with adults and certainly cannot avoid visual as well as sometimes physical contact and interaction with the child. Inducing a controlled regression is antithetical to the forward developmental thrust of the child. The child rarely consciously suffers to the same extent as an adult, nor does he or she seek treatment on their own. Their cognitive organization precludes a full understanding of and cooperation in what is involved in undertaking analysis, although many children, even prelatency ones, get the general idea. The transference never develops in the relatively uncontaminated way that it does in adult analysis. One is presented with a complex, constantly changing group of reactions from the child to the analyst as a real object, an adult from whom he or she looks for some of the usual responses they might expect from a helpful adult. The analyst is much more frequently an object of displacement of current feelings toward the parents, still very present and active in the child's day-today life. The analyst is also a transference object with whom the child will indeed repeat earlier patterns of relationship to his primary objects, but the shifting complexities of these varying reactions make it much more difficult to tease out those which are transference repetitions. Far less often will the analyst become so much the focus of drive derivatives and conflicts that a transference neurosis as such develops, although that also can and does occur with some children (for example, P. Tyson 1978). All of these are differences that deserve extensive discussion, but I will limit myself to further discussing the role of transference later in the paper.

What then is it that constitutes analysis in the treatment of the prelatency child? Predominantly I would say that it is the maintenance of an analytic stance in the sense that what one seeks to bring about is an analytic process. We try to identify recurrent ways of reacting and connect that to feelings. We identify sources of anxiety, mostly in relation to the here and now as it presents in the analysis. We try to point out defenses as well as identify affects. The defenses may have a somewhat more limited range and may be manifested more in action than in verbal terms, but externalizations, identifications with the aggressor, undoing, reaction formations, and denial are all identifiable. Indeed, there are good examples of most of these in the cases presented here. There is probably somewhat more of an educational aspect and of attempts to foster ego development through trying to enhance verbalization and self-observation. These may also operate in adult analysis but to a far lesser degree. There is very much that is different about prelatency analysis, but there is also an essential core of commonality, and it is that core that defines whether or not we consider it analysis. But we should not minimize the divergences.

The child must be brought for consultation by his or her parents. With the prelatency child, the analyst's emphasis must be on the degree of distress the parents see the child feeling or feel themselves because of the child's impact on them. It is more difficult for the prelatency child's parents to accept the recommendation for analysis, not only because of the time and money involved, but also because of the increased pressures on the family, particularly in the case of the young mother who has other young children. Parental guilt is probably maximal in recognizing disturbance in a very young child. One is more likely to see a latency-age child referred because of difficulties in school functioning, social functioning, and so on. Parents in that case, as they often do, can blame the teacher or bad friends or devise a host of other rationalizations for the nature of the child's difficulties. Prelatency parents, however, mostly blame themselves, consciously or otherwise.

I think that parental self-blame is one of the reasons all of the cases presented here involve specific traumas that the child had undergone or was about to undergo: reconstructive surgery for hypospadius, ureteral implantation following numerous intrusive procedures, a visual handicap necessitating months of patching of a good eye, and a child who had repetitive experiences of respiratory arrest related to a sudden infant death syndrome. Parental and grandparent death occurs in others. It is easier for the parents of such children to attribute the disturbance to the trauma, and under those conditions to accept a recommendation for analysis. Of course, other children enter analysis, but the analyst must always be prepared to deal sensitively with the parents' feelings about the recommendation. Not only does parental guilt operate, but parents may fear that they will lose their child's affection, that their child will become very involved with another adult, that they may be exposed to even more unpleasant feelings emanating from the child, especially early in treatment, as well as a host of other considerations. All of these concerns may be encountered by the analyst in contact with the parents and must be dealt with. Even that reaction, so common at any age, that equates the frequency of the sessions with the degree of illness, wherein a recommendation for analysis means their child must be very sick, requires education and sensitive handling of parents. One of the big advantages of places such as Hampstead and the Cleveland Center, among others, is that analysts there have not only the opportunity to observe a child over time and to properly identify those disturbances for which analysis is indicated, but also time to allow the parents to come to understand the recommendation and to enlist and hopefully maintain their support. Time spent in consultation that helps the parents recognize their anxieties and educates them is time very well spent and absolutely necessary if a child is to get into analysis.

Maintaining the analysis for as long as the analyst might think advisable is another problem much related to these same concerns. The parents' wish is to be relieved of the burden. They want to feel less guilty in the sense of feeling that their child is now well. They want to recapture the child emotionally in the sense of becoming once again the focus of a child's feelings without the intrusion of the analyst. Mostly, of course, they wish to get past the personal pain of having had a child in distress, a factor which often can lead to premature interruptions, also illustrated in several of the cases. In fact, we often have difficulty in determining what is premature and what is an appropriate termination. We do not have the guideline of resolution of a transference neurosis. We rely instead on a resumption of the child's developmental process so that what appears in the various components of levels of drive organization, the nature of object relationships, the nature of defenses, indeed, all the lines of development, seem to have reached a phase appropriate level.

In the group of cases presented here, analysis began within a range of two years, nine months to four and a half. They range in duration from somewhat less than six months to five years. They are all what has been termed "pieces of analytic work," a term originally used in connection with adolescent analysis but obviously appropriate for most child analyses. The analyst looks to do that which is possible to help resume progressive development, but is always left with unanswered questions about what later development may bring.

Having made some general comments, I would now like to turn to consideration of some specific developmental issues as they related to prelatency analysis. All of these children were taken into analysis because of an assessment that suggested their developmental progression was significantly interfered with and that, in all likelihood, if there were no intervention, the interference would become more widespread or fixed. Whether or not it is done consciously, the child analyst assesses the developmental level of the child by means of the concepts initially presented by Anna Freud in her suggestions for assessment according to lines of development (1963; 1965). This involves all of the various mental structures and functions — that is, the level of drive organization, the balance between the libidinal and aggressive drives, the level of ego organization in terms of the varying ego functions such as the capacity to regulate and control drive discharge, the level of object relationships, the level of thought processes, the relationship and adaptation to reality (including conflicts over the reality of sexual identity), an assessment of the intactness of the so-called autonomous ego functions, and the assessment to the extent possible of the ego's capacity to synthesize. All need to be considered. In addition, one will have assessed the appearance of superego precursors, or the level of organization of superego functioning. In particular, one will be assessing the balance in relationship between these varying structures and functions.

This assessment is not easy in a prelatency child, particularly because of the rapidly changing shifts that occur in a developing but incomplete psychic organization in relation to both drive and ego organization; there are new and higher levels of organization coexisting with earlier drive and ego configurations. The rapid changes between progressive and regressive movements in children this age are well known but complicate the assessment of whether or not a degree of fixation or regression might be spontaneously reversed. This is by no means an easy task. In the process of such an assessment we are immediately impressed with the child's dependency on the parents for providing information, which means the analyst is also very much dependent upon information provided by the parents. Here we need not be overly influenced by the information supplied but, at the same time, make careful note of it. For example, many parents will tend to overemphasize what they view as traumatic situations and may retrospectively distort and reorganize events around the assumption that a particular event was traumatic. Several of the cases offer this possibility, including not only the emphasis on surgical or other medically invasive procedures and congenital problems, but also early object losses. Important as these events are and even though they may prove to be significant pathogenic factors in the subsequent analytic work, the analyst must not organize his thinking too early around such conclusions. Even when such events have been significantly pathogenic, they will be reshaped, reorganized, and reexperienced in successful developmental phases.

In addition to the historical data provided by the parents, the analyst attempts to carefully evaluate the relationship and interaction of the parents with the child and to identify factors in the parents that might facilitate or impede specific aspects of development. This parental influence is not constant throughout development but depends upon the parents' psychological functioning at any given time and their own conflicts in relation to the child's evolving developmental stages. Here again there are many illustrations of this in the cases presented. We have one case in which gender preferences of the parents influence attitudes toward gender-related activities, for example, taking pleasure in cross-dressing, encouraging the boy's passivity or play with girls' toys. In another case there is an example of a mother who highly sexualizes much of the child's interaction with her. The temptation to intervene with the parents in order to correct such ways of relating is great, whether the temptation is to refer them to treatment, clearly preferable but, as the cases indicate, by no means always acceptable, or to give advice during consultations with the parents.

We need to keep in mind that powerful as the effect is of such parental styles, the relationship between parent and child is not an entirely passive one from the child's side. The child has at each phase of development a significant capacity to influence environmental responses to him. Some children evoke parental responses to provide a great deal of preoedipal satisfaction and therefore are less likely to seek any more developmentally advanced level of gratification. Such behaviors will be obvious as the analytic situation evolves, with the child attempting to get the analyst to directly gratify early drive derivatives. Hopefully, most children amenable to analysis will also manifest their ability to experiment with new ways of reacting to objects other than their parents. One can at times see higher levels of functioning in relation to the analyst even while the child continues to satisfy the expectations of the parents. In order for this to be possible, we need a clear capacity in the child for distinguishing and responding differently to other adults from the way he responds to his parents. This is a developmental consideration that plays a particularly important role in prelatency analysis and will be discussed in relation to the capacity to use the analyst as a transference object as it coexists with the ability to react to the analyst as a new and separate object.

Before turning to that subject, however, I want to touch upon one other factor in assessing development during consultation. The analyst feels much more comfortable when there is time to follow the child's development, at least over a short period of time, before coming to definitive conclusions about the possibility for progressive development or about the specific limitations or regressions in given areas. Because of the rapidly fluctuating changes, observations over time are necessary in order to properly evaluate the relative fixity of any developmental unevenness, arrests, fixations, or regressions.

Let me turn to the capacity of the child to perceive and react to other adults differently from the way they react to the parent. This capacity involves a number of complex developmental issues, but clearly, for the child to develop transference, there needs to be a relatively stable differentiation between self and objects and a relatively stable internalized representation of the primary objects. In short, the child should have achieved object constancy if he is to have the capacity to develop transference to repeat in interactions with others earlier response to the parent. We are accustomed to thinking of this as being achieved around thirty-six months, but of course this is not an either/or proposition. It is a process that extends over time, one in which younger children certainly may have varying degrees of this capacity. Parallel to this capacity is the capacity to differentiate clearly between the parents and significant other adults the child encounters. The child carries over some expectations of what to expect from adults along with the capacity to recognize that not all adults are the same. In addition to what this requires in terms of self-object differentiation, it requires the capacity to integrate good and bad representations of the same object and to retain them in the absence of the object. I have already indicated that this is not an all or nothing proposition.

Several of the cases contain examples of children who have inadequate integration of these representations. This is particularly striking in several cases in which there has been severe trauma, for example, in the child who had multiple experiences of respiratory arrest in relation to her sudden infant death syndrome. Her mother had to repeatedly resuscitate her, something inevitably experienced as an intrusion and an aggressive act on the part of the mother. Another is the child with a congenital urinary tract defect who had undergone several urethral catheterizations with cystoscopy and an intravenous pyleogram. Such children inevitably experience their own intensified aggressive feelings toward the mother, and these can interfere with the integration of good and bad object representations as well as their self representation. This, however, does not mean that they have not achieved any degree of object constancy. Indeed, both of these children clearly developed transference reactions which were quite specific, suggesting that they have fairly stable psychic representations, even if those representations are unintegrated and in conflict. Stable psychic representation means that the possibilities for intrapsychic conflict are present in the child, whether that be intersystemic or intrasystemic. Most children who are taken into analysis will have these capacities present to some degree even when there are indications of fixations or regressions that lead to unresolved problems in separation-individuation. For example, several of the cases presented involve children who are unable to separate from the parent in a variety of settings, such as going to nursery school; in fact, many of the cases present children who require the parent's presence for varying lengths of time at the beginning of the treatment. In spite of these indications of incomplete separation-individuation, all of these children clearly perceive the analyst as an object different from the parent as well as a transference object. For some, the separation-individuation problem may be a temporary regression, while in others trauma may have upset the normative process.

Without belaboring the point, this area lends a particular coloring to analysis of young children—the interplay between the analyst as someone with whom one repeats earlier patterns of reacting with the parent, onto whom one displaces current reactions to the parents based on the common qualities of being adults, and, at the same time, someone who is new and different from the parents and with whom one can experiment with new ways of interacting.

A study group at what was then the Downstate Psychoanalytic Institute, under the chairmanship of Peter Neubauer, M.D., made a series of presentations concerning this subject beginning in 1971. Sandler, Kennedy, and Tyson (1980) wrote along similar lines a few years later. In the varying cases presented, this particular aspect—that is, the interplay between the analyst as transference object and the analyst as the object of newly evolving or presenting levels of drive organization and, in that context, as a new object—is very striking. In at least half of the cases presented today, the analyst appears as the object of positive oedipal wishes which seem to be presenting in the analytic situation before they present in the relationship with the parent. Interestingly this occurs unmistakably with the young boy Dr. Phyllis Tyson describes when she becomes the object of evolving oedipal wishes. In others, the analyst becomes the focus of aggressive competitive oedipal wishes. Dr. Gavalya's case in particular illustrates a young girl with whom there are clearly transference enactments. At the same time she perceives the analyst as a new object unlike her kosher mother, one with whom she can explore behaviors in a manner different than she does at home. In none of these cases does the analyst have to do anything in order to see this particular intermingling in differentiation between the past and what is possible in the present, and for that matter the future. The analytic situation as such provides the milieu, analytic neutrality, within which the child will perceive a different kind of response from an adult. Within the confines of the analytic stance, the analyst is friendly, interested, noncritical, encouraging expression of various moods, feelings, and behaviors, occasionally setting limits where necessary, and not overly permissive. Surely this is for most children a new experience. In successful analytic work, we hope that these elements of new levels of object relationship within the context of new levels of drive organization will be carried from the analytic situation back to the primary family.

The subject of the child's use of the analyst as a therapeutic object touches upon questions of the sex of the child in relationship to the sex of the analyst, particularly with certain kinds of disturbances. We all know that theoretically the sex of the analyst should make no difference in a well-conducted analysis, at least in a well-conducted analysis of an adult. Presumably, in that situation, it may influence what transference manifestations appear first, but eventually all of the transference manifestations should appear. The condition for that is in part that degree of anonymity of the analyst that relates to avoidance of active interventions of various kinds with the patient, the relative silence of the analyst, especially early in treatment, and a host of other factors that constitute good analytic technique. Even under such conditions, most analysts will agree that there may be different sequences of transference manifestations and perhaps different degrees of the intensity of the transference being influenced by the sex of the analyst. Even Freud wrote that women analysts would evoke certain kinds of transference manifestations from their female patients and that a different view of the preoedipal mother was afforded than might present to a male analyst.

How then does this apply to prelatency analysis? In the material of the cases presented we have a dramatic example well worth some discussion. There are two boys, both of whom have cross-gender preferences; one is treated by a female analyst, Dr. Tyson, and the other by a male analyst, Dr. Haber (Dr. Haber's paper was published in the *Journal of the American Psychoanalytic Association* in 1991, 39:107–29). I have already suggested that both of these children seem to have reached oedipal levels of organization in the course of the analysis wherein the analyst was the primary object of newly evolving drive organizations at the oedipal level. Yet if one looks closely, one would be struck by factors that may indicate that these two boys have had different experiences. The mother of the boy Dr. Tyson treated developed a brain tumor when he was six months of age which left her with what Dr. Tyson referred to as "a relatively impassive nature." She was not able to relate to Johnny affectively, and she died when he was just over two. The following two months were spent in foster care. After the mother's death, a punitive and neglectful caretaker, who was also described as seductive, entered the scene when the father was hospitalized with back trouble. It was not until Johnny was three that a stepmother arrived on the scene. There is much much more involved in this case, but for making the point I am discussing, Johnny had a tenuous attachment to his mother and then lost her. He became very attached to his father, partially to replace his lost mother. The father himself seems to have sought comfort and affection in what were stimulating interactions with Johnny, including showering and sleeping with him. When first seen, Johnny stated that he doesn't like girls, he only likes men. Early in treatment Johnny was flirtatious and says, "I'm beginning to like girls a little." Indeed, he goes on in the course of treatment to become very much involved with Dr. Tyson now as the object of oedipal wishes.

Was this affected at all by Dr. Tyson's being female? Or for that matter, by other aspects of the whole degree of responsiveness of the analyst, who seems to maintain her analytic stance in dealing with the wide range of emotions with which Johnny confronts her? I at least get the impression of an analyst who liked this little boy, enjoyed playing and interacting with him while at the same time being his analyst. Given the degree of deprivation that he had experienced in the first three years of his life, he responds to a warm, appropriate interaction with a mothering person. I have the impression that this is a significant factor. Infant research has demonstrated the organizing effect that the mother's affective responses to the child, particularly pleasurable ones such as smiling, laughing, and so on, have in eliciting such responses from the child. This child's mother developed a brain tumor when he was six months of age and her affective responses were thereafter limited. It is even possible that her symptoms affected this prior to that age. Johnny seemed to have been deprived of this kind of interaction in relation to his separation-individuation phase. It suggests that, in this case, the real interaction with the analyst would be a more significant factor. That is to say, there would be more weight on the factor of the analyst as a therapeutic object or a corrective emotional experience. This in no way detracts from all the rest of the analytic work much more oriented to dealing with his conflicts. I know that Dr. Tyson herself is well aware of this as a factor in treatment and has indeed written about the subject (P. Tyson, 1980). Yet she does not really mention it in relation to this case, which, for me, would be a far more convincing one than the one described in her published paper. Johnny needed to experience a loving relationship with a woman who would be accepting, noncritical, and nonintrusive. He found this in his analyst and then was able to bring these feelings back into his relationship with his stepmother. Having already said I would not discuss the cases in any

Melvin A. Scharfman, M.D. / 255

great depth individually, I will stop at this point, although there is much more that could be discussed.

I would like to turn to the boy whom Dr. Haber had in analysis as a contrast (Haber 1991). Stanley's background was quite different. He was described as coming from a matriarchal background with a mother who presumably had wanted a girl. When Stanley was thirty months of age, the mother's younger brother was in a severe motorcycle accident. This brother was in a cast for some time and then was again casted after subsequent surgery. Stanley reacted with fear and withdrawal. Three months later the grandfather wore a bandage over his eye. Stanley became phobic of bandages after this. When he was three, Stanley was again traumatized by the death of his grandfather, who apparently lived in the same house and with whom Stanley had felt a good deal of closeness. Along with many other factors, these events seemed to have reinforced Stanley's feeling that being a male was dangerous and that it would be preferable and safer to be a girl. He sought the closeness he felt his sister had with his mother by wanting to be a girl. Stanley perceived women as clearly more powerful and favored in all ways—the powerful and dangerous preoedipal mother. This perception was probably intensified by the symbolic castration of his grandfather and his uncle. During the phallic period this may in turn have interfered with adequate progression in the late separation-individuation phase. It is also clear that he failed to have much positive interaction with what he could perceive as a masculine father. In fact, his identification seemed female. That this was also defensive against castration anxiety was indicated by the high value he put on his penis. In the course of the analysis, again, by no means taking anything away from the centrality of interpretations that were done, Stanley developed a warm, playful interaction with and attachment to his analyst. Again, the analyst seemed very much to enjoy this boy. When oedipal feelings seem to appear late in the analysis, they are of an openly competitive and rival-rous nature and include, among other things, the wish to steal the analyst's strength by homosexual submission and then by more direct competition.

Once again, oedipal themes begin to appear seemingly with the analyst as their object before they become as apparent in the boy's interplay with his father. He seems to take some of the positive feelings of closeness with Dr. Haber back to his father, with whom he is then able to develop a different kind of rela-tionship. Having seen Dr. Haber as a powerful man who could deal effectively with his dangerous mother, Stanley is able to see his father as potentially more of a model of masculinity and to evoke that kind of a response from his father. Here again, I have the impression that the sex of the analyst played a silent but im-portant role in this analysis. The boy does not show indications of having experienced early maternal deprivation or excessive seduction in his early childhood of the type found in some trans-vestites or homosexual men I have seen who seem to have a pri-mary feminine identification. Stanley's dynamics seem compat-ible with those of some other homosexual men, those in whom conflict and a defensive retreat to homosexuality is more central. In that light, the resolution of his difficulties focused around conflict resolution. This boy clearly identified with Dr. Haber as a man, and it would not have been quite the same experience had his analyst been a woman.

Both Dr. Tyson and Dr. Haber are cautious about the future outcome, and rightly so. We cannot know what adolescence will bring, but both boys have a more easily accessible heterosexual resolution than would have been possible without analysis. Inci-dentally, genetic factors do not seem to be major ones in these cases as presented. As already mentioned, the sex of the analyst is one factor that operates in many child analyses about which not too much is said or written, yet it sometimes seems to play an important role. It may well be that on the basis of careful assessment, analytic treatment with an analyst of one sex or another might be more facilitating for a given child. Certainly it is an area that we need to study and about which we need to learn a great deal more.

Thus far I have largely dealt with factors operating in the analysis without considering one of the central aspects that determine analysis, namely, interpretation, particularly interpretation within the transference. Very much related to that is the question of the use of transference manifestations in reconstruction and what role that plays in the analysis of a prelatency child. I know that it is Hansi Kennedy's role to discuss the technical aspects of the analysis of a prelatency child, so I will attempt to provide something of the developmental background for the technical aspects of the analysis, at least from my perspective. At the same time I hope that she will share with us some of her views of the developmental aspects as they influence the technical aspects. Obviously the two are so closely interconnected that the separation is a somewhat artificial one.

Let me begin by pointing to something we all know. The analyst interprets in verbal terms to the child, whether that interpretation is of a defense, of a feeling the child is not conscious of, or of an event from the past as it appears in the present. For the most part we interpret that which is not conscious, whether unconscious drive representation, ego function, or superego, as well as affects. We need to look at the relationship between our interpretation, made in verbal terms, and what the child understands. More broadly, how does the child react to our interpretation? Is the reaction to the verbal content of the interpretation, to the words the analyst uses, or is it to a much broader context? In considering the prelatency child we need to be very much aware of such developmental issues as the level of cognitive organization, the nature of memory organizations, the way the child is able to understand him or her self, the way he or she understands other people and the relationship between the two. Katherine Rees (1978) has discussed this in an article about the child's understanding of his past. Much of what she presents as an attempt to apply some of Piaget's conceptual framework to how the child will be able to utilize reconstruction is also applicable to how the child reacts to interpretation.

I would like to quote from that article, to use it as a background for discussion about reactions to interpretation:

> For example, the child (from about four to six years) who is still in the intuitive, preoperational phase of thinking tends to see the world as an extension of his wishes and needs, finds it hard to take into account more than one aspect of an object, and is tied to his own immediate perceptions. In interaction with others, he therefore will tend to see only surface appearances, overt behavior, and global affects; he will "center" on only one striking feature, and find it hard to take into account two different aspects of another person or himself. He does not yet see things from another's point of view, and has little inclination to explain himself, to search for causes, reasons, or antecedents. He reasons by transduction, and does not see logical cause-and-effect connections. He tends to react to the immediate present state, and is not able to comprehend the transformations which lead from one event or state to another event or state. He cannot yet quite think of himself and others as stable beings who remain the same over time and circumstance. And he is not able to observe his own thought processes and retrace his lines of thought.

We can add to this a number of other factors that operate in this situation. Prelatency children tend to be more concerned with the present than with the past and tend to express themselves in motor activity as well as verbally. Interpretations or interventions which support the ego's cognitive functions by putting into words thoughts, feelings, or events which the child is not able to verbalize aid the growth of the secondary process thinking. There are many examples of such interventions in the cases presented. To give just one, Dr. Epstein (whose presentation is not included in this volume) describes the boy he is seeing, B., as engaged in ongoing erotic play with his mother. The analyst comments, "You're having a great time playing that game with Mom—it seems exciting." The analyst continues a little later: "It's a lot of fun and exciting to play that." He then describes how B. ignores this but lies down on top of his mother and laughs. He gets his mother to spread her legs, gets between her legs, asks her to sit up, then pushes her down, and then repeats this. Not only is such an intervention aimed at putting into words the excitement the child feels, but the confirmation comes in play rather than verbally. Prelatency childrens' sense of time is also quite different from that of an older child, an adolescent, or an adult. We know that at least with many young children the line between fantasy and reality is not always a clear one; magical thinking exists, and primary process thinking is often very much present. This suggests that an interpretation that focuses on the child's present interaction between analyst and child, or parent and child, can be effective in identifying conflicts, sources of anxiety and defenses, but cannot be too complex. Trying to introduce causes or connections too early can minimize the effectiveness of an intervention. Genetic interpretations are not always easy for the child to fully grasp because, for much of the time, the present condenses and encompasses the past. Other factors could be added to this list, but I think the general idea is clear. We cannot assume that all of our interpretations will be understood by a child at this age in the way we intend them, nor can we always look for verbal kinds of confirmation. Even if we get such a verbal confirmation, we do not necessarily know what intrapsychic use the child makes of an intervention. This is a subject that requires much investigation and integration with relevant technical applications.

The Technique of Psychoanalysis with the Prelatency Child

Hansi Kennedy

A review of the literature on technique suggests that child analysts are moving away from the mere delineation of differences and similarities between adult and child psychoanalysis. They are developing a theory of technique based on developmental considerations. There is nothing surprising about this: it reflects a general trend in psychoanalytic theory, vividly illustrated by the contributions of A. Freud, Hartmann, Kris, Mahler, and others who gave new and wider perspectives from which to view normal and pathological development. Today, our efforts are more concerned with defining the limits of the psychoanalytic method and with considerations of those therapeutic interventions that aim to redress delays or severe distortions in child development.

A study of some more recent contributions on technique which focus on these issues—for example, those of Kestenberg (1969), Maenchen (1970), Olch (1971), Neubauer (1972), Solnit (1975), Glenn (1978), Ritvo (1978), Sandler, Kennedy, and Tyson (1980), and Harley (1986)—reflects a consensus of opinion regarding the essential features of clinical child analysis. In fact, M. Harley's Marianne Kris lecture (1985) at Chapel Hill looked at these questions from a historical perspective with a clarity that I will not even try to emulate. Instead, I will address some of the more controversial issues in the analyst/child/parent interaction which, I believe, assume special significance in work with prelatency children.

If ready agreement can be reached among authors on a comprehensive but global definition that child psychoanalytic technique is signified by the analyst's interpretive approach to the child's intrapsychic life with due consideration to his developmental status, disagreement and controversy arise as soon as the meaning of the three components of this statement are narrowed down.

What is referred to as "the analyst's interpretive approach" can encompass wide-ranging differences of technique. An application of technique which is geared to the needs of the individual patient and his level and mode of functioning can be firmly based on the bedrock of psychoanalytic theory; however, adherence to a more rigidly defined, strictly interpretive stance may require the analyst to remain personally distant and aloof in his interactions with the child. Both approaches may work if not carried to extremes, but it is my personal belief that every child analyst practices within a technical framework allowing adaptation to the child's needs and level of functioning even if he or she does not theorize about it. This will be most needed in the treatment of prelatency children, who confront the analyst with different tasks and different problems than older children.

Anna Freud's general dictum that the aim of child analysis is to restore the child to the path of normal development is particularly relevant in terms of the developmental status of the prelatency child's intrapsychic world. A significant landmark on his developmental path will be the negotiation of the oedipal phase, an ontogenetic point of demarcation at which the child's intrapsychic world attains a crucial degree of structural autonomy. We postulate that substantial structural changes occur with entry into latency. Massive repression leads to the "infantile amnesia," perhaps insufficiently talked about nowadays, resulting in a more effective "censorship" or "repression barrier" (Kennedy et al. 1985). We associate this major occurrence with concomitant changes in the structure of the superego and a more definite compartmentalization in the mind between unconscious and preconscious systems. In addition, Piaget's work has alerted us to important changes in cognitive functions which occur at this same time and which have important implications for psychoanalytic technique (A-M. Sandler 1975; Rees 1978).

Developmentally, the preoedipal (and even the oedipal) child's "intrapsychic world" is still in a relatively fluid state, and to some extent his internal and external worlds remain open systems. Frustrations, prohibitions, and conflicts, even though they may originate internally, are experienced predominantly in relation to the external world. Even after parental prohibitions have become internalized, the primitive defenses at the child's disposal will tend to relocate conflicts as if they were still between himself and the external world.

Such defensive maneuvers, aimed at reducing tension and maintaining feelings of well-being, also have a bearing on the child's object relationships, both internally and interpersonally. The stability of self and object representations is constantly undermined by a lack of synthesis of contradictory images of the object, kept alive by unresolved ambivalence and fueled, in turn, by the impact and intrusion of the external world. Until "good self" and "benign object" representations are firmly established and provide internal sources of support and protection, the child is much more dependent on external feedback to maintain internal equilibrium. And likewise, external experiences in interaction with the primary objects (and perhaps their extensions in the transference) will have a more profound effect on the building up of stable, cohesive, and benign self- and object-representation.

In the treatment of prelatency children, the ready availability of id content in the clinical material is particularly helpful to the analyst. Feelings, wishes, and fantasies are more openly and freely expressed; and this eases the task of understanding the underlying content that is not consciously known to the child but is not truly repressed in a dynamic sense. This advantage, however, has to be weighed against the young child's greater vulnerability: his internal controls are insufficiently stabilized to safeguard him against overwhelming feelings and wishes. This vulnerability is a frequent source of resistance and can undermine the effectiveness of interpretations whenever these are experienced as too dangerous or painful for the child to bear. The analyst's interpretations, ostensibly aimed at strengthening the ego, may threaten ego functions that are precariously established, and not just impulse control, although this is a very prominent technical problem in our work with under-fives. Interpretations, if not carefully worded and adapted to the child's level of functioning, can be misconstrued by him and threaten his reality testing, his self-esteem, and even his capacity to maintain object differentiation. A three-year-old, for example, who made a slip and called his therapist "mummy," could not allow himself to hear the therapist's appropriate transference interpretation because he felt humiliated by his inability to maintain proper object boundaries.

In extreme forms such difficulties are encountered only in children with specific delays in ego development, but they are met with, in lesser degree, in work with all preoedipal children. The advance to the oedipal level itself presupposes important developmental achievements in drive organization, object relationship, and ego functioning. These provide the ego with new flexibilities in dealing with wishes, fears, and internalized prohibitions and with more scope to react appropriately to interpretations of defense, resistance, and transference.

The importance of the move into the oedipal phase was stressed in each of the cases presented here, but the developmental issues to which I referred in these introductory remarks, and their important implications for technique, touch significantly on the assessment of whether our patients have reached the oedipal level and regressively retreated from it or whether this important developmental progression is negotiated for the first time during the analysis. Equally, we must consider differences in the nature of oedipal transference in children who are in the process of negotiating the oedipal phase and in those who are regressively reliving oedipal relationships and conflict in analysis.

Although the very interesting cases present a variety of referral problems, including differences of age (from two years, nine months to four years, six months), of developmental stage reached at the beginning of treatment, and of length of respective analyses (from five months to four years), they have a striking feature in common: They have all been subject to the impact of a physical condition or illness on their early development. Five of the children had medical histories, and the mother of the sixth had a physical illness. Dr. van Dam's case suffered from SIDS (Sudden Infant Death Syndrome), needed to be on a monitor for the first year of her life, and experienced many life-threatening episodes. The same conditions prevailed for her brother, born when she was two and a half years old, and thus relived by both the family and herself when she began treatment at two years, nine months. Dr. Epstein's case (not included in this volume) was born with a congenital hypospadius and Dr. Gavalya's with a congenital urinary tract defect; both children were exposed to many exciting and anxiety-provoking examinations and painful surgical interventions. Dr. Haber's (not included in this volume; see Haber 1991) patient's chronic ear infection from the age of six months as well as the regular injections for allergies against which he fought vehemently were still continuing when he entered analysis at three years, nine months. Dr. Nover's patient Jenny had an organically based eye defect, diagnosed also at six months. It led to her good eye being patched for a large part of her waking hours, and she too protested and struggled against it with vehemence. Dr. Tyson's patient Johnny had no impingement of a personal physical condition, but a tragic impingement of his mother's illness. She had a brain tumor, removed surgically six months into her pregnancy with Johnny, and although still alive in his infancy, she could not care or relate to him and died when he was two years old. As a result, he had multiple caretakers and suffered many separations and object losses in his early years.

It is not difficult to draw some general conclusions about the impact of such major and prolonged physical problems on the whole family. They color the child's perception of his world as potentially frightening, painful, and hostile, contaminate the mother-infant relationship, and mobilize undue aggressive investment in self- and object-representation. All are preconditions for complicating the separation-individuation process, irrespective of the more individually determined dangers of pre-oedipal libidinal fixations.

Most of the children showed considerable unevenness in their ego development, being precocious in some aspects such as verbal or reasoning capacities, yet prone to express themselves in an action mode because of lack of impulse control and aggressive conflicts.

Important reasons for recommending analysis usually were the pervasive difficulties affecting most areas of the child's life and the primitive inflexible defenses leading to stalemates in the mother-child relationship and defeat of the parents. In spite of these severe problems, in several cases it was difficult to gain parental support for the analysis, and this, in turn, had repercussions on the analytic work.

We cannot dispense with parental cooperation in child analysis, least of all in work with prelatency children. The degree and nature of the analyst's involvement with the parents is the subject of much discussion in the literature on technique and is an area of considerable controversy. What is the parents' role in their child's analysis and how can it be accommodated? If we exclude the parents too much we create serious difficulties for the preschool child in engaging in the analytic work. The parents may wittingly or unwittingly accentuate the child's loyalty conflicts or extend punitive, denigrating, or hostile attitudes toward the child in the analyst's direction. But parental intrusiveness in the child-analyst relationship can be equally detrimental, encroaching on the child's budding needs for autonomy and undermining therapeutic expectations that the therapist is available for the child and will keep his confidences. For the analyst there is a danger that too little contact with the parents may blur his view of the child's overall functioning (for example, the analysis is going well, but the child's adjustment is deteriorating everywhere else) and, conversely, that too much external information may contaminate his view of the analytic material.

For the parents, in addition to the external strains related to time and money, their child's analysis will touch on many of their internal concerns. In the mother, the need for her young child's treatment mobilizes guilt and fears of having failed or damaged the child; and her narcissistic hurt and feeling of inadequacy will be heightened by having to hand over her child to a therapist, who conveys that he understands her child better than she does (Furman 1969). This will be even more painful if the analyst succeeds in engaging the child quite soon in an intimate and close relationship on whatever basis.

If the child is currently engaged in an openly defiant, hostile, or sadomasochistic relationship to the mother, he may grasp immediately the opportunity to engage positively with the analyst because this represents an attack on the mother. When the child's aggression toward her is defended against by excessive clinging or controlling, the opposite may occur. The child may insist that the mother stay in the room or make constant visits to the waiting room or insist on her symbolic presence in the consulting room by keeping hold of her handbag or her chair, and so on.

One could say that the new relationship to the analyst is so intimately linked with current as well as past interactions in parent-child relationships that, psychologically speaking, in the treatment of prelatency children, the mother or father or both are always present in the consulting room.

This implies that, as therapists, we all feel more comfortable if the parental presence in the consulting room is metaphoric rather than actual; but the recognition may have some bearing on the tenacity and speed with which we pursue our efforts to bring about a physical separation.

The youngest child, Betty (age two years, nine months), could be separated in the first session from her psychoanalytically enlightened mother, with whom a separation strategy had been carefully discussed in a preliminary interview. But one could not fail to be impressed with the skillfully handled first contact with the child, partly through nonverbal actions, partly through verbalization, which enabled the child to move from sitting on mother's lap unbuttoning her blouse and averting eye contact with her therapist to playing with him while mother left, ostensibly to feed the parking meter. To quote Dr. van Dam, "I felt that it was important to separate mother and child during treatment sessions as soon as practicable for the sake of the unfolding of the therapeutic process to afford the child separation and privacy from the parent and to foster her ability to reveal herself with more ease."

By contrast, Dr. Epstein had to conduct the analysis of his patient (age three years, two months) with the mother in the consulting room for more than two years, and not as a passive observer but an active participant in a highly eroticized relationship with her son aimed at excluding the analyst. She not only colluded with the boy's enactment of his defensive fantasies of having omnipotent and exclusive possession of her, but also responded with excitement in playing this role. Every effort was made to work this through in the shared sessions as well as in sessions with mother alone.

In order to maximize the benefit that analysis can provide for the prelatency child, parents need to be actively involved in the analytic work with a young child. It is not enough to meet the analyst to give information or to discuss conflicting feelings about the continuation of the treatment. The child's developmental needs also have to be met by the parents. Regular work with them offers unique opportunities to facilitate their understanding of the child's current feelings and conflicts and will lead to better handling of the child. In this way it is possible to create an environment for our patients which genuinely supports the analysis and enables the parents to retain confidence in their parenting roles. Even more important, it may also create a home milieu that can support the patient's gains after the treatment is over.

There are various ways to work with parents toward these ends. Sometimes they need to be present in the consulting room for shorter or longer periods and be part-recipients of the analyst's interpretations, tempered as they may have to be for both mother and child. Additional individual sessions with the mother are even more important in this situation, to work through her reactions and her feelings and enable her to respond appropriately to the analyst's handling of the separation issue. Sessions with the parents, however, are best not traded off against the child's treatment time, which would be diminished as a result.

Whatever contact the child analyst has with the parent must be regarded as a part of the work with the child. When, for example, Rachel (age four years, six months) had a temper tantrum when her mother announced in the waiting room before her session that "we almost fell asleep on the way here," Dr. Gavalya told the mother that Rachel wanted to speak for herself about her own sleep.

The child must always remain the primary patient, and this implies that he must be kept in the picture regarding any contact with the parents, who soon learn to put this into practice as well. Of course, the child analyst will not give details of the child's fantasy material to the parents, but the danger of making a child feel threatened by possible breaches of confidence through contact with the parents is, I believe, often exaggerated with young children. While omnipotent thinking is still dominant, children are not surprised that parents know what they are thinking or feeling and indeed sometimes feel relieved by this knowledge. Their concept of secrets is usually first built up around "family secrets" that should not be talked about to outsiders. The so-called secrets that emerge in analysis are revelations that the young patient does not want to know about himself; and this may be even more important than having the parents know about them. There are different levels of knowing, and it is particularly important to bear in mind the fact that the superego is still largely dependent on parental approval or disapproval. When forbidden wishes are not taken up in the context of a conflict in the analysis, a young child may have to resort to complaining to the parents about the naughty things the analyst is telling her to do or gauge the parents' reaction in seeking their protection in the consulting room.

Parental secrets, which must not be conveyed to the child, are unwelcome burdens for the child analyst and hamper his freedom to interpret. This is quite different, I believe, from obtaining extra-analytic information about the child which can be kept as a potential resource and used when appropriate. It is interesting but not really surprising that, under favorable conditions, when the analysis and the work with the parents go well, there is remarkable overlap between the child's and the parents' material on a week-to-week basis; this does not occur to anything like the same extent with older children or if different therapists work with child and parents.

I want to move from the direct analyst/parent relationship to the analyst/child one. The young child only gradually develops the capacity to contain the analytic material inside the session; he has a tendency to carry the product of the analytic work into the home even if the analyst tries to curb this tendency through the symbolic action of keeping toys, drawings, and so on in the consulting room. But the child's tendency to "spill over" or to "act out" in this way affects the interactions with his parents and, in turn, adds to the analyst's difficulty in distinguishing between current reality, defense, or transference in the child's material. These problems are underlined by the child's mode of communication. The prelatency child's verbal statements are still partly tied to primary process thinking. The analyst will have to learn to understand the child's idiosyncratic language and also to "tune in" to the meaning of his nonverbal communications. This includes observing the child's behavior and giving meaning to it. For example, in the first session, while obeying Betty's demand to sharpen pencils, Dr. van Dam explained that he was there to help her not only with the pencils, but also with many other things, like her feelings and thoughts about her mother and her brother. Betty then made scribbles and asked the analyst to erase them. The meaning of such symbolic actions could be open to different interpretations.

Containment in the session of the child's enactments, his "acting in," faces us with even greater difficulties than his acting out. When a child is prone to wrecking the consulting room or to attacking the analyst physically in sudden eruptions of rage or panic, attention tends to be diverted from the analyzing function. Such outbursts frequently arise in response to the child's frustrated attempts to control the therapist and failure to coerce the therapist into acting a specific role (as in Dr. Nover's case).

So-called role-play is an important part of the analytic work with young children but may challenge the analyst's wish to adhere to a rigid set of technical rules. The main consideration in determining whether and for how long the therapist should comply with the patient's demand actively to play a role in his scenario must always depend on what the therapist's involvement will mean to the child and what purpose it is serving in the analytic work. A fine balance has to be kept between eliciting fantasy material in a mode natural to the child's level of functioning and self-expression and providing too much gratification or excitement in doing the analytic work itself. We aim in child analysis to facilitate a move from action to verbalization, ostensibly to help the child gain better ego control. But we may sometimes overlook the young child's cognitive need to experience or to "replay experiences" in a concrete, action-based modality which may enhance his capacity to gain mastery and better integration.

In several of the cases presented, the trauma of surgery or of other medical interventions was reenacted with the analyst in circumstances in which passive was turned into active. One child gave shots to his analyst in a doctor's game; another child stuck an embroidery needle into her therapist's finger with obvious delight, accompanied by reassurances that it would not hurt. The children carried out imaginary surgery resulting in either death or recuperation. We know that this kind of play in the service of mastery occurs in and outside analysis. When it is brought into the analysis by the child as a reflection of his current concern, the analyst, through verbalizations and interpretations, transforms the action play into a meaningful communication. In this way an analytic process becomes established in the form of a dialogue between patient and analyst. In the course of the dialogue the fantasies, past and present, associated with the surgery will appear in the analytic material in different forms and contexts. The analyst's interpretations allow the child to view the effects of his past traumatic experiences from a new perspective. The language of this dialogue between child and analyst is communication through both play actions and words.

Fantasy play with toys permits a degree of distancing and displacement which is often preferred by the analyst to action play. When Betty wanted her therapist to give her a bath and started to undress, the analyst, for obvious reasons, diverted her by encouraging her to bathe the doll instead. She accepted this and gave the doll a bath with only minimal assistance from her analyst. Sometimes Betty assigned to the analyst the role of being her baby brother on the monitor, so that his fate was in her hands. She would then either "fix" the monitor or pull out the plug on him. In this context the analyst could interpret her wish to stop her brother's breathing and her resulting fear as one of the reasons for her bedtime difficulties, to which Betty retorted, "I know that."

Some children need to maintain a rigid distinction between pretend play and real-life experiences. They have to protest if the therapist steps out of the role of play and interprets. The therapist may have to concede and formulate his interpretations within the framework of the play scenario to keep the analytic work going (Kelly 1970). While this may be a quite acceptable technique in the early stages of treatment, the analytic aim would still be the direct address of the patient's feelings, fantasies, and conflicts. We assume that the capacities for self-awareness and insightful understanding are increased by acknowledgment of full proprietarial ownership.

What should not be overlooked in adjusting technical interventions to the appropriate cognitive level of the child is that play interaction may be an important or even necessary adjunct to interpretation and working through if the ego mode is action based and still tied to concrete experience.

Thirteen months into Rachel's treatment a termination date was set. It prompted Rachel to become very bossy and provided opportunity to talk about her intense need for control in the past. She listened intently to Dr. Gavalya's interpretations, who also playacted for Rachel the scenes in the car and at home when she had temper tantrums if mother acknowledged her as Rachel instead of a make-believe character. To this Rachel responded with great delight, saying, "I can hardly believe it, I can hardly believe it, but I remember, it is true."

Apart from making important links between separation anxiety and her defensive need to control, this clearly helped Rachel to organize her experiences in a time sequence, to look for motivation, cause and effect, all in the service of improved self-awareness. This form of reconstruction enables the child to gain a new perspective of current feelings, from the vantage point of recent ego achievements (Kennedy 1972).

This was illustrated also in Dr. Haber's case (Haber 1991): "Stanley appreciated genetic interpretations as long as the word 'baby' was included. He appreciated the time relationships, because his narcissism was not injured by the implication that now he was older and smarter."

I have used action and play as synonyms because in the context of the analytic material they are both enactments of a sort. In one of the cases the child referred to her activities in the session as work, without, I think, reference to the analyst's endeavor. Playing can be a serious activity for the young child, and its illusory quality may encompass features in the child's fantasy life with which we can work in analysis.

I have so far omitted any reference to transference in describing these child/analyst interactions. In a shorthand way, we may describe all these aspects of the interpersonal relationship as "transference," and this would be simple enough. But there are many complexities in an issue such as this (Scharfmann 1978; Tyson and Tyson 1986).

How do we categorize role-play in which the analyst is assigned the role of mother, brother, doctor, or the child himself and related to effectively within a scenario which appears to be based on fantasied or real experiences in his current or past life? Some of the role casting is quite enduring and is probably based on a splitting of ambivalence; but some more fleeting images of a good, caring, neglectful, or frightening mother suggest an externalization or unintegrated object representations linked with memories of the past. In several cases the child's positive attachment to the analyst was linked to the temporary absence of the parents; in other cases fluctuations between positive and negative feelings corresponded to similar swings in the child's relationship to the parents. All these could be described as spillovers or extensions of the child's current relationship to the parents where, strictly speaking, the parent of the present is also the transference object of the past. This statement emphasizes what I have said earlier, namely, that the preoedipal and oedipal child's current conflicts, whether external or externalized, still involve the primary objects, and that earlier conflicts continue as live issues or, in modified form, as part of these relationships.

Sometimes children also externalize aspects of their intersystemic conflicts as, for example, described by Rachel's therapist. "She not only projected onto me her sense of being unclean, but also made me do all the things she wished to do but feared doing. I understood this game to be an expression in the transference of her need to deal with those parts of herself which were not acceptable to her parents." And one could add, "Because they were not acceptable to her parents, they were also not acceptable to her budding superego."

Transference evolves as part of the analytic process, and this will result, on occasion, in the child experiencing transferences to the analyst with greater intensity than the corresponding relationships with the parents. This is not at all unusual in the transition to the oedipal phase, which may unfold first, and quite intensively, in relation to the therapist and from there "extend" to the parents. But this is still different from the revival of preformed object related fantasies when these are freed from repression and reexperienced in relation to the analyst.

Such conceptual refinements need not trouble us too much in our clinical work. One conclusion we should draw from it is that the prelatency child's "transference material" should not be interpreted only in relation to the analyst and the parent of the past, but also in relation to the here and now feelings toward the parents.

Although there was hardly any mention of countertransference in the case reports, some authors (Kohrman et al. 1971) have drawn attention to a ready intensification of countertransference reactions in child analysis. Child analysts are prone to overidentify with their child patients or to have rescue fantasies often mobilized by their direct contact with parents. Phyllis

Tyson referred to her considerable technical difficulties of "juggling Johnny's positive transference and his stepmother's negative transference in a way that remained therapeutic and enabled the analysis to continue," but she did not spell out the countertransference involvement in dealing with these difficulties.

Like transference, countertransference has undergone considerable conceptual expansion (Marcus 1980; R. Tyson 1986) since Freud's original formulations, so much so that nowadays one sometimes listens to case reports in which the analyst's feelings are the main criteria for interpretation of the patient's material. While our understanding of the analytic material is obviously not entirely based on our empathic identification with the child, the need to be "in tune" with our young patients is underscored by having to rely quite heavily on observing and interpreting behavior and other nonverbal material. We also have to monitor carefully our reactions to the child's destructive and aggressive enactments and provide "containment" for both ourself and for the child, as ego auxiliary support.

What the Sandlers (J. Sandler 1976; J. and A-M. Sandler 1978) have described as "free floating responsiveness" to the patient's wish to actualize his unconscious fantasies focuses on another aspect of the extended meaning of countertransference, one that may have special relevance for what we have been discussing. They describe how fantasies involving self and object interaction in the patient's intrapsychic life tend to be actualized in relationships with external objects, especially in the transference. It is not unlike the way we viewed the child's scenario for his role-play, except that the adult has to find more subtle ways of imposing role responses from his analyst, and that the child's scenario is more transparent. Countertransference, in this sense, can indeed become an aid in the analysis of the prelatency child provided the child analyst carefully monitors his spontaneous contributions to the role-play.

Ritvo (1978, 298) questions the degree to which young children can enter fully into the analytic process. "The analyst uses his conceptualizations of the analytic process and his understanding of the phenomena of transference, resistance, defense, etc., to initiate, guide and intensify the process." As a result, the child's conflicts find more direct expression of repetitions of past experience in the transference, but the analyst's role as the knowing and informing one will not readily give way to self-exploration and insight.

Mangham (1981) traces the origin of pleasurable affects associated with insight to affective experiences in the mother-child interaction in infancy. I expressed similar ideas (Kennedy 1984) when I suggested that the genesis of affective awareness and self-understanding has to be sought in the experience of being and feeling understood. The infantile prototype of the later feeling of being understood by the analyst originated in the infant's affective experience of his mother's appropriate responses through her more sophisticated understanding to his needs. This analogy can be taken further; just as the mother understood what the infant needed before he could do so, so the child analyst's insights into his patient's wishes, fantasies, and conflicts usually precedes the patient's "higher level of knowing." This should remind us that, in the initial phases of treatment, some children perceive our interpretations merely as "friendly noises" and also highlight the experiential components of the interaction between the child and the analyst. Quite a number of our child patients need the affective experience of "feeling understood" before they can feel safe enough to participate in the often painful endeavor to increase self-understanding.

Many will find my approach to the technical problems in the analysis of prelatency children quite controversial. Indeed, it may once again raise doubt about whether this work is truly analysis. For this reason I was interested to read Dr. Kestenberg's reply to the same question raised at the end of a panel discussion on "Technical Problems in the Analysis of the Preoedipal and Preschool Child" some eighteen years ago (Olch 1971). A. Maenchen, who was chairman of the panel, agreed with Dr. Kestenberg's statement that "since we analyze the developing ego and superego, the defenses and wishes, and help the child to remember and integrate, we can call it analysis" (550). We can be even more positive in answering this question today. The required technical adaptations discussed are necessitated by the developmental status of the prelatency child and can readily be encompassed in our earlier definition of child psychoanalytic technique.

Therapeutic results are potentially far-reaching and often obtained much quicker. This is due to the fact that the analytic work not only helps the child in dealing with conflicts and finding new solutions and adaptations but also promotes the consolidation of structural development itself. This is especially significant in the treatment of the preoedipal child, in whom the therapeutic efficacy linked with the assistance that can be given to developmental processes that are still in a state of flux is substantial.

A. Freud (1965, 229) drew attention to the fact that the child makes his own selection for therapeutic use from the full range of possibilities that are contained in the child analytic setting.

I have said earlier that our efforts today are more concerned with defining the limits of the psychoanalytic method and with considerations of therapeutic interventions that aim to redress developmental disturbances.

The cases presented at this symposium could all be classified as developmental disturbances and in some instances as accumulative traumatization. The impact of major and prolonged physical conditions or illnesses in their early life profoundly affected these children's development and complicated the separation-individuation processes. Parental conflicts often reinforced these difficulties.

Anna Freud (1974) suggested that the ego can change only what it has done and not what has been done to it. She referred here to her frequent attempts to distinguish between neurotic conflict and developmental disturbances. In the former, "interpretation of the repressed, of transference and resistance, enables the child's ego to replace pathological conflict solutions by more adaptive ones." In the latter, the child will at best learn "to cope better with the after-effects of what has happened to him. But child analysts . . . are reluctant to accept the humiliating fact that the developmental damage which they understand so well and reconstruct so efficiently, can be beyond their power to cure, by truly analytic means" (1976, 259).

This would explain some of the difficulties encountered in the analysis of some of these patients, the need for extending the treatment over several years, and some reservations on the analyst's part about the successful conclusion of the analysis. Perhaps it is precisely in cases such as these that applied psychoanalysis and psychoanalytic treatment become one and the same thing.

References

Aichhorn, A. (1955). *Wayward Youth*. New York: Meridian Books

Alpert, A., P. Neubauer, and A. Weil. (1956). Unusual variations in drive endowment. *Psychoanal. Study Child* 11:125-63.

Anthony, E. J. (1957). An experimental approach to the psychopathology of childhood encopresis. *Brit. J. Med. Psychol.* 30:146-75.

Aruffo, R. N., S. Ibarra, and K. R. Strupp. (2000). Encopresis and anal masturbation. *J. Amer. Psychoanal. Assn.* 48:1327-54.

Bornstein, B. (1949). The analysis of a phobic child: Some problems of theory and technique in child analysis. *Psychoanal. Study Child* 3:181-226.

Buxbaum, E. (1983). Vulnerable mothers—vulnerable babies. In *Frontiers of Infant Psychiatry,* edited by J. D. Call, E. Galenson, and R. L. Tyson, 1:86-94. New York: Basic Books.

Cohen, D. J., et al. (1987). Analytic discussions with oedipal children. *Psychoanal. Study Child* 42:59-83

Edgcumbe, R. M. (1984). Modes of communication. *Psychoanal. Study Child* 39:137-54.

———. (2000). *Anna Freud: A View of Development, Disturbance and Therapeutic Techniques.* London: Routledge.

Fraiberg, S. (1969). Libidinal object constancy and mental representation. *Psychoanal. Study Child* 14:9-47.

———. (1980). *Clinical Studies in Infant Mental Health: The First Year of Life.* New York: Basic Books.

Freud, A. (1963). The concept of developmental lines. *Psychoanal. Study Child* 18:245-65. Also in *The Writings of Anna Freud,* 6:62-87. New York: International Universities Press, 1965.

———. (1965). *Normality and Pathology in Childhood: Assessments of Development.* New York: International Universities Press.

———. (1970). The symptomatology of childhood: A preliminary attempt at classification. *Psychoanal. Study Child* 25:19-41.

———. (1972). The Widening Scope of Psychoanalytic Child Psychology, Normal and Abnormal. *The Writings of Anna Freud,* 8:8-23.

———. (1974). A Psychoanalytic View of Developmental Psychopathology. *The Writings of Anna Freud*, 8:57-73.
———. (1976). Changes in Psychoanalytic Practice and Experience. *The
Writings of Anna Freud*, 8:176-85.
———. (1981). Insight: Its presence and absence as a factor in normal
development. *Psychoanal. Study Child* 36:241-50.
Freud, S. (1905). A case of hysteria. *S.E.*, 7:7-122.
———. (1905). Three essays on the theory of sexuality. *S.E.*, 7:123-243.
———. (1909). Analysis of a phobia in a five-year-old boy. *S.E.*, 10:3-
149.
———. (1931). Female sexuality. *S.E.*, 21:223-43.
———. (1933). Femininity. *S.E.*, 22:112-35.
Furman, E. (1957). Treatment of under-fives by way of their parents.
Psychoanal. Study Child 12:253-62.
———. (1969). Treatment via the mother. In *The Therapeutic Nursery School*, edited by R. Furman and A. Katan, 64-123. New York:
International Universities Press.
Gadpaille, W. (1980). Biological factors in the development of human
sexual identity. *Psychiatric Clinics of North America* 3:3-20.
Galenson, E., M. Robert, and H. Roiphe. (1976). The choice of symbols.
J. Amer. Acad. of Child Psychiatry 15:83-96.
———, and H. Roiphe. (1976). Some suggested revisions concerning
early female development. *J. Amer. Psychoanal. Assn.* 24:29-57.
Garrand, S., and J. Richmond. (1952). Psychogenic megacolon manifested
by fecal soiling. *Pediatrics* 10:747-83.
Glenn, J. (1977). Psychoanalysis of a constipated girl: Clinical observations during the fourth and fifth years. *J. Amer. Psychoanal. Assn.*
25:141-62.
———. (1978). The psychoanalysis of prelatency children. In *Child
Analysis and Therapy*, edited by J. Glenn, 163-205. New York: Aronson.
Green, R. (1982). Prenatal androgens, postnatal socialization and psychosexual development. In Androgens and Sexual Behaviors, W. Pardridge
(Moderator), *Annals of Internal Medicine* 96:448-501.
Greenacre, P. (1945). Urination and weeping. *Amer. J. Orthopsych.* 15:81-
88. Also in *Trauma, Growth, and Personality*. New York: Norton,
1952.
Grossman, W. I., and W. A. Stewart. (1976). Penis envy from child wish
to developmental metaphor. *J. Amer. Psychoanal. Assn.* 24 (Suppl):193-
212.

Grunes, M. (1984). The therapeutic object relationship. *Psychoanalytic Review* 71:123–45.

Haber, C. H. (1991). A three-year-nine-month-old boy with a gender identity disorder. *J. Amer. Psychoanal. Assn.* 39:107–30.

Hall, J. W. (1946). The analysis of a case of night terror. *Psychoanal. Study Child* 2:189–227.

Harley, M. (1986). Child Analysis 1947–1984. *Psychoanal. Study Child* 41:129–54.

Hartmann, H. (1952). Mutual influences in the development of the ego and the id. *Psychoanal. Study Child* 7:9–30.

Katan, A. (1946). Experiences with enuretics. *Psychoanal. Study Child* 2:241–55.

Kelly, K. (1970). A precocious child in analysis. *Psychoanal. Study Child* 25:122–45.

Kennedy, H. (1972). Problems in reconstructions in child analysis. *Psychoanal. Study Child* 26:386–402.

———. (1979). The role of insight in child analysis. *J. Amer. Psychoanal. Assn.* Suppl., 27:9–28.

———. (1984). The "baby at the breast" experience: Memory or fantasy? Some further thoughts on reconstruction. *Bull. Hamp. Clinic* 7:15–24.

———. (1985). Growing up with a handicapped sibling. *Psychoanal. Study Child* 40:255–74.

———, G. Moran, S. Wiseberg, and C. Yorke. (1985). Both sides of the barrier: Some reflections on childhood fantasy. *Psychoanal. Study Child* 40:275–83.

Kernberg, O. F. (1966). Structural derivatives of object relationships. *Int. J. Psycho-Anal.* 47:236–53.

Kestenberg, J. (1969). Problems of technique of child analysis in relation to the various developmental stages: pre-latency. *Psychoanal. Study Child* 24:358–83.

Kleeman, J. E. (1976). Freud's views on early female sexuality in the light of direct child observation. *J. Amer. Psychoanal. Assn.* 24(5):3–27.

Kohrman, R., et al. (1971). Technique of child analysis: Problems of countertransference. *Int. J. Psychoanal.* 52:487–97.

Kohut, H. (1976). Creativeness, charisma, group psychology: Reflections on the self-analysis of Freud. In *The Search for the Self,* edited by Paul H. Ornstein, 2:793–843. New York: International Universities Press.

———. (1984). *How Does Analysis Cure?* Chicago: University of Chicago Press.

Lehman, E. (1944). Psychogenic incontinence of feces (encopresis) in children. *Amer. J. Dis. Child.* 68:190–99.

Lewin, B. D. (1971). Metaphor, mind and mannikin. *Psychoanal. Q.* 40:6–39.

Loewald, H. W. (1960). On the therapeutic action of psychoanalysis. *Int. J. Psycho-Anal.* 41:16–33.

Maenchen, A. (1970). On the technique of child analysis in relation to stages of development. *Psychoanal. Study Child* 25:175–208.

Mahler, M. S. (1965). On the significance of the normal separation-individuation phase. In *Drives, Affects, Behavior,* edited by M. Shur, 2:161–69. New York: International Universities Press.

———. (1968). *On Human Symbiosis and the Vicissitudes of Individuation.* Vol. 1, *Infantile Psychosis.* New York: International Universities Press.

———. (1972). The rapprochement subphase of the separation-individuation process. *Psychoanal. Q.* 41:487–506.

———, F. Pine, and A. Bergman. (1975). *The Psychological Birth of the Human Infant: Symbiosis and Individuation.* New York: Basic Books.

Mangham, C. A. (1981). Insight: Pleasurable affects associated with insight and their origins in infancy. *Psychoanal. Study Child* 36:271–77.

Marcovitz, E. (1973). Aggression in human adaptation. *Psychoanal. Q.* 41:487–506.

Marcus, I. M. (1980). Countertransference and the psychoanalytic process in children and adolescents. *Psychoanal. Study Child* 35:285–98.

McDevitt, J. B. (1971). Preoedipal determinants of an infantile neurosis. In *Separation-Individuation: Essays in Honor of Margaret S. Mahler,* eds. J. B. McDevitt and C. F. Settlage, 201–26. New York: International Universities Press.

———. (1979). The role of internalization in the development of object relations during separation-individuation phase. *J. Amer. Psychoanal. Assn.* 27:327–43.

———. (1985). Pre-oedipal determinants of an infantile gender disorder. Paper read at the Philadelphia Society Scientific Meeting, December 5, 1985, Philadelphia.

Meyer, J., and C. Dupkin. (1985). Gender disturbance in children. *Bull. Menninger Clinic* 49:236–69.

Money, J., and A. A. Erhardt. (1972). *Man and Woman, Boy and Girl.* Baltimore: Johns Hopkins University Press.

Neubauer, P. (1972). Psychoanalysis of the preschool child. In *Handbook of Child Psychoanalysis,* edited by B. Wolman, 221–53. New York: Van Nostrand Reinhold.

Novick, K. K. (1974). Issues in the analysis of a preschool girl. *Psychoanal. Study Child* 29:319–40.

———. (1983). Modes of communication in the analysis of a latency girl. *Psychoanal. Study Child* 38:481–500.

———, and J. Novick. (1987). The essence of masochism. *Psychoanal. Study Child* 42:353–84.

Olch, G. (1971). Reporter 1971 Panel: Technical problems in the analysis of the preoedipal and the preschool child. *J. Am. Psychoanal. Assn.* 19:543–51.

Parens, H. (1979). *The Development of Aggression in Early Childhood.* New York: Aronson.

———. (1979). Developmental considerations of ambivalence, Part II: An exploration of the relations of instinctual drives and the symbiosis-separation-individuation process. *Psychoanal. Study Child* 34:385–420.

———. (1980). An exploration of the relations of instinctual drives and the symbiosis-separation-individuation process. Part 1: Drive motivation and psychic development—with special reference to aggression and beginning separation-individuation. *J. Amer. Psychoanal. Assn.* 28:89–114.

———. (1984). Toward a reformulation of the theory of aggression and its implications for primary prevention. In *Psychoanalysis: The Vital Issues,* eds. J. E. Gedo and G. H. Pollock, 87–114. New York: International Universities Press.

———. (1985). Discussion of J. D. McDevitt's "Pre-oedipal determinants of an infantile gender disorder." Presented to the Philadelphia Psychoanalytic Society, December 5, 1985, Philadelphia.

———. (1989). In *The Course of Life,* vol. 2: *Early Childhood,* eds. S. Greenspan and G. Pollock, 129–61. New York: International Universities Press.

———, L. Pollock, J. Stern, and S. Kramer. (1976). On the girl's entry into the Oedipus complex. *J. Amer. Psychoanal. Assn.* 24 Suppl:79–108.

Person, E. (1986). The omni-available woman and lesbian sex: Two fantasy themes and their relationship to the male development experience. In *Psychology of Men,* eds. G. Vogel, F. Lane, and R. Liebert, 71–94. New York: Basic Books.

Pine, F. (1985). The interpretive moment. In *Developmental Theory and Clinical Process,* edited by F. Pine, 148–59. New York: Aronson.

Rees, K. (1978). The child's understanding of his past: Cognitive factors in reconstruction with children. *Psychoanal. Study Child* 33:237–59.

———. (1978). Reconstruction with children. *Psychoanal. Study Child* 33:295–305.

Ritvo, S. (1978). The psychoanalytic process in childhood. *Psychoanal. Study Child* 33:295–305.

Sandler, A-M. (1975). Piaget and psychoanalysis. *Int. Rev. of Psychoanal.* 3:43–48.

———. (1984). Problems of development and adaptation in an elderly patient. *Psychoanal. Study Child* 39:471–89.

———. (1985). On interpreting and holding. *J. of Child Psychotherapy* 11:3–16.

Sandler, J. (1960). On the concept of the superego. *Psychoanal. Study Child* 15:128–62.

———, and A-M. Sandler. (1978). On the development of object relationship and affect. *Int. J. Psychoanal.* 59:285–96.

———, H. Kennedy, and R. L. Tyson. (1980). *The Technique of Child Analysis: Discussions with Anna Freud.* Cambridge: Harvard University Press.

Schafer, R. (1960). The loving and beloved superego in Freud's structural theory. *Psychoanal. Study Child* 15:163–90.

Scharfman, M. (1978). Transference and the transference neurosis in child analysis. In *Child Analysis and Therapy,* edited by J. Glenn, 275–307. New York: Aronson.

Schwarz, H. (1950). The mother in the consulting room. *Psychoanal. Study Child* 5:343–57.

Settlage, C. F. (1971). On the libidinal aspects of early psychic development and the genesis of the infantile neurosis. In *Separation-Individuation: Essays in Honor of Margaret S. Mahler,* edited by J. B. McDevitt and C. F. Settlage, 131–54. New York: International Universities Press.

———. (1977). The psychoanalytic understanding of narcissistic and borderline personality disorders: Advances in developmental theory. *J. Am. Psychoanal. Assn.* 25:805–33.

———. (1980). Psychoanalytic development thinking in current and historical perspective. *Psychoanal. and Contemp. Thought* 3:139–70.

———. (1989). The interplay of therapeutic and developmental process in the treatment of children: An application of contemporary object relations theory. *Psychoanal. Inq.* 9:375–96.

———, J. Curtis, et al. (1988). Conceptualizing adult development. *J. Am. Psychoanal. Assn.* 36:347–69.

Shane, M. (1967). Encopresis in a latency boy: An arrest along a developmental line. *Psychoanal. Study Child* 22:296–314.

Solnit, A. J. (1975). *Psychoanalytic Study of the Child*, Monograph Series, no. 5. *Studies in Child Psychoanalysis: Pure and Applied*. New Haven: Yale University Press, pp. 1–13.

―――. (1987). A psychoanalytic view of play. *Psychoanal. Study Child* 42:205–19.

Sperling, M. (1965). Dynamic considerations in the treatment of enuresis. *J. Amer. Acad. Child Psychiatry* 4:19–31.

Spitz, R. A. (1957). *No and Yes: On the Genesis of Human Communication*. New York: International Universities Press.

Sterba, E. (1949). Analysis of psychogenic constipation in a two-year-old. *Psychoanal. Study Child* 3:227–52.

Stoller, R. (1976). Primary femininity, *J. Amer. Psychoanal. Assn.* 24 Suppl.:59–78.

―――. (1968). *Sex and Gender*. New York: Science House.

Strachey, J. (1934). The nature of the therapeutic action of psychoanalysis. *Int. J. Psycho-Anal.* 15:127–59.

Thomas, A., and S. Chess. (1977). *Temperament and Development*. New York: Brunner/Mazel.

Tyson, P. (1978). Transference and developmental issues in the analysis of the prelatency child. *Psychoanal. Study Child* 33:213–36.

―――. (1980). The gender of the analyst in relation to transference and countertransference manifestations in prelatency children. *Psychoanal. Study Child* 35:321–38.

―――. (1989). Infantile sexuality, gender identity and obstacles to oedipal progression. *J. Amer. Psychoanal. Assn.* 37:1061–68.

―――. (1996). Neurosis in childhood and in psychoanalysis: A developmental reformulation. *J. Amer. Psychoanal. Assn.* 48:143–65.

―――, and R. L. Tyson. (1990). *Psychoanalytic Theories of Development*. New Haven: Yale University Press.

Tyson, R. L. (1986). Countertransference evolution in theory and practice. *J. Amer. Psychoanal. Assn.* 34:251–74.

―――. (1991). Psychological conflict in childhood. In *Conflict and Compromise*, edited by S. Dowling, 31–48. Madison, Conn.: International Universities Press.

Tyson, R. L., and P. Tyson. (1982). A case of "pseudo-narcissistic" psychopathology: A re-examination of the developmental role of the superego. *Int. J. Psychoanal.* 63:283–93.

———. (1986). The concept of transference in child psychoanalysis. *J. Amer. Assn. Child Psychiatry* 25:30–39.

van Dam, H. (1980). Ages four to six—the Oedipus complex revisited. In *The Course of Life,* vol. 1, edited by S. Greenspan and G. Pollock, 573–87. Adelphi, Md.: U.S. Department of Health and Human Services.

Warson, S. R., et al. (1954). The dynamics of encopresis (workshop). *Amer. J. Orthopsychiat.* 24:402–15.

Weil, A. P. (1970). The basic core. *Psychoanal. Study Child* 25:442–60.

Winnicott, D. W. (1958). *Through Paediatrics to Psycho-Analysis.* New York: Basic Books.

———. (1965). *The Maturational Processes and the Facilitating Environment.* New York: International Universities Press.

———. (1968). Playing: its theoretical status in the clinical situation. *Int. J. Psycho-Anal.* 49:591–599.

———. (1971a). *Playing and Reality.* London: Tavistock.

———. (1971b). *Therapeutic Consultations in Child Psychiatry.* London: Hogarth Press.

———. (1977). *The Piggle.* New York: International Universities Press.

Selected Works on Child Analysis

Bornstein, B. (1935). Phobia in a two-and-a-half-year-old child. *Psycho-anal. Q.* 4:93–119.

———. (1949). The analysis of a phobic child: Some problems of theory and technique in child analysis. *Psychoanal. Study Child* 3:181–226.

Bornstein, S. (1935). A child analysis. *Psychoanal. Q.* 4:190–225.

Edgcumbe, R. (2000). *Anna Freud: A View of Development Disturbance and Therapeutic Techniques*. London: Routledge.

Edwards, M. (1967). Libidinal bases in the analytic treatment of a preschool child. *Psychoanal. Study Child* 22:199–215.

Etezady, M. H. (Ed.) (1993). *Treatment of Neurosis in the Young: A Psychoanalytic Perspective*. Northvale, N.J.: Jason Aronson.

Freud, A. (1922–80). *The Writings of Anna Freud*. Vols. 1–8. New York: International Universities Press.

Furman, E. (1956). An ego disturbance in a young child. *Psychoanal. Study Child* 11:312–35.

———. (1962). Some features of the dream function of a severely disturbed young child. *J. Amer. Psychoanal. Assn.* 10:258–70.

Furman, R. (1968). Excerpts from the analysis of a child with a congenital defect. *Int. J. Psycho-Anal.* 49:276–79.

Geleerd, E. R. (Ed.) (1967). *The Child Analyst at Work*. New York: International Universities Press.

Glenn, J. (1977). Psychoanalysis of a constipated girl: Clinical observations during the fourth and fifth years. *J. Amer. Psychoanal. Assn.* 25:141–61.

Glenn, J. (Ed.) (1978). *Child Analysis and Therapy*. New York: Jason Aronson.

Haber, C. H. (1991). The psychoanalytic treatment of a preschool boy with a gender identity disorder. *J. Amer. Psychoanal. Assn.* 39:107–29.

Kennedy, H., and G. S. Moran. (1984). The developmental roots of self-injury and response to pain in a 4-year-old boy. *Psychoanal. Study Child* 39:195–212.

———. (1991). Reflections on the aim of child analysis. *Psychoanal. Study Child* 46:181–98.

Kestenberg, J. S. (1969). Problems of technique of child analysis in relation to the various developmental stages: Prelatency. *Psychoanal. Study Child* 24:358–83.

Kolansky, H. (1960). Treatment of a three-year-old girl's severe infantile neurosis—stammering and insect phobia. *Psychoanal. Study Child* 15:261–85.

Levinson, L. (1993). Verbalization and play in the treatment of a five-year-old boy. In *The Many Meanings of Play: A Psychoanalytic Perspective.* Edited by A. J. Solnit, D. J. Cohen, P. B. Neubauer, 155–71. New Haven: Yale University Press.

Neubauer, P. B. (1972). Psychoanalysis of the preschool child. In *Handbook of Child Psychoanalysis,* edited by B. B. Wolman, 221–52. New York: Van Nostrand Reinhold.

Novick, K. K. (1974). Issues in the analysis of a preschool girl. *Psychoanal. Study Child* 29:319–40.

Omwake, E. B., and A. J. Solnit. (1961). "It isn't fair"—the treatment of a blind child. *Psychoanal. Study Child* 16:352–404.

Pearson, G. H. J. (Ed.) (1968). *A Handbook of Child Psychoanalysis.* New York: Basic Books.

Rees, K. (1987). "I want to be a daddy!" Meanings of masculine identifications in girls. *Psychoanal. Q.* 56:497–522.

Sandler, J., H. Kennedy, and R. L. Tyson. (1980). *The Technique of Child Psychoanalysis: Discussions with Anna Freud.* Cambridge: Harvard University Press.

Silverman, M. (1985). Sudden onset of anti-Chinese prejudice in a four-year-old girl. *Psychoanal. Q.* 54:615–19.

Smirnoff, V. (1971). *The Scope of Child Analysis.* London: Routledge and Kegan Paul.

Tyson, P. (1978). Transference and developmental issues in the analysis of a prelatency child. *Psychoanal. Study Child* 33:213–36.

———. (1980). The gender of the analyst—in relation to transference and countertransference manifestations in prelatency children. *Psychoanal. Study Child* 35:321–38.

Tyson, R. L. (1978). Notes on the analysis of a prelatency boy with a dog phobia. *Psychoanal. Study Child* 33:427–58.

von Klitzing, K., Phyllis Tyson, Dieter Bürgin. (2000). *Psychoanalysis in Childhood and Adolescence.* Basel: Karger.

Yanoff, J. A. (2000). Barbie and the tree of life: The multiple functions of gender in development. *J. Amer. Psychoanal. Assn.* 48:1439–65.

Journals

Bulletin of the Anna Freud Centre
Published quarterly from 1978 through 1995, when publication ceased.
Child Analysis
Published annually by the Cleveland Center for Research in Child Development.
Kinderanalyse
Published quarterly in Stuttgart, Germany
Editor: Prof. Dr. med. Dr. phil. Jochen Stork, Biedersteiner Str. 29, 80802 Munich, Germany

Index

aggressive conflicts, 197; anal sadism of, 199–200, 202, 203–5; background, 194–95; behavior problems of, 193; castration themes, 205, 207, 208; compared to Mary Lou, 232–38; early analysis of, 196–98; limits and discipline lacking, 193, 194–95; marital problems of parents of, 194, 195–96; and oedipal issues, 204, 205–9; play about pooping, 198–201; presenting problem, 231–32; separation anxiety, 196–97, 201–3; stools withheld by, 196, 197–98; termination, 209–10

aggression: and gender, 93; nondestructive and phallic, 93, 94–95

Aichhorn, A., 1

American Psychoanalytic Association, xiv

analysis. *See* psychoanalysis

analyst: attitude of prelatency child toward, 1, 3; dyadic or triadic conflicts, 7; function of, for patient, 40–41; gender of, in relation to child, 253–58; interpretation by, 156, 157–58; and the presence of the parents, 269; as therapeutic object, 157, 158;

as transference object, 249–50, 251–53

Anna Freud Centre, xiii–xiv

Anthony, E. J., 211

Association for Child Psychoanalysis, x

behavior modification, 97

Betty: analyzability of, 29; anxiety experienced by, 38; birth of brother, 10, 11; button incident, 13–14; case presentation of, 7–9; concern about control, 38–39; conflicts of, 22, 23–24, 30–31; denial of, 17; developmental history of, 9–26; dyadic stage, 22, 23, 29–30; emotional availability of mother to, 37, 38; interpersonal conflicts, 31; "monitor" confused with "monster," 23; move from preoedipal to oedipal, 29–30; neatness of, 16–17; negative images of mother for, 36–37, 39; nonverbal communication of, 18–19, 32; parallel developmental process, 40; pathological identification with aggressor, 36–37, 39–40; relationship with Aunt Florence, 8–9, 36; repression and denial, 31; separation from mother, 30,

Betty (*continued*)
269-70; as sibling of handicapped child, 11-12; and Sudden Infant Death Syndrome, 9-10, 33, 34, 36, 38; swearing by, 24-25; symbolic actions of, 31-32, 272-73; toilet training, 10-11; uncontrolled aggression of, 7-8, 30, 31, 33-42

Billy (patient of Dr. J. B. McDevitt), 90-91, 92, 93, 94, 95

child analysis. *See* prelatency analysis
child development, x; impact of physical condition or ailment on, 266-68; and object relations, 264-65; oedipal phase, 263; and the preoedipal state, 264; and repression, 263-64
children, blind, 154
Cleveland Center for Child Development, xiii-xiv, 246
Cohen, Donald J., 6
communication, nonverbal, 2-4; and play, 4-5; and the presence of the parent, 2, 3
countertransference, 277-78

Dora, xi, 4
Downstate Psychoanalytic Institute, 252
dyadic stage, 30

Edgcumbe, R. M., 4
elderly, psychoanalysis for, ix
Emmett: ambivalence of, 73; anger toward mother, 84-85; being bad played by, 73; castration anxiety of, 73, 75, 76, 77-78, 79-80, 92;

compared to other boys who wished to be girls, 90-93, 95-96; defenses against hostility of, 85-86; evaluation of, 71-73; fear of loss and abandonment, 91; hostile destructiveness of, 92-93; identification with mother, 73; masochistic maneuvers of, 73; mother's anger, 72, 90-91; need to control, 71; negative Oedipus complex, 73, 75, 79; oral sadism of, 87; other forms of treatment for, 96-98; phallic narcissism of, 80; positive Oedipus complex, 77, 79-80, 84; problem with aggression, 71; rage of, invested in mother representation, 92, 94; relationship with father, 83, 87, 90; switch fantasies of, 95-96; technique in analysis of, 77-78; termination of analysis, 89; themes in play of, 74-75, 80-83, 86, 88, 91-92; and transference, 77, 79-80; treatment alliance formed by, 78; wish to be a girl, 71, 95; women in fantasies of, 95
encopresis, x-xi, 211-12
"Encopresis in a Latency Boy" (Shane), 211
Epstein, Dr. R. A., 260, 266, 270

fantasy. *See* play
femininity, 212-13
Freud, Anna, 211, 262; on the aim of child analysis, 263; and analytic interpretation and prelatency children, 156; and the child's involvement in analysis, 280; and child development, x, 246; and the difference between

neurotic conflict and developmental disturbances, 281; on the function of the analyst for prelatency children, 40

Freud, Sigmund: and the age range suitable for analysis, xi; on analytic influence, 1; on the gender of analysts, 253; and infantile sexuality, 32; and Little Hans, 92; mentioned, 14, 212, 278; on nonverbal communication, 4

Galenson, E., 4
Gavalya, Dr. Alicia, 252, 266, 275
gender disturbance, 94–95
Glenn, J., 262
Greenacre, P., 212
Grossman, W. I. and W. A. Stewart, 160

Haber, Dr. C. H.: mentioned, 267; Stanley analyzed by, 90, 92, 93, 94, 254, 256, 257, 275–76
Harley, M., 262
Hartmann, H., 262

infantile amnesia, 264

Jenny: analysis, 1-8 months, 133–42; analysis, 9-21 months, 142–48; analyst's role explored by, 133–34; analyst viewed by, 138–39, 150–51; copying tasks set by, 134–35, 146–47; dependency longings, 138; diagnostic picture, 131–32; different diagnosis of, 155; displacement, 141–42; effect of visual handicap and patching, 153–54; family background, 128–33; fear of body damage

and castration, 135, 136, 143–45; feelings about eye patch, 135–36; and object relationship, 158–61; oral incorporation, 136–37, 159; other strains on development of, 154–55; paradox of, 133; positive oedipal strivings, 145–48; presenting problem, 127–28; response to analytic interpretations, 158–59; self as imperfect and defective, 135; and self observation, 156–57; and separation, 139–41, 147–48, 159, 161; technical considerations, 148–52, 155–56; themes of looking and seeing, 134–35, 137–38; transference of, 150, 152

Johnny (Dr. Galatzer-Levy's patient): analyst's response to, 121–22; analytic alliance, 106–9; background, 101–3; and books, 101–2, 105, 111; competing with men to protect women, 118–20; drawings by, 117; fear of father, 119; fire eyes fantasy of, 101, 104, 105, 108–9, 123–24, 125; identification of conflict and defense, 109–14; initial interviews, 103; and Janet, 116, 117, 118, 119; Moym and Gump characters of, 107–8, 126; stories told by, 105–6, 111–12, 114–16, 125; termination, 122–26; toilet training, 102, 109–11, 117–18; and transference, 114–16, 122–23; witches in stories of, 105–6, 124

Johnny (Dr. Tyson's patient): adoptive mother of, 44–45, 48, 61; aggressive behavior of, 44,

tations, 35; and transference, 250–51
Oedipus complex, xiii
Olch, G., 262

parents: and confidentiality, 271–72; guilt of, 245–46; involvement in prelatency analysis, 1–2, 248–49; and psychoanalysis of prelatency children, 97–98; role in prelatency analysis, 268–69, 270; separation from, 2–3; as source of information, 6–7
Piaget, Jean, 156, 259, 264
Pine, F., 158
play: and the drives, 5–6; and the inner life, 5; integrative problem of, 5; interpretations of, 242–43; limitations of, 241–42; as nonverbal communication, 4–5; in prelatency analysis, 241, 273–77; replaced by fantasy, 5; seductions offered to analyst by, 242; verbalization in, 96
prelatency. *See* prelatency children
prelatency analysis: aim of, 263; analytic stance and goals in, 244; analytic work carried home by child in, 272; availability of id content in, 265; case reports lacking, ix; and the child's ability to respond differently to other adults, 249–50; and the child's vulnerability, 265–66; countertransference in, 277–78; and developmental issues, xiv–xv, 239, 247–50, 262, 263; and feeling understood, 279; and interpretation within the transference, 258–61; and nonverbal

communication, 272–73; and the oedipal phase, 266; and parental guilt, 245–46; parental influence in, 248–49; play in, 241, 273–77; and the psychoanalysis model, 241; role-play in, 273–74; shortage of analysts for, ix, xiv; success of, 100–101, 281; technical considerations, 26–27, 96, 279–81; and termination, 246–47; theoretical predispositions in, 99–100; and transference, 243–44, 258–61, 277
prelatency children: and the categorization and organization of experience, 33; choice of symptoms of, 91; and defense analysis technique, 33; denial and repression by, 31; and the distinction between fantasy and reality, 6; externalization by, xiii; and formation of object and self constancy, 33; looseness of definition of, ix–x; other forms of treatment for, 97, 100; responses to interpretations, 156–57; and secrets, 271–72; symbolic representation and associative processes of, 32–33; therapeutic results among, xv; verbalization of fantasies, 96
preoedipal children. *See* prelatency children
psychoanalysis: and age, xi–xv; elements in model of, 240–41; patient's response to interpretation in, 156; of prelatency children (*see* prelatency analysis); and theoretical prejudices, 99–100; training in, 239–40